DREAMING GLOBAL CHANGE, DOING LOCAL FEMINISMS

In a world where frontiers are militarised and classifications systems defining rights and belonging are reinforced, transnational feminist agendas are fundamental. We use the concept of 'scholarships of hope' to analyse the diversity of feminist struggles and imaginaries in diverse geopolitical locations.

Dreaming Global Change, Doing Local Feminisms explores subversive practices of knowledge production that challenge Eurocentric scientific models and agendas. The book also explores the tensions and challenges of doing transnational feminist theory at the crossroads between feminist scholarship and feminist activism.

In conjunction, these chapters provide a solid analysis framed by feminist methodologies opening complexities and contradictions of individual and collective feminist and trans identity struggles in Argentina, Belarus, Pakistan, Sweden, Taiwan and Turkey. These identities and struggles are rooted in transnational and local genealogies that go beyond the narratives of the West as the origin for democracy and human rights, providing powerful agendas for alternative futures.

Lena Martinsson is Professor in Gender Studies at the University of Gothenburg, Sweden. Her main research interests are political subjectivity, social movements and transnationalism in the field of feminist and post/decolonial studies. Her recent publications include: Martinsson, L., Griffin, G., and Nygren K.G., (eds.). (2016) *Challenging the Myth of Gender Equality in Sweden*. Bristol: Policy Press, and Reimers, E., and Martinsson, L., (eds.). (2017) *Education and Political Subjectivities in Neoliberal Times and Places: Emergences of Norms and Possibilities*. London: Routledge.

Diana Mulinari is Professor in Gender Studies at the University of Lund, Sweden. She works within the field of studies of racism in the tradition of Black/Chicano and decolonial feminists. Her recent publications include: Mulinari, D., and Neergaard, A., (2017) Theorising racism: Exploring the Swedish racial regime. *Nordic Journal of Migration*. 7(2), and Rätzhel, N., Mulinari, D., and Tollefson, A., (2014) *Transnational Corporations from the Standpoint of Workers: Thrown Together, Working Apart*. London: Palgrave Macmillan.

DREAMING GLOBAL CHANGE, DOING LOCAL FEMINISMS

Visions of Feminism. Global North/ Global South Encounters, Conversations and Disagreements

Edited by Lena Martinsson and Diana Mulinari

LONDON AND NEW YORK

First published 2018
by Routledge
2 Park Square, Milton Park, Abingdon, Oxon OX14 4RN

and by Routledge
711 Third Avenue, New York, NY 10017

Routledge is an imprint of the Taylor & Francis Group, an informa business

British Library Cataloguing-in-Publication Data
A catalogue record for this book is available from the British Library

Library of Congress Cataloging-in-Publication Data
Names: Martinsson, Lena, editor. | Mulinari, Diana, 1954- editor.
Title: Dreaming global change, doing local feminisms : visions of feminism : global North/global South encounters, conversations and disagreements / [edited by] Lena Martinsson and Diana Mulinari.
Description: 1 Edition. | New York : Routledge, 2018.
Identifiers: LCCN 2017049665| ISBN 9781138555990 (hardcover) | ISBN 9781138556010 (pbk.) | ISBN 9781315149820 (e-book)
Subjects: LCSH: Feminism–Cross-cultural studies. | Women's rights–Cross-cultural studies. | Women–Political activity–Cross-cultural studies.
Classification: LCC HQ1155 .D74 2018 | DDC 305.42–dc23
LC record available at https://lccn.loc.gov/2017049665

ISBN: 978-1-138-55599-0 (hbk)
ISBN: 978-1-138-55601-0 (pbk)
ISBN: 978-1-315-14982-0 (ebk)

Typeset in Bembo
by Taylor & Francis Books

CONTENTS

ILLUSTRATIONS

Figures

Tables

CONTRIBUTORS

Editors

Lena Martinsson is Professor in Gender Studies, University of Gothenburg, Sweden. Her main research interests are political subjectivity, social movements and transnationalism in the field of feminist and post/decolonial studies. Her recent publications include Martinsson, L., Griffin, G., and Nygren K.G., (eds.). (2016) *Challenging the Myth of Gender Equality in Sweden*. Bristol: Policy Press, and Reimers, E., and Martinsson, L., (eds.). (2017) *Education and Political Subjectivities in Neoliberal Times and Places: Emergences of Norms and Possibilities*. London: Routledge.

Diana Mulinari is Professor in Gender Studies at the University of Lund, Sweden. She works within the field of studies of racism in the tradition of Black/Chicano and decolonial feminists. Her recent publications include: Mulinari, D., and Neergaard, A., (2017) Theorising racism: Exploring the Swedish racial regime. *Nordic Journal of Migration*. 7(2), and Rätzhel, N., Mulinari, D., and Tollefson, A., (2014) *Transnational Corporations from the Standpoint of Workers: Thrown Together. Working Apart*. London: Palgrave Macmillan.

Contributors

Erika Alm (PhD) is a Lecturer in Gender Studies at the University of Gothenburg, Sweden. Her research interests are in the areas of gender, sexuality and identity, and she has worked extensively on the meanings of intersex and trans experiences, activisms and identities. Recent publications include: Alm, E., and Martinsson, L., (2016) The rainbow flag as friction: Transnational, imagined communities of belonging among Pakistani LGBTQ activists. *Culture Unbound: Journal of Current Cultural Research*. 8(3), and Alm, E., Bremer S., and Nord, I., (eds.).

(2016) Cisnormativitet och feminismer [Cisnormativity and feminisms]. *Tidskrift för genusvetenskap*. 37(4).

Selin Çağatay holds a PhD degree in Comparative Gender Studies. She is a Visiting Lecturer at the Department of Gender Studies at the Central European University and the Department of European Studies at Eötvös Loránd University, Budapest, Hungary. Her main research interests include women's and feminist activism in Turkey and worldwide (with a focus on the Middle East), gender regimes, intersectionality studies, Turkish political history, and women's paid and unpaid labour. Her recent publications include: Çağatay, S., (2017) Laicism, women's rights, gender politics: Thinking today's Turkey in its historical and global context [in Turkish], *Birikim*, no. 333–334 (January–February), and Çağatay, S., (2016) From 'daughters of the Republic' to contentious citizens: Kemalist women's activism in historical perspective. In: Bumbaris, A., Helfert, V., Richter, J., Semanek B., and Sigmund, K., (eds.). *Frauen- und Geschlechtergeschichte un/diszipliniert? Aktuelle Beiträge aus der jungen Forschung (Studien zur Frauen- und Geschlechtergeschichte; 11)*, Bozen: StudienVerlag.

Mia Liinason (PhD) is Wallenberg Academy Fellow and Associate Professor in Gender Studies at the University of Gothenburg, Sweden. She is interested in analysing the relationship between resistance and power in feminism as a transformative project. Recent publications include: Liinason, M., (2017) *Equality Struggles: Feminist Movements, Neoliberal Markets and State Political Agendas in Scandinavia*. London: Routledge, and with Sabine Grenz (2016), "Women's/gender studies and contemporary changes in academic cultures: European perspectives", a guest-edited section in *Women's Studies International Forum*, 54.

Tiina Rosenberg is Professor of Performance Studies at Stockholm University and was previously Professor in Gender Studies at Stockholm University and at Lund University. Rosenberg has written extensively on performing arts, feminism and queer theory. Her most recent books include: Rosenberg, T., (2016) *Don't Be Quiet, Start a Riot: Essays on Feminism and Performance*. Stockholm: Stockholm University Press, and Rosenberg, T., (2017) *Mästerregissören: När Ludvig Josephson tog Europa till Sverige* [The Master Director. Bringing the Arts of Europe to Sweden]. Stockholm: Atlantis.

Olga Sasunkevich (PhD) is an Assistant Professor in Gender Studies at the University of Gothenburg. She obtained her doctoral degree in East European History from Greifswald University in 2014. She is currently finalizing her research project "De-essentializing ethnicity: 'Karta Polaka' and the process of ethnicization in the Belarus–Poland border region". Her next project is dedicated to feminist and LGBTQ-activism in contemporary Russia. She is the author of Sasunkevich, O., (2015) *Informal Trade, Gender, and the Border Experience: From Political Borders to Social Boundaries*. London: Ashgate/Routledge.

Chia-Ling Yang is an Assistant Professor at the Graduate Institute of Gender Education at National Kaohsiung Normal University in Taiwan. Her research interests include women in civil society, the social welfare movement in Taiwan, and migrant Chinese workers in Sweden. Her recent publications include: Yang, C.-L., (2017) The political is the personal: Women's participation in Taiwan's Sunflower Movement. *Social Movement Studies*. 16(6), and Yang, C.-L., (2016) Encounters between the 'oppressed' and the 'oppressor': Rethinking Paulo Freire in anti-racist feminist education in Sweden. *Race, Ethnicity and Education*. 19(4).

ACKNOWLEDGEMENTS

Our special thanks go to the many feminist and trans activists who have shared their time and knowledge with us in solidarity with their struggles.

The foundation for this book was funded by the Swedish Research Council as part of the projects 'Dreaming Change: Women and the creation of civil societies in Europe, Asia, and Latin America' and 'Futures of genders and sexualities: Cultural products, transnational spaces and emerging communities'.

1

INTRODUCTION

Transnational feminism: a working agenda

Lena Martinsson and Diana Mulinari

> Stories matter. Many stories matter. Stories have been used to dispossess and to malign, but stories can also be used to empower and to humanize. Stories can break the dignity of a people, but stories can also repair that broken dignity.
>
> Chimamanda Ngozi Adichie [1]

> Do works that matters. Vale la pena.
>
> Gloria Anzaldúa

> At a challenging moment in our history, let us remind ourselves that we the hundreds of thousands, the millions of women, trans people, men and youth who are here at the Women's March, we represent the powerful forces of change that are determined to prevent the dying cultures of racism, hetero-patriarchy from rising again. We recognize that we are collective agents of history and that history cannot be deleted like web pages
>
> Angela Davis, *Women's march, Washington, January 21, 2017*[2]

Adichie, Anzaldúa and Davies; three writers that have inspired, nurtured and comforted us during these turbulent times. The three of them strongly believe in the power of words and the responsibility that goes with the wording. These quotes embody the fundamental topics explored in this anthology: the diverse, and constantly changing, role of *transnational feminism* as a theoretical and political agenda within social theory more generally, and within gender studies more specifically, and the other role of feminist transnational struggles in the creation of *scholarships of hope*.

The work presented in this anthology is inspired by transnational feminist studies in its critique of Western academic knowledge regimes and their emphasis on the relationship between Eurocentric, imperialist and colonial power and the politics of knowledge. The politics of knowledge and the link between modernity and colonialism has brought optimism and hope for some during the centuries, while bringing despair, exclusion, exploitation and loss of communities, histories and visions for the future for others (cf Fanon 1961/1963). However, today the notion of European modernity as an origin of democracy, welfare, women- and LGBT-friendly gender regimes and societal development has been subverted and challenged globally (Puar 2007; Massad 2008; Rivera Cusicanqui 2012). Some of us experience an academic and societal context in the West, where a discursive production of dystopic futures located within the frame of white nostalgia in remembrance of a modern past is on the rise; a good example of how highly political the emergence of hope and dystopia is.

The connection between the European Enlightenment and conquest, the link between modernity and colonialism, and the on-going production of dystopia as well as of hope and political imaginaries are therefore important topics in this anthology. We hope to (de)place and thereby limit the dystopic notion of a modern past and search for other emergences, stories, communities, convivialities and possible political imaginaries and hope.

The book takes as its starting point the diversity of feminists' knowledge production as embodied in the intervention of Black feminist scholar Angela Davis in the Women´s march in Washington in January 2017 quoted above, but also in the variety of feminist, queer and trans knowledge evolving from struggles and visions outside the scope of Western media; for example, #NiUnaMenos – "Not One Less", the Latin American feminist mobilisations and campaigns against all forms of hetero-patriarchal violence.

Transnational feminism

The term *transnational feminism* is a contested one, meaning different things to different activists and researchers. Some scholars argue that the term transnational feminism runs the risk of being appropriated and depoliticised within neo-liberal academic landscapes as a commodity to be consumed, marginalising its historical roots within activism and feminist political struggles (Sudbury and Okazawa-Rey 2009; Conway 2011). It is in this context that feminist genealogies – the way feminists read their past to understand their present – are fundamental.

In resisting processes of Western cultural appropriation and academic institutionalisation, we want to locate this anthology within forms of knowledge production that are both situated in specific places and trans-located. The tradition of transnational feminism does not advocate the rejection of generalisation in social (feminist) theory. However, it does take a point of departure in the centrality of situated knowledges, which is, according to Donna Haraway and in contrast to relativism, "partial, locatable, critical knowledges, sustaining the possibility of webs of connections called solidarity in politics and shared conversations in epistemology perspectives" (Haraway 1988: 854). It also takes its points of departure in acknowledging the relevance of outside/within positions (Collins 1999; Trinh 2011) and the need for 'dirty theory' (Connell 2009: 207). We think of dirty theory as ways of doing the theoretical, where intellectual labour is understood as an embodied practice in which those (embodied) scholars/activists search for forms of writing the social that transcend the rigidity of mono-vocal analytical models, a rigidity that often reinforces the framework of Eurocentric knowledge. In other words, 'dirty theory' aims to engage in analytical work that challenges the reproduction of Western academic classification systems.

Our use of a transnational feminism frame is inspired by the work of what are today considered two canonical interventions in the field: *Scattered hegemonies: postmodernity and transnational feminist practice* (Grewal and Kaplan 1994) and *Feminist genealogies, colonial legacies, democratic futures* (Alexander and Mohanty 1997). We are also inspired by what we consider a landmark in transnational feminist studies, Jacqui Alexander's intervention in *Pedagogics of crossing* (Alexander 2006), which underlines the need for gender studies to explore transnational frameworks that foreground questions of colonialism, political economy and racial formation. Her emphasis on the need to re-conceptualise modernity to account for the hetero-normative, and – we want to add – gender-binary, regulatory practices of modern state formations, is an important contribution to the ways in which gender and sexual regimes are conceptualised within gender studies today (cf Spade 2011).

The field of transnational feminism is not a monolithic one and covers diverse theoretical frameworks and political debates. To a certain extent the field reproduces the tension between transnational feminism as a conceptual framework and transnational feminism as a field of study (Naples and Bickman 2014). It also reproduces the tension between the more post-structuralistically oriented framework of *Scattered Hegemonies* and the emphasis on global capitalism and labour in the work of Alexander and Mohanty (Swarr and Nagar 2010; Patil 2017). We are inspired by a transnational feminist tradition that has put the issue of racism at the core of feminist theory and that understands and reads racism through an analysis of colonialism, imperialism and nation-state building. Transnational feminism is, as we read the tradition, a call to de-centre the colonising voice of Western feminism, a call to provincialise Europe and challenge European universalism. It is a call for the development of Southern theory.

Despite the differences in form and content, transnational feminism as a theoretical framework evolved as a response and a critique of notions of global feminism. A transnational feminist agenda challenges fantasies of global feminism as a powerful metaphor of shared sisterhood between women, a fantasy evolving from a theoretical understanding of power narrowly regulated through the binary opposition between victims (women) and perpetrators (men). Global feminism often fails to mention the experiences of colonialism, racism, imperialism and class exploitation, experiences that have shaped the theoretical interventions of Black, Women of Colour, Indigenous, Postcolonial and Decolonial feminism.

Postcolonial feminist scholar Chandra Mohanty's (1997) well-known, and for us very important, arguments about the making of the theoretical subject of Western feminism has challenged a Eurocentric tradition of gender studies narrowed to the analytical categories of gender and sexuality. We are particularly concerned with

Western feminism's complicity in Eurocentric notions of personal autonomy and freedom and of personhood solidly located in the self-sufficient, non-dependent individual adult (cf Mahmood 2012). Or, rather, we are concerned with the suppression of other epistemologies, a suppression that seems to be a necessary condition for the (apparent) universality of Western feminist theory.

Following the work of Mohanty, transnational feminism underlines the need to pay attention to borders in order to transgress them (Mohanty 2003: 18). The tradition provides a thinking of space inspired by feminist geographers, such as Doreen Massey (Massey 2013; Meegan 2017) in her exploration of the relationship between space, gender and power. Close to this tradition is also the queer scholar Jasbin Puar (2007), who challenges the naturalisation of spatial constructs and borders and the constantly re-centring of the West and Europe as the progressive centre of democracy, where sexual rights become a national trait. We have also been influenced by concepts such as necropolitics, which identifies and names processes of control of specific groups and populations, what postcolonial thinkers Achile Mbembe and Libby Meinties (2003) identify as necropolitical regimes where specific populations (often racialised) are marked for death. Borders, border-work and border-struggles are concepts used here to focus on the on-going materialisation or production of space, territories and categories as well as on the struggles that challenge or transform them (cf, Mohanty 2003; Reeves 2014; Trinh 2011). The concept of border is not only referring to borders between nations. Borders, as we use the concept, also appear in divides like subject-object, north-south, religious-secular. Borders are racialised, classed and gendered and with the materialisation of gender, class and race follow borders. Borders go between as well as inside communities and individuals.

Drawing on Mohanty's work and emphasising situated knowledge is not contradictory to acknowledging global processes. We are aware of the structural transformations of gender relations on a global level – such as the feminisation of labour and migration – and how, as feminist scholars argue, this has changed the ways by which gender issues and gender subjectivities enter the public political arena. Most feminist scholars are also concerned with issues of nation-state belonging, migration and the effects of climate change, and agree that globalisation is generating a new agenda for national and supra-national policy-making regarding gender. The globalisation of capital, transnational production, biotechnology, and the acceleration in the flow of cultural products and people are all gendered and have affected and transformed the lives of women and men in both similar and in different ways (Kaplan et al 1999; Basu et al 2001; Salzinger 2003; Ferree and Tripp 2006). We are also well aware of the role of the International Monetary Fund in continuing to impose structural adjustment programmes on Third World countries and the role of the World Bank in imposing neo-liberal models and regulating (unfair) trade in the last three decades (Sparr 1994; Lindio-McGovern and Wallimann, 2009; Rätzhel et al 2014).

We understand these global processes as possible illustrations of what British cultural studies scholar Stuart Hall captured in the notion of the West and the Rest

(Hall, 1996). In the different chapters of this book, the neo-liberal normativity reiterated around the world, and the role of capitalist formations and the state and their relationship to one another, are two interrelated and recurrent themes. However, in this book we also claim the necessity to challenge the impact of these global processes and their representations in order to shine a light on the many complex forms of transforming counter-hegemonic border-struggles that are going on when these processes are reiterated.

We will provide ample examples of how the neo-liberal model, which is one of many global processes today, is imposed on or embraced (in contradictory ways) by feminist and trans★ movements' struggles. We try to explore these connections as well as cultural representations of neo-liberalism and the role and representations of the state and the nation from below, from the situation on the ground. What do transnational and neo-liberal aid and donors imply for those on the ground; how does this affect how the work is oriented? What happens to neo-liberal or transnational discourses when they are reiterated? How are they transformed and articulated alongside other norms and discourses? Instead of understanding neo-liberalism as a single dominant global order, we look for its many emergences, its sometimes contradictory role and its both predictable and unpredictable articulations alongside local norms and discourses (cf Rofel 2007). We ask what role feminist scholarship and activists play, in this neo-liberal situation, in creating arenas through which visions of social justice can be named and practices of social injustice challenged.

Instead of focusing on what could be understood as processes of neo-liberal globalisation, and other global forces 'spreading' around the world, we are interested in the emergence of a transforming, complex and contradictory transnational sphere. This transnational sphere becomes a space in its own right (Alvarez et al 2014). As such it is also a space in which there exist many different positions, frictions, new and old borders between different communities and hierarchies as an effect of colonialism, imperialism, racialisation and nationalisation. To discuss the transnational space makes it possible to discern alternative communities, migrant movements as well as hierarchies and borders marked by colonialism, racism, gender and class constructions on a level beyond nations but still recognising the impact of the constructions of nations and of local and global discourses. It is a way of abolishing an idea of a global community, which, as Trinh T. Minh-ha critically states, has "overcome frontiers" (2011: 1). Trinh also illuminates the complexity of migration and refugeeism, which, in profound ways, transform and challenge any simple understanding of a transnational space. She describes migration and refugeeism, the home as far away and at the same time "right here", as a displacement that takes on many faces: "The source has been travelling and dwelling on hybrid ground" (2011: 12, 46).

A transnational feminist agenda, as we read it, has its critical starting point, on the one hand, in methodological globalism – closely related to Mohanty's concept of methodological universalism (2003) – where borders and differences seem to be erased by strong global forces and notions of a global community are created. On the other hand, it has its starting point in a critique against methodological nationalism, which is at the core of Western scholarship with its focus on nation states. We also find four important traits in transnational feminist work. Firstly, instead of focusing on global processes or nations, transnational feminists explore the shared location of specific categories of people – migrant female workers, LGBT communities etc. – across national frontiers and in contrast to a universal global community. Secondly; a transnational feminism is a theoretical framework, which makes it possible to study the becoming, reiteration and transformation of colonial, racist and gendered positions beyond nations. Thirdly, transnational feminism theorises gender and sexuality as social relations and classificatory systems, as well as the forms of identities and communities evolving from these categories in similar contexts across the world – in the floor-shops of neo-liberal globalisation, within migratory movements, in on-going border-crossings and in diaspora communities. Finally, transnational feminism is both a theoretical tradition *and* a commitment to political practice, which, while recognising different locations and exploring privileges, emphasises the need for and the possibility of building solidarity and shared communities of struggle. The tradition challenges the binary opposition between theory and activism and underlines the centrality of collective practices in the production of feminist knowledge (Blackwell et al 2015), providing solid and original models of activist scholarship. We find the contribution of transnational feminism, with its aim of social justice, more important than ever.

A position at the margins

For some of us, the sociologist Raewyn Connell (2006) has also been an important influence. She proposes a new path for social theory, by developing a critical dialogue with social theorising in the margins, defined in terms of socio-political locations situated in a hierarchical relation to hegemonic centres. She uses the notion of Southern theory to underline relations of authority, exclusion, inclusion and hegemony between intellectuals and institutions in the centre and those in the periphery. Connell identifies four strategies through which what she defines as the Northerness of general theory is created: the claim of universality; reading from the centre; gestures of exclusion and grand erasure (Chakrabarty 2000; Connell 2006). Connell's discussion reiterates or connects to what many other scholars have pointed to. Cultural theorist bell hooks (1984) writes that a particularly insightful standpoint comes from living life in the margins, as opposed to in the centre. In her analysis, hooks defines the margins in terms of US racial formation. According to this analogy the periphery is where intellectual authority is denied and where intellectual contributions are obscured or appropriated, and the centre is where work becomes legitimated, paradigmatic, and sometimes canonised. Scholarship in the centre influences future work and sets the guidelines for academic 'quality' and is legitimated as Theory.

As feminist human geographer Robin Peace (2009) suggests in her reading of Southern theory, however, the metropole is perhaps more nuanced than Connell suggests. Moreover, there is a risk of developing deterministic connections between alternative ways of creating knowledge and specific (essentialised) ethnic and geographic locations, as well as creating monolithic categories of the varied and contradictory experiences of different regions. A subaltern episteme location, Grosfoguel (2008) argues, is not automatically socially located in the oppressed side of power relations.

There is also a problematic continuity between Eurocentric social theory and postcolonial approaches when it comes to the marginalisation of feminist scholarship. Reina Lewis and Sara Mills (2003) suggest that, to a certain extent, this exclusion is a product of the institutionalisation of postcolonial theory as an academic discipline reproducing 'Theory' coded as male, from Edward Said to Homi Bhabba (even if Spivak (1988, 1999) is sometimes included in this list of people doing 'theory'). This orthodox understanding of theory, more than an exclusion of the analytical category of gender, marginalises the work of feminist scholars on imperialism and racism.

Gender has seldom been taken into account in postcolonial approaches even if gender metaphors are at the core of the colonial and postcolonial understanding of nationhood and belonging. However, feminist scholarship shows that Eurocentred capitalism spread through colonisation, and through this process, binary gender hierarchies were introduced (Oyewumi 2005). The feminist philosopher Maria Lugones calls the latter the coloniality of gender (Lugones 2010).

Feminist scholarship with its historical roots in critical theory broadly defined (Calhoun 1995; Mama 2009) has been, from its very beginning, sensitive to the production of theoretical intervention that re-examines its own categories and frameworks, exploring the relationship between power and regimes of truth. The field has successfully explored the relationship between specific social positions and authoritative voices illuminating the ways through which academic knowledge is created and reproduced, convincingly arguing that science is often coded as male, white, Western, hetero- and cis-normative.

While conducting ethnographic fieldwork in Taiwan, Pakistan, Germany, Turkey, Belarus, Sweden and Argentina with a joint focus on feminist, queer and trans movements and other counter-hegemonic gender/feminist struggles, we have kept this critique against Eurocentrism and against notions of a global community in mind. Mohanty, Anzaldúa, Trinh, and Spivak are some of the post- and decolonial researchers that have been crucial during the research process. They have made it possible for us, theoretically and empirically, to develop our analysis in a productive and critical dialogue with our research subjects.

These ambitions are also interwoven in the way we write and from where we write. The question *What are 'we' doing here?* has followed each of the contributors in this anthology, both regarding the problematic duality between feminist activism/feminist academic scholarship and resisting the risk of being conceptualised as an 'expert' on a specific country, region or culture. The transnational framework and the critique against Eurocentrism (Amin and Chakrabarty 1996) has forced us, especially those of us living in Europe, to ask "what are we doing here?", when travelling and doing research elsewhere. The scholars in the anthology are strongly engaged in anti-racist struggles and solidarity with migrants in Europe, and our connections to the local contexts we explore are based in diverse forms of activist scholarship. We are committed to the grounding of theory in everyday life and accept the challenge and dilemmas of 'taking sides' when producing analysis that we hope is relevant in the knowledge production towards inclusive and democratic alternatives to hetero-capitalism.

We are inspired by a tradition of transnational feminism, which both acknowledges the diverse forms of privilege and the politics of borders and racial classification systems at their core *and* the possibility and the need for developing forms of solidarity within and through diverse struggles. Methodologically, the authors in this anthology never speak for others. Most of the activists that they have met are highly articulate. What these scholars try to do is to learn from transnational feminist experiences in order to unlearn privilege and to contribute to the production of knowledge that make feminists' words and worlds possible.

Central to the anthology is an understanding, following postcolonial scholar Manuela Boatca (2006), that the strength of (semi) peripheries in late capitalism is their transformative epistemological and cultural potential. This potential is mirrored not only in challenging neo-liberalism but in transgressing the core principles of capitalism, as in the World Social Forum in Porto Alegre, which proposed, according to the sociologist Boaventura de Sosa Santos, an epistemological alternative to the capitalist monoculture of knowledge (de Sousa Santos 2004: 13).

Still, feminist theory continues to be 'spoken' in a specific form of English dialect. Feminist theory, while an important part of Western critical production of knowledge, does not necessarily transcend the parochial events and life-forms located between New York and London. Central to this anthology is an understanding of the coloniality of power, particularly of the central role of gender and sexuality within colonialities of power. Another important aspect here is anthropologist McClintock et al's (1997) assertion that imperialism cannot be fully understood without a theory of gender power, and philosopher Lugones's (2000) exploration of the historical legacy of the colonial gender system today.

Transnational feminism is discussed in connected as well as different ways in the book. In her chapter "Dreaming of home: A feminist strategy for importing the Nordic model to Taiwan", Chia-Ling Yang challenges the Orientalist reading of East Asian welfare states and demonstrates how Confucianism is used as a legitimated cultural tradition by state feminists demanding state-financed care in line with what they define as the Nordic model of welfare services. Different transnational philosophies, with different histories, of societal organisation are articulated together.

In her chapter "The social democracy is gone: Performing feminisms in times of right-wing populism", Tiina Rosenberg focuses on how the welfare system that was asked for in Taiwan has been seriously reduced in the Scandinavian countries with the decreased power of the social-democratic vision, a context that demands feminist coalitions that are transnational at their core.

In the chapter "In, against (and beyond?) the state", Selin Çağatay reads transnationalism through a time-space location, when feminists in Turkey translated their local goals into universal ones in order to be considered worthy of belonging to the European Union. From the perspective of mainstream gender and politics scholarship, feminist politics in Turkey seems to be in decline. However, the author shows how, despite being excluded and marginalised by the state, feminist politics is a crucial constituent of the democratic social opposition, remaining a powerful force in public spaces. This presence/absence calls for a critical reconsideration of the state-civil society-transnational governance as the dominant framework within which to analyse feminists' engagement in the politics of gender.

In her chapter "Make/in room: Pakistani Khwaja Sira organising in transnational surges and neoliberal times", Erika Alm warns against tendencies to construct universal gender variant subjects unmarked by, for example, class and locality. She argues for the need of studies that look at the co-constitution of transnational and local conditions for gender variant activism, and critically examines the use of transnational concepts such as transgender. She also asks what it means that many small organisations in the South are dependent on financial support from Northern and Western donors or that the funding available is connected to medicalising interventional programmes like HIV/AIDS prevention programmes. And how does the role of the state change in the void of transnational NGOisation?

In her chapter "Transnational messiness, political subjectivity and feminism across borders: In conversation with three Pakistani activists", Lena Martinsson challenges the Eurocentric idea of a great democratic movement spreading out globally, through looking at the frictions, messiness, complexity and multidimensional reiterations of global discourses among subaltern activists struggling for women's and workers' rights in Pakistan.

In the chapter "Putting (left) politics back into (Western) feminist theory: Conversations with feminist activists and scholars in Argentina", Diana Mulinari argues that the Latin American legacies of struggle against colonialism and imperialism are fundamental to the ways that feminism articulates itself in Argentina, or rather in the ways that feminist activists name themselves vis a vis the Global North.

Finally, in the chapter "Women resisting border regimes: Two case studies from Eastern and Northern Europe", Mia Liinason and Olga Sasunkevich explore border regimes both in Northern Europe and Eastern Europe, and analyse the transnational regime at the core of practices of intimacy, labour, economy and reproduction for the construction of the state and the nation.

The ownership and meaning of feminist theory and the relationship between women's movements of social protest and feminism as a field of knowledge remain contested issues globally. These questions at are the core of this anthology.

Scholarships of hope

> The project of indigenous modernity can emerge from the present in a spiral whose movement is a continuous feedback from the past to the future – a "principle of

> hope" or "anticipatory consciousness" that both discerns and realizes decolonization at the same time.
>
> *(Rivera Cusicanqui 2012: 106)*

As already mentioned at the beginning of this introduction, some of us find ourselves in academic contexts in the Global North where the discursive production of dystopic futures is located within the framework of white nostalgia, often in remembrance of an ethnically homogenous past that never actually existed (Wekker 2017). The nostalgic element lies not least in a still-living vision about a modern rational developmental linearity. In the context of the cruelty of European refugee policies and the success of right-wing xenophobic parties (Mulinari and Neergaard, 2017; Reimers and Martinsson 2017), the nostalgic discourse of European modernity continues to create borders between an 'us' and a 'them' where hope for a rational and well-organised future sticks to some bodies, positioned as white and 'European', and not to others.

We would like to suggest that this dystopic nostalgic reading and narrating risk creating closures, from which it is nearly impossible to explore the complexity, ambivalence and the fractures within and between social relations and diverse actors and social meanings that would create the space not only for resistance but also for successful political struggle (Sullivan and Tuana 2007).

Feminist scholarship on resistance has moved within a dual agenda, either with a focus on the success of women's movements and struggles or with a problematisation of these struggles, focusing on the paradoxes through which, despite a rhetoric of social transformation, new hierarchies of power are re-created and reinforced. Different norms and discourses produce hope and imaginaries as feminist scholars Mia Liinason and Marta Cuesta (2016) show through the emergence of a Swedish Black and queer feminism, which underlines an anti-capitalist agenda and challenges the banal nationalism at the core of mainstream Swedish feminism.

Without denying the need for identifying discursive appropriation and serious analysis of these dangerous times, it is also highly important to meet the everyday interactions, the emerging forms of sociability, the 'banal sociality', as well as the interactions of many unpredictable and contradictory practices of transgressing norms, discourses and practices (Laclau and Mouffe 1985; Mouffe 2013) together with others that follow with living with difference in a transnational time. The category of hope (Bloch 1995; Dinerstein, 2014) explores and names the openness of society towards alternative futures and realistic utopias (Wright 2010).

Even if, and we will soon come back to that, we acknowledge how the production of hope is a double-edged sword, we also understand this production as unavoidable in a political struggle. For us as researchers, it is therefore necessary to understand and follow how hope becomes possible, how it orients some agendas and stops others. Discursively, the production of hope is connected or sticks to some bodies and positions and not to others.

Feminist cultural critic Sara Ahmed (2004, 2017) writes about how the word feminism fills one with hope and energy. It also provides strength and creates a powerful feminist subjectivity. In relation to the hegemonic situation, hope might orient us towards an alternative goal. But hope is also part of hegemonic discourses and thereby stabilises them. Hegemonic discourses always produce hope about the future in order to become dominant. One example is the hope that continues to follow the discourse on European modernity.

However, while we understand that norms and structures are deeply embedded in our identities and societies, and that we need to stay with the social conflicts, we want to study the emergence of hope not just as stable reiterations of discourses but as part of a sociability where the role of frictions and messiness for political agency and imaginary, on a transnational and a translocal level, play an important, transformative role (cf Tsing 2005). We are convinced that human agency, even if it is conditioned, is powerful. Human agency is far from predictable when visions and hopes of social justice are created. As transnational feminists it is necessary to move from the arrogance of certainity to acknowledging pluralism, unpredictability and situated knowledge.

Some texts have been of special importance for us in our theoretical understanding of how hope becomes possible and visible in a world where inequalities and social injustice increase. Gloria Anzaldúas's iconic text "La conciecia de la mestiza" from 1987 is of significant importance for some of the chapters in this book. Anzaldúa writes about a position of mestiza, 'travelling' from one culture to another, being situated outside, as well as inside her diverse cultures and communities. Instead of conceptualising these different experiences and positions as a problem of homelessness, Anzaldúa writes about this location of being in between as a political possibility to deconstruct hegemonic paradigms. In her writings, the mestizo identity is transformed from being an oppressive racial category to a central location for a (feminist) counter-hegemonic movement. The exploration of contradictions, intersections and border-works as a possible tool in resistance and epistemologies of hope is also distinct in Trinh's work (2011) and is also present in Walter Mignolo's (1999) concept of *border thinking*. As he states, "to engage in border thinking requires engaging in conscientious epistemic, ethical and aesthetical political projects. It requires first of all delinking from hegemonic epistemology" (Mignolo 1999: xvii).

Feminist political philosopher Judith Butler (1993) is also important for some of us in trying to understand the complexity of everyday life as well as how we understand the performativity of artistic performances. We are aware of how Butler's writings on the importance of mistakes in the on-going repetitions of norms risk to make it, as Sara Ahmed has pointed out (2004), possible to understand political agency, as well as politics and hope, as superfluous. Change seems to come simply by mistake, in more or less passive reiterations. However, it might be possible to also read this moment of mistake as a political space, a space for a resistant political subjectivity to emerge. Through the mistakes, the wrong emotions, or actions, situations can emerge where it becomes possible for groups or individuals to perceive that life could be lived in other ways, and society organised differently. The subject can experience different normative orders, and thereby different possibilities, or obstacles. Butler's discussion of the importance of all those who are placed outside the norm suggests that they are not only abjected, but are always challenging the hegemonic order, showing that there is something else as well. These positions, the possibility to 'talk back', opens up space for counter-hegemonic political strategy.

Another contribution, fundamental for us when thinking about scholarships of hope is the work of Black feminists; intersectionality as a theoretical intervention has inspired vital feminist work and nurtured and inspired feminists' struggles (Collins 1991; Anthias and Yuval-Davis 1992). With an intersectional perspective, it is also possible to understand how we are talked to, or interpellated, in different ways. It is possible to both be understood by others, as well as by oneself, as both superior and supressed (Mouffe 2013; Martinsson and Reimers 2017). The academisation of the term intersectionality in Europe has obscured the centrality of intersectionality as central to scholarship on hope. Inscribed into a Black feminist tradition of doing theory in the flesh (Moya 2002), the concept provides a naming of the process of social injustice at the core of the creation and reproduction of specific forms of femininity and masculinity. The term identifies a matrix of domination but also identity formations that, when politicised, open for different futures.

It is not just hope as important for political struggle that interest us. Hope is also about the possibility to come together, to build communities and practice conviviality. Cultural theorist Paul Gilroy suggests that it is important, perhaps vital, to ask what kind of knowledge might nurture the ability, the desire and the possibility of living with difference in a globalised world. In his own words:

> We need to know what sort of insight might actually help increasingly differentiated societies and anxious individuals to cope successfully with the challenges in dwelling comfortably in proximity with the unfamiliar without becoming fearful and hostile.
>
> *(Gilroy 2004: 3)*

He uses the notion of 'conviviality' for the forms of everyday interaction that make ways of living with difference and hybridity taken for granted. The author questions, like we do, the static boundaries of race/ethnicity/culture and emphasises the ambiguity and shifting nature of identities and the multiple nature of self. He further asserts that, while it is true that in the United Kingdom notions of race and belonging have become more important when reflected in hostility and panic about asylum seekers and fear of 'black' criminality, race as a classification system dividing people hierarchically has, according to Gilroy, become almost irrelevant in their everyday interactions for many (mostly) urban Britons. Against a backdrop of unresolved and dangerous conflicts, the author locates hope for the future in "the spontaneous tolerance and openness evident in the underworld of Britain's convivial culture" (2004: xii) Against political and scientific assumptions that solidarity and diversity cannot co-exist, the author identifies the great diversity inside central British social institutions such as the NHS (National Health Service) with its vibrant cultural interaction. Alongside media tales of crime and racial conflict there are emerging patterns of convivial modes of interaction that transcend narrow patterns of mosaic pluralism.

Following classical social theory, Gilroy stresses the relational aspects of human encounters. For him, 'conviviality' is a social pattern that designates the process(es) of cohabitation and interaction that have made multiculturalism an ordinary feature of social life in urban areas of European postcolonial societies. A focus on conviviality signifies analyses that encompass simultaneously conflict and friendliness, both situations of boundary markings and crossings.

In line with these scholars and perspectives, and in order to make other stories and other lives, and other convivial communities possible and liveable, we find it fundamental to critically deconstruct notions of stable cultures and authentic radical subjects (Narayan 2000). The notion of the radical authentic subject, such as 'the worker', 'the woman', 'the trans-person', just to mention a few, recreates an image of homogenous societies or cultures or resistant subjects with unitary identities. It not only makes the hope of living with differences and in conviviality, as Gilroy outlines it, impossible. It also hinders an understanding of the complexity of the emergence of political subjectivities or political agency expressed by, for example, Anzaldúa, Rivera Cusicanqui and Trinh.

The same critique could also be turned against discussions about appropriation, re-establishing ideas of stable 'identities' and 'cultures' that are possible to appropriate. In a Western context in which feminism and queer struggles are appropriated by right-wing xenophobic agendas (Puar 2007; Mulinari 2016), an over-focus on this appropriation and institutionalisation can lead to an understanding and reproduction of political struggle in a way that marginalises human agency, on-going border-crossing transformation as well as the possibility to live with differences and transformations, and instead reproduces ideas on stability and essentialism (Roseneil and Frosh 2012). This does not imply that we do not see the need to acknowledge the centrality of diverse forms of strategic essentialism in the political articulation of struggles for social justice. We also underline, again, the importance of situated knowledge.

Sara Ahmed writes that politics without hope is impossible and hope without politics is a reification of possibility (2004: 184). We are, like Ahmed, interested in what this affective hope does, how it circulates, but also how it emerges, becomes possible as well as dangerous. Chantal Mouffe (2003) focuses on the importance of passion for political mobilisation and for creating a possible we. "Democratic politics", writes Mouffe, "needs to have real purchase on people's desires and fantasies. To be able to mobilise passions towards democratic designs, democratic politics must have a partisan character" (2005: 6). This has been one important perspective for some of us in this book. Possible vision orients or mobilises passions that represent an alternative to the existing hegemony. Hope is therefore a necessary emotion of passion for social movements and different organisations, an unavoidable dimension in political struggle (cf Mouffe 2003: 85). It makes a counter-hegemonic agenda possible (Mohanty 2013), or maybe it creates an emotional understanding that societies and our societal positions are possible to transform and that society as well as our individual identities can emerge in a different way.

It is very important for us to acknowledge that the production of hope can of course be both problematic and dangerous. In an affective economy it sticks to some lucky bodies, like some white Euopean ones, and leaves others untouched, without hope (cf Ahmed 2004). It can reproduce conservative ideologies and recreate exclusions.

Let us take some examples. Walter Mignolo's (2009) strong criticism of coloniality veiled as modernity makes it possible to understand how hope, as part of modernity, naturalises Europe as the centre of modernity and a 'hopeful' development. A concrete example is a strong notion in Sweden that Sweden is the most modern, developed and gender-equal nation in the world. The gender equality norm creates a notion of a problematic 'then', a before when it was worse and a hope about the future where a 'he' and a 'she' finally will be equal, a modern linear development. This story also creates the modern Sweden, and Europe, in contrast to what is then constructed as the traditional and non-modern Other. The focus on the relation between 'him' and 'her' contributes also to a hetero-normative, binary and cis-normative regime of truth. The gender equality norm produces hope for some Swedish heterosexual cis-bodies while others are excluded or untouched by hope (Martinsson et. al 2016).

Neo-liberal normativity is probably not successful just because of its economic principles (cf Brown 2015). It is important to remember that neo-liberalism also produces hope for societal and individual transformations. Neo-liberal orientations mobilise different political *We* and different regimes of hope. To exemplify: Neo-liberal ideologies assume that the market can solve nearly all problems, such as the problem with poverty both in the North and in the South, through micro credits. The poor person should become an entrepreneur. Thousands of organisations have adhered to this belief, and therefore changed their orientation, during the last decades (Bernal and Grewal 2014). Gender inequality can be solved because the female perspective is good for business and that becomes the reason not to discriminate. The schools will develop the best pedagogy for success if they are allowed to compete in an educational market (Biesta 2009; Ball 2012). The market offers what seems to be a rational solution, making politics and democratic ambition unnecessary.

It is, to take a last example, of course crucial to remember that fascism and populist right-wing movements are build on an ideology which also carries hope for some – hope about re-establishing a nostalgic dream of a white glorious past, a hope which creates fascist communities of belonging.

These conflicting emergences of hope are evident in several of the chapters in this book. Erika Alm's chapter on local and transnational gender variant activism addresses the consequences of NGOs being oriented by medical and neo-liberal Western discourses. For example, universalistic notions create a chasm between 'modern', middle-class mobilising of the transnational category of transgender and gender variant communities that do not meet the criteria of this category, such as

Khwaja Siras. Khwaja Sira activists experience push back when trying to enter the transnational arena. There is also a discrepancy between the aims and fantasies of NGOs and Khwaja Sira's own hopes and imaginaries for the community. However, since Khwaja Sira activism is based in local intervention and grounded in extended gender variant communities, the chapter also shows the dynamics in Khwaja Sira activism, as activists navigate strategies of redistribution and inclusion, assimilation and resistance in a translocal context that is far more complex than colonial notions of political subjectivities in the global South account for.

Tiina Rosenberg writes about possible hope and resistance among feminist performers at a time where Trump has a global audience and populist right-wing movements fill the void after the decrease of the power of European social democrats. She focuses on the performativity of the performance, the possibility for the feminist and anti-racist activist to affect, as well as on a hope for what Rosenberg, rather than intersectionality, calls a multi-solidarity activism.

Diana Mulinari explores how the connection (and the fractures) between hope and political struggle is understood and given different meaning by feminist activists in Argentina. She identifies the centrality of genealogies in the doing of hope and shows how these activists name their hope in both opposition and collaboration with the powerful legacy of the Latin American left. In her reflection on the forms of collaboration between trans and human rights activists, the author also explores how central fractured identities, made up of diverse experiences of exclusion, are for a politics of hope.

Selin Çağatay explores the impact of "the multiplicity of sites and agendas of feminist struggles and of shifting power configurations and alliances between feminisms and other actors of gender politics" (p. 59, this volume) in Turkey. She especially focuses on the role of counter-publics for the on-going transformation of politics.

Lena Martinsson discusses, through close ethnographic work among activists' struggle for workers' and women's rights in Pakistan, the potential of transnational discursive-material messiness and contradictory interpellations for the emergence of political space and subjectivity. She challenges the notion of what is defined as Western and European knowledges as well as neo-liberal discourses as smoothly reiterating global forces and thereby connecting the messiness to emergences of hope and imaginaries.

Mia Liinason and Olga Sasunkevich explore hope at the level of the everyday, in the forms of transgression that are rarely articulated or spoken about but that in their powerful silence challenge national narratives about borders and create new forms of intimacy. Hope seems to inscribe itself in feminist activists' ability to translate or to re-frame women-friendly models within traditional cultural norms. The authors argue that the women they followed during fieldwork refused to conform to norms around sexual desire, authentic subjectivity and 'rational' legitimised economic action, and suggest that this visualises a multi-levelled resistance against territorial, socio-spatial and symbolic borders of the nation, the state, the neo-liberal economy and hetero-/homo-normativity.

For Chia-Ling Yang, or rather for her informants, hope emerges in feminist articulation of a Nordic model with Confusianism. It is the reinvention of religious worldviews towards a feminist understanding of social needs which creates strategies of possible and successful forms of politics of care, with a vision of another sort of society.

An epistemology of hope departs from acknowledging the contingent and conditional forms of both transnational as well as translocal gender and sexuality regimes. It also departs from a powerful focus on methodological interventions that provide nuanced and rich analyses on the complexity and contradictions "on the ground".

Notes

1 https://thewritelife.com/chimamanda-ngozi-adichie/ downloaded, September 3, 2017
2 www.theguardian.com/commentisfree/2017/jan/22/angela-davis-womens-march-speech-countrys-history-cannot-be-deleted, downloaded, September 3, 2017

References

Ahmed, S., (2004) *The Cultural Politics of Emotion*. London: Routledge.

Ahmed, S., (2017) *Living a Feminist Life*. Durham, MC: Duke University Press.

Alexander, J., (2006) *Pedagogies of Crossing: Meditations on Feminism, Sexual Politics, Memory and the Sacred*. Durham, MC: Duke University Press.

Alexander, M.J., and Mohanty, C.T., (eds). (1997) *Feminist Genealogies, Colonial Legacies, Democratic Futures*. New York: Routledge.

Alvarez, S.E., de Lima Costa, C., Feliu, V., Hester, R., Klahn, N. and Thayer, M. (eds.). (2014) *Translocalities/Translocalidades: Feminist Politics of Translation in the Latin/a Américas*. Durham, NC: Duke University Press.

Amin, S., and Chakrabarty, D., (eds.). (1996) *Subaltern Studies*. Delhi: Oxford University Press.

Anthias, F., and Yuval-Davis, N., (1992) *Racialized Boundaries*. London: Routledge.

Anzaldúa, G., (1987) La conciencia de la mestiza. In: Conboy, K., Medina, N., and Stanbury, S., (eds.). *Writing on the Body: Female Embodiment and Feminist Theory*. New York: Columbia University Press. pp.77–91.

Ball, S.J. (2012) *Global Education*. New York: Routledge.

Basu, A., Grewal, I., Kaplan, C., and Malkki, L., (2001) Globalisation and Gender. Special issue of *Signs*. 26(4), pp.943–948.

Bernal, V., and Grewal, I., (eds.). (2014) *Theorizing NGOs: States, Feminisms, and Neoliberalism*. Durham, NC: Duke University Press.

Biesta, G., (2009) *Good Education in an Age of Measurement: Ethics, Politics, Democracy*. Boulder, CO: Paradigm Publisher.

Blackwell, M., Briggs, L., and Chiu, M., (2015) Transnational Feminisms Roundtable. *Frontiers: A Journal of Women Studies*. 36(3), pp.1–24.

Bloch, E., (1995) *The Principle of Hope*. Vol. 1. Cambridge, MA: MIT Press.

Boatca, M., (2006) Semiperipheries in the World System: Reflecting Eastern European and Latin American Experiences. *Journal of World System Research*. 12(2), pp.321–346.

Brown, W., (2015) *Undoing the Demos: Neoliberalism's Stealth Revolution*. Cambridge, MA: MIT Press.

Butler, J., (1993) *Bodies that Matter*. New York: Routledge.

Calhoun, C., (1995) *Critical Social Theory: Culture, History, and the Challenge of Difference. Twentieth-Century Social Theory*. Cambridge, MA: Wiley-Blackwell.

Chakrabarty, D., (2000) *Provincialising Europe: Postcolonial Thought and Historical Difference*. Princeton, NJ: Princeton University Press.

Collins, P.H., (1991) *Black Feminist Thought: Knowledge, Consciousness and the Politics of Empowerment*. New York: Routledge.

Collins, P.H., (1999) Reflections on the Outsider Within. *Journal of Career Development*. 26(1), pp.85–88

Connell, R., (2006) Northern Theory: The Political Geography of General Social Theory. *Theory and Society*. 35(2), pp.237–264.

Connell, R., (2009) *Southern Theory: The Global Dynamics of Knowledge in the Social Sciences*. Cambridge: Polity Press.

Conway, J.M., (2011) Activist Knowledges on the Anti-Globalization Terrain: Transnational Feminisms at the World Social Forum. *Interface*. 3(2), pp.33–64.

de Sousa Santos, B., (2004) *The World Social Forum. A User's Manual*. Madison, WI: University of Wisconsin.

Dinerstein, A.C., (2014) *The Politics of Autonomy in Latin America: The Art of Organising Hope* (Non Governmental Public Action Series). London: Palgrave Macmillan.

Fanon, F., (1961/1963) *Los condenados de la tierra* [*The Wretched of the Earth*]. Mexico D.F.: Fondo de Cultura Economica.

FerreeM.M., and Tripp, A.M., (eds.) (2006) *Global Feminism: Transnational Women's Activism, Organizing, and Human Rights*. New York: New York University Press.

Gilroy, P., (2004) *After Empire: Melancholia or Convivial Culture?*London: Routledge.

Grewal, I., and Kaplan, C., (eds). (1994) *Scattered Hegemonies: Postmodernity and Transnational Feminist Practices*. Minneapolis,MN: University of Minnesota Press.

Grosfoguel, R., (2008) World-system analysis and postcolonial studies: A call for dialogue from the coloniality of power approach. In: Krishnaswamy, R. and Hawley, J.C. (eds.). *The Postcolonial and the Global*. Minneapolis, MN: University of Minnesota Press. pp. 94–104

Hall, S., (1996) The West and the rest: Discourse and power. In: Hall, S., Held, D., Hubert, D., and Thompson, K. (eds.). *Modernity: An Introduction to Modern Societies*. Malden, MA: Blackwell.

Haraway, D., (1988) Situated Knowledges: The Science Question in Feminism and the Privilege of Partial Perspective . *Feminist Studies*. 14(3), pp.575–599.

hooks, b., (1984) *From Margins to Center*. Boston, MA: South End Press.

Kaplan, C., Alarcón, N., and Moallem, M., (1999) Introduction. In: Kaplan, C., Alarcón, N., and Moallem, M., (eds.). *Between Women and Nation: Nationalisms, Transnational Feminisms, and the State*. Durham: Duke University Press. pp.1–15

Laclau, E., and Mouffe, Ch., (1985) *Hegemony and Socialist Strategy*. London: Verso.

LewisR., and Mills, S., (2003) *Feminist and Postcolonial Theory: A Reader*. London: Routledge.

Liinason, M., and Cuesta, M., (2016) *Hoppets politik: Feministisk activism I Sverigeidag*. [*Politics of Hope: Feminist Activism in Sweden Today*]. Göteborg: Makadam förlag.

Lindio-McGovern, L., and Wallimann, I., (eds.). (2009) *Globalization and Third World Women: Exploitation, Coping and Resistance*. Farnham and Burlington: Ashgate.

Lugones, M., (2000) *Colonialidad del poder, eurocentrismo y America Latina. In Colonialidad del saber, eurocentrismo y ciencias sociales*. [*The Coloniality of Power, Eurocentrism and Latin America. In the Coloniality of Knowledge, Eurocentrism and Social Sciences*]. Buenos Aires, Argentina: CLACSO-UNESCO.

Lugones, M., (2010) Toward a Decolonial Feminism. *Hypatia*. 25(4), pp.742–759

Mahmood, S., (2012) *Politics of Piety: The Islamic Revival and the Feminist Subject*. Princeton, NJ: Princeton University Press.

Mama, A., (2009) Challenging patriarchal pedagogies by strengthening feminist intellectual work in African universities. In: Sudbury, J. and Okazawa-Rey, M. (eds.). *Activist Scholarship: Antiracism, Feminism and Social Change*. Boulder, CO: Paradigm Publishers

Martinsson, L., Griffin, G., and Nygren, K.G., (eds.). (2016) *Challenging the Myth of Gender Equality in Sweden*. Bristol: Policy Press.

Martinsson, L., and ReimersE., (2017) Introduction: Making trouble with neoliberalism, education and political subjectivity. In: Reimers, E. and MartinssonL. (eds.). *Education and Political Subjectivities in Neoliberal Times and Places: Emergences of Norms and Possibilities*. London: Routledge. pp. 1–13.

Massad, J.A., (2008) *Desiring Arabs*. Chicago: Chicago University Press.

Massey, D., (2013) *Space, Place and Gender*. Oxford: Polity Press.

MbembeA., and MeintiesL., (2003) Necropolitics. *Public Culture*. 15(1), pp.11–30.

McClintockA., Aamir, M., and Shohat, E., (1997) *Dangerous Liaisons: Gender, Nation, and Postcolonial Perspectives*. Minneapolis, MN: University of Minnesota Press.

MeeganR., (2017) Doreen Massey: A Geographer That Really Mattered. *Regional Studies*. 51(9). pp.1285–1296.

Mignolo, W., (1999) *Local Histories, Global Designs: Coloniality, Subaltern Knowledges and Border Thinking*. Princeton, NJ: Princeton University Press.

Mignolo, W.D., (2009) *The Idea of Latin America*. Oxford: Blackwell Publishing.

Mohanty, C.T., (1997) Women workers and capitalist scripts: Ideologies of domination, common interests, and the politics of solidarity. In: Alexander, M.J. and Mohanty, C.T., (eds.). *Feminist Genealogies, Colonial Legacies, Democratic Futures*. New York: Routledge. pp.3–29.

Mohanty, C.T., (2003) *Feminism without Borders*. Durham, NC: Duke University Press.

Mohanty, C.T., (2013) Transnational Feminist Crossings: On Neoliberalism and Radical Critique. *Signs: Journal of Women in Culture and Society*. 38(4), pp.967–991.

Mouffe, C., (2003) Politik och passion [The politic and passion]. *Ord & Bild*. 3, pp.85–93.

Mouffe, C., (2005) *On the Political*. London: Routledge.

Mouffe, C., (2013) *Agonistics: Thinking the World Politically*. London: Verso.

Moya, P., (2002) *Learning from Experience: Minority Identities, Multicultural Struggles*. Berkeley, CA: University of California Press.

Mulinari, D., (2016) Gender equality. Anti-feminism and the Sweden Democrats. In: Martinsson, L. et al (eds.) *Challenging the Myth of Gender Equality in Sweden*. London: Policy Press.

Mulinari, D., and Neergaard, A., (2017) From racial to racist state? Reimagining the Nation. In: A. Ålund, C-U. Schierup, and A. Neergaard (eds.) *Reimagining the Nation: Essays on Twenty First Century Sweden*. Frankfurt am Main: Peter Lang. pp.257–285.

Naples, N., and BickmanJ., (2014) *Border Politics: Social Movements, Collective Identities, and Globalization*. New York: New York University Press.

Narayan, U., (2000) Essence of culture and a sense of history: A feminist critique of cultural essentialism. In Narayan, U., and Harding, S. (eds.). *Philosophy for a Multicultural, Postcolonial and Feminist World*. Bloomington and Indianapolis, IN: Indiana University Press. pp.80–100.

Oyewumi, O., (ed.). (2005) *African Gender Studies: A Reader*. New York: Palgrave Macmillan.

Patil, V., (2017) From Patriarchy to Intersectionality: A Transnational Feminist Assessment of How Far We've Really Come. *Signs*. 42(4), pp.847–867.

Peace, R., (2009) Southern Theory: The Global Dynamics of Knowledge in Social Science. *New Zealand Geographer*. 65, pp.84–85.

Puar, J., (2007) *Terrorist Assemblages: Homonationalism in Queer Times*. Durham, NC: Duke University Press.

Rätzhel, N., Mulinari, D., and Tellefson, A., (2014) *Transnational Corporations from the Standpoint of Workers. Thrown Together. Working Apart*. London: Palgrave Macmillan.

Reeves, M., (2014) *Border Work: Spatial Lives of the State in Rural Central Asia.* Ithaca, NY: Cornell University Press

Reimers, E., and Martinsson, L., (2017) Political subjectivity, political struggle and political education in times of precarisation. In Reimers, E., and Martinsson, L., (eds.). *Education and Political Subjectivities in Neoliberal Times and Places: Emergences of Norms and Possiblities.* London: Routledge. pp.118–129.

Rivera Cusicanqui, S., (2012) Ch'ixinakax utxiwa: A Reflection on the Practices and Discourses of Decolonization. *The South Atlantic Quarterly.* 111(1), pp.95–109.

Rofel, L., (2007) *Desiring China: Experiments in Neoliberalis, Sexuality, and Public Culture.* Durham, NC: Duke University Press.

Roseneil, S., and Frosh, S., (2012) *Social Research after the Cultural Turn.* London: Palgrave Macmillan.

Salzinger, L., (2003) *Genders in Production: Making Workers in Mexico's Global Factories.* Berkeley, CA: University of California Press

Spade, D., (2011) *Normal Life. Administrative Violence, Critical Trans Politics, and the Limits of Law.* Durham, NC: Duke University Press.

Sparr, P., (1994) Feminist critiques of structural adjustment. In: Sparr, P. (ed.). *Mortgaging Women's Lives: Feminist Critiques of Structural Adjustment.* London: Zed Books. pp.13–40.

Spivak, G., (1988). Can the subaltern speak? In: Nelson, C., and Grossberg, L. (eds.), *Marxism and the Interpretation of Culture.* Urbana, IL: University of Illinois Press. pp. 271–313.

Spivak, G., (1999). *A Critique of Postcolonial Reason: Toward a History of the Vanishing Present.* Cambridge, MA: Harvard University Press.

Sudbury, J., and Okazawa-Rey, M., (2009) *Activist Scholarship: Antiracism: Feminism and Social Change.* New York: Routledge.

Sullivan, S., and Tuana, N., (eds.). (2007). *Race and Epistemologies of Ignorance.* New York: SUNY series.

Swarr, A.L., and Nagar, R., (ed.). (2010) *Critical Transnational Feminist Praxis.* Albany, NY: State University of New York Press

Trinh T., M., (2011) *Elsewhere, Within Here: Immigration, Refugeeism and the Boundary Event.* London: Routledge.

Tsing, A.L., (2005) *Friction: An Ethnography of Global Connection.* Princeton, NJ: Princeton University Press.

Wekker, G., (2017) *White Innocence: Paradoxes of Colonialism and Race.* London: Duke University Press.

Wright, O.E., (2010) *Envisioning Real Utopias.* London: Verso.

2

TRANSNATIONAL MESSINESS, POLITICAL SUBJECTIVITY AND FEMINISM ACROSS BORDERS

In conversation with three Pakistani activists

Lena Martinsson

Introduction

During my fieldwork among participants in social movements in both Pakistan and in Sweden, I have encountered an endless amount of national, transnational, as well as translocal, situations of messiness, frictions and paradoxes. Many of these messy situations are possible to relate to dominant transnational discourses, conditions or norms, recognised around the world. Some of these discourses reiterate the notion of a vantage point, a place or *a centre*, like Europe (Brah 2003); some re-establish religious/secular divides or the North/South divide, the postcolonial order or neoliberalism. Some messy situations are caused by new information or cultural artefacts plugged into local contexts and discourses. The contexts, discourses, as well as the information and cultural artefacts, can then become transformed in far from predictable ways (cf. Chakrabarty 2007). Often this messiness is problematic but sometimes it makes lives more liveable, making other lives recognisable, thereby challenging hegemonic norms, borders and (Western) ignorance.

This chapter focuses on the struggles of workers' and women's rights activists in Pakistan and how they are part of entanglements of connections with organisations, artefacts, discourses and people, like myself, from the Global North. The aim is to focus on messy and contradictory conditions, situations and interpellations and to ask what this messiness might imply for possible political subjectivities, necessary disturbances in colonial understandings, hopes and visions and for the emergence of a decolonial, transnational feminism.

Theoretical perspective and material

The concept of messiness refers to a theoretical perspective on what happens in frictions between, and in the permanent contradictory articulations of, norms, discourses and materialities. The ambition is to stay with the frictions and more or less unpredictable mergings in order to challenge notions on strong binaries, or on a modern linearity, between a Global North and a Global South, between subject and object, between political subjectivity and activism and a passive, subaltern mass. I abandon the search for clear explanations and ideal types and do not merely focus on reproductions of strong norms and dominant discourses.

Several scholars have been of crucial importance for my way of thinking about messiness. Hybridity and complex intersectionality are different concepts and attempts to capture the on-going (re)emergence of societies and identities of political conflicts and subjectivities, or as Trinh T Minh-ha puts it:

> Yet, never has one been made to realise as poignantly, as in these times how thoroughly hybrid historical and cultural experiences are, or how radical they evolve within apparently conflictual policy-oriented rationales and resisting the simplifying actions of nationalist closures. The named 'other' is never to be found merely over there and outside of oneself, for it is always over here, between Us, within our discourse, that the "other" becomes a nameable reality. Thus despite all the conscious attempts to purify and exclude, cultures are far from being unitary, as they have always, owed their existence more to differences, hybridities and alien elements than they really care to acknowledge.
>
> *(Trinh 2011:45)*

Gloria E. Anzaldúa is another important decolonial scholar who, like Trinh T Minh-ha, finds some sort of hope in the differences, the movements and changes. Anzaldúa is not least famous for her writing about the *mestiza*, "a product of the transfer of the cultural and the spiritual values of one group to another [...] and how the mestiza undergoes a struggle of flesh, a struggle of borders, an inner war [...] like all people, we perceive the version of reality that our culture communicates, like others having or living in more than one culture we get multiple, often opposing messages" (1987:78). Even if Anzaldúa, in this very early text, seemingly reproduces an idea about culture as a unity one can be transferred from, it is important to recognise how she transforms the idea of the position of mestiza from a problem into a possibility. Instead of psychic restlessness, writes Anzaldúa, the new mestiza "creates a tolerance for contradictions" and the ambivalence turns into something else, "a mestiza consciousness", which challenges the "unitary aspects of each new paradigm" and "breaks down the subject and object duality". And she states: "A massive uprooting of dualistic thinking in the individual and collective consciousness is the beginning of a long struggle" (1987:77–80). Anzaldúa acknowledges the importance of a "divergent way" of thinking.

A third scholar whose work has been important for my way of understanding the fluidity and messiness that is interconnected with strong discourses and hegemonies is Chantal Mouffe (2013) and her work with Ernesto Laclau (1985). Mouffe writes about the importance of contradictory interpellations, that one is always talked to, understood by others and by oneself through different norms and discourses, that in relation to each other could be highly contradictory and full of frictions. In these contradictions, in these situations of messiness, where I find a resonance between her work and Anzaldúa's, a political situation exists that might make it possible to experience the possibility of creating other sorts of societies and identities than the ones that are recognisable at the moment. However, as both Mouffe and Avtar Brah (2003), who also focuses on multidimensional situations and subjectivities, so clearly state, a 'border position', as this contradictory, intersectional interpellation might also be called, does not ensure an emergence of a radical political subjectivity or agency. What all these researchers have in common is the interest in new possible emergences of political possibilities.

In this chapter, the place from which I start is not a single culture or discourse. The place, or the space, is neither Pakistan nor Sweden. If it is a space it is a transnational one. I understand it as a space where (dis)connections are made, not in single national localities but somewhere in between or beyond these. Let me elaborate on this while presenting my main informants and our different positions in this transnational space. Grace Bibi, Sughran Khaskhelly and Sunita Devi are three activists, from three different religious communities: Christian, Muslim and Hindu.[1] They are part of a network of three very closely related organisations, Pakistani NGOs (hereafter I will call this network for the Organisation) working against bonded labour, i.e. the debt slave-system in Pakistan. I met them both as a researcher and as an activist engaged in a small anti-slavery organisation in Sweden (hereafter called the Swedish support organisation) which, among other things, supports the Organisation. Even if I keep my position as a researcher apart from the position as an activist fairly well, there are a lot of unavoidable methodological and messy leakages between them. For example, the activist transnational struggle for workers' rights is what once brought me into this field of research. We and our organisations are struggling on what I would like to call a 'messy', transnational arena, where norms, discourses, people, cultural products such as human, women's and children's rights, flags, languages, and not least money are moving around the world, constantly connecting and disconnecting in a transformative and far from predictable way.

It is easy however to also describe our positions in a stable way, with strong borders. Grace, Sunita and Sughran live in a nation marked by colonial history. Grace and Sunita have experiences of inhabiting subaltern positions, which, according to the influential postcolonial researcher Gayatri Chakravorty Spivak, refers to:

> …those who do not give orders; they only receive orders. That comes from Antonio Gramsci, who made the word current. He was looking at people who were not in fact working-class folks or victims of capitalism. He was looking at people who were outside of that logic because he was himself from Sardinia, which was outside of the High Italy of the north. But "subaltern" also means those who do not have access to the structures of citizenship. I am

> now talking about India today, where the largest sector of the electorate is the rural landless illiterate. They may vote but they have no access to the structures of citizenship. So that is a subaltern
>
> *(Interview, Paulson 2016)*

The subaltern is outside the system, and becomes objectified. In Spivak's well-known essay "Can the subaltern speak?", her point was not that the subaltern could not speak, but that no one listened (Spivak 1988). When meeting bonded labourers I have, in line with Spivak, myself thought about them as subaltern in a material way. They are not part of the capitalist society; they are only meant to produce for others, not take part in consumption. Grace, while positioned as an illiterate, formerly bonded labourer, and I, as part of a colonising imperialistic Europe and a global middle class, embody in many ways these different positions. Even Sunita comes from a family with long experience of being excluded, without access to society, education and recognition as equal citizens. Her family has, through hard work and activism, succeeded in the struggle to get education for their children. Sugrhan, from a small town in the countryside, belongs to the working class. The four of us are identified with different racialised positions and live in very different national contexts. It is impossible to escape from these positions, from these relations of power and inequalities. It is also impossible for us to escape our different localities and nationalities and from the colonial conditions and discourses.

The Pakistani researcher Shahnaz Rose writes that Pakistani women's lives cannot be separated from the history of colonialism and postcolonialism: they are a product of it. The British colonisation had a big impact on how Pakistani women could live their lives, and women have become the symbol for the nation after independence and after its partition from India in 1947 (2006, cf Shaheed and Shaheed 2011). Even the position 'Western women' is a colonial and postcolonial product of the North/South divide, supposed from a Eurocentric perspective to be tantamount to individuality and freedom in contrast to what is presumed to be the Other. The idea about who we are, or are supposed to be is, in other words, a local, national, translocal and transnational condition. The transnational space may be abstract and difficult to grasp, but it is important to acknowledge that we are not just guests in each other's houses/nations. We are in-between, and beyond and dependent on each other in how we understand our lives and societies. But, and I will come back to this, it is a messy space of its own, a space of discursive/national and normative border troubles (Trinh 2011; Rivera Cusicanqui 2012). Therefore, the focus on the transnational sphere does not mean that the national or local history is of no importance. As is very well explored in Diana Mulinari's and Erika Alm's chapters in this book, the national or local history is of the deepest importance and full of conditional or frictional resonances as it is (Greiner and Sakdapolak 2013), but the transnational sphere needs to be discussed as a space in its own right, not least because of its messiness and importance for feminist investigations and interventions.

The positions described above also describe borders and divides between religions, religion/secularism, North/South and different classes. But there are also many connections. The three main participants and I have a lot of common interests. Sughran and I share a critical perspective on capitalism and a deep interest in economy and change. With Grace, I share an interest in politics. Grace, Sunita and I all share an interest in, and struggle for, education. All four of us are engaged in the struggle against slavery in different parts of the world, and as Sughran said when I asked her on Facebook if it was okay for me to use her name, and her pictures, she answered with help from Google Translate: "sure you use my name & pictures & i hope if our ideas are spread against capitalism & fever for socialism". Even if our positions are very different, we have made similar political analyses. It was possible for her to recognise herself in my struggle and for me to recognise myself in hers, to follow her and her comrades' lead (Anzaldúa 1987:85). The transnational materiality, such as the Internet and Google Translate, made this moment of reciprocal recognition possible.

Apart from the three already mentioned, I have interviewed approximately 50 women and 15 men struggling for change in the countryside in Pakistan. I have listened to discussions and speeches in women's meetings and I have been a guest researcher at Lahore College for Women University at the Department for Gender and Development Studies, where NGO-based work is an especially important subject. I have also established contacts and interviewed city-based women, feminist and LGBT organisations in Lahore, Islamabad, Mirpurkhas and Karachi. In parallel with this I have, as already mentioned, been a member of the Swedish support organisation that, among other things, has invited activists from Pakistan to come to Sweden in order to inform people in the West, who are often ignorant about the political and pedagogical work being done by these Pakistani activists.

Contradictory messages

As a young bonded labourer on a brick kiln, Grace Bibi was one day reached by a pamphlet she could not read because of her illiteracy. Someone else let her know that the pamphlet said it was no longer permissible to have bonded labourers. The pamphlet had a huge impact on Grace and her community. "I wanted to do some good with my life after that", Grace told me. "Something had happened to me", she said. I understood it as a moment of change, a moment where it became possible for her to understand herself in a new way, not just as a debt slave, but as another sort of subject. She was talked to, or interpellated, differently. Maybe it is also possible to say that this new interpellation, in contrast to how she was usually placed and talked to and how she usually understood herself, made Grace aware of a political conflict, of how some exploited others. She became a sharper political subject, wanting 'to do good' (Butler 1990; Mouffe 2013; Martinsson and Reimers 2017). Her way of 'doing good' was to walk to other brick kilns together with a female friend to agitate and inform others. I have also been told that she went into the brick kilns and found out who were debt slaves, or bonded labourers. She protected the released debt slaves from their former 'owner' and became an important voice and leader. Together with some other former bonded labourers and people with knowledge of the legislation and with experience from trade unions, she founded an organisation against bonded labour. After a few years her organisation became part of a national network of similar organisations, which I call the Organisation. The Organisation gained international support, and became part of a transnational activist movement and of transnational support and struggle. My point is that Grace was both talked to, as a slave and as a citizen and thereby as someone with rights, at least officially. Two strong contradictory discourses about who she was, and thereby how life could be lived, had reached her and inner discursive border-struggle became possible. Maybe it was to these struggles Grace referred when I asked her about where she got the power to start her struggle and she pointed at her breast and said: "from here".

I have heard similar stories about messy transformative moments from other women living outside society, not counted as citizens worthy of protection, education and healthcare, learning about the concept of women's rights. "First we understood that men have rights, and then we learned that we also have rights", two interviewed women with experience of being bonded labourers living in the desert explained to me. They also expressed that it was a special moment to learn about this and that they remembered it very well. Others have talked about moments like these by saying that "everything changed". These stories of moments of change are of course hiding processes of change and contradictions going on for shorter or longer times. Grace, for example, had grown up with a father who had been critical of the system; she knew that it was wrong. She knew that she had more competences than being a slave. She could sing and created pieces of poetry. She, as well as the women in the desert, was already in a challenging, messy and transformative situation living between different discursive messages. But these stories about transformative moments are interesting, as they can be understood as an interruption by a legal system they maybe did not really know existed, or that it existed for them. They got another message from a parallel authority. The contradictory interpellations were strong (Mouffe 2013), creating discursive border struggles and thereby political space.

Of course, to be aware that there is a state that should recognise you is not the same as being recognised. To not be recognised, when you know you should, is an interpellation in itself. The state and the bounded labourer system are not the only ones who produce possible subject positions, even if they may be the strongest. Many of the subaltern persons I have met are talked to in different ways. I have visited groups of women who have been talked to as debt slaves as well as entrepreneurs by neo-liberal NGOs offering them micro credits, and, by other NGOs, as workers and activists who should abolish slavery through education. They meet patriarchal norms as well as norms on women's rights. In this messy situation it becomes possible to transform a situation into something new (Anzaldúa 1987). I have visited two villages where the women have assembled in order to improve conditions in their villages. They meet over religious borders and collect money in order to be less dependent both on NGOs, which come and go, and on the landlords or owners of the looms they have usually borrowed money from. They are critical against the government, which does not give them the education and healthcare they now know they have a right to; the governmental schools are either unsafe for their girls to go to, or of poor quality. In other words, they know they do not get the things they have a right to, or that they are not listened to and recognised by the state, which should support and protect them. Now they struggle for change, struggle against the hegemonic subject-object divide reiterated both nationally and transnationally. Naturalised positions of subordination have become political and the critique, both against international NGOs coming and going and a non-present state, has been possible to articulate, and an alternative identity has thereby emerged. It is an insecure situation, in which it becomes easy to be exploited again and again in different ways.

In the transnational, as well as the national, processes of transformation, and for feminists in the Global North as well as in Pakistan there is a need to recognise these political subjects and their struggle, and take part in transforming the subject-object divide. One of many ways to do this is to understand political subjectivity and develop an awareness of political conflicts as something that happens in and between different discourses and not as something that is just told or taught to someone. This understanding challenges the idea of political modernity as something coming from the Global North. To understand the discursive messiness as a politically unpredictable space opens up space for the many border struggles, transformations and emergences (cf. Rofel 2007; Rivera Cusicanqui 2012; Leve, 2014).

To acknowledge the messiness, and challenge the notion of a one-dimensional political development from North to South, it is of course important to also scrutinise dominant representations of subaltern groups as object for change and reinstallations of privileged subjects, an ambition the philosopher Antonio Gramsci himself had (Green 2002). Let me give an example of this from a land report on Pakistani people experiencing poverty, published by the Swedish International Development Cooperation Agency, (hereafter SIDA), in order to evaluate the Swedish civil society strategy in practice:

> All three Reality Checks raise important questions about whether any strategy of supporting improvements in children's rights or workers' rights as supported by SFOs can have any real impact in Pakistan unless there is a significant improvement in the delivery of government services, especially in health, education, social security, and workers' rights. While it is important to talk about "child rights" and "child protection," what does this mean in a context where children do not have the opportunity to access basic schooling?
>
> *(Goyder et al. 2014:5)*

The interpellation here to the government to achieve something is, of course, immensely important, and rights need to be recognised by someone in order to be rights. The absence of healthcare and schooling among groups in subaltern positions are expressions of a dehumanising process. However, there is also another narrative in the quotation, a reiteration of a discourse that reinstalls the privileged and the state as those capable of doing something, of being subjects. The idea that until government services are in place, the people who are not recognised as citizens should be unaware of their rights, is another way, as Spivak might have put it, to maintain the idea about the passive mass and the importance of it being 'rescued' (cf. Lundahl 2014:16). The need for the subalterns to be rescued, and their presumed inability to struggle for their own cause, can be compared to another discourse, which hinders subalterns from acting, to hinder, in this case, subaltern children to travel to meetings organised by transnational NGOs or to go to school. In interviews with activists, I have heard several examples of how people from the upper classes tell activists to stop giving poor children education, and Pakistani activists being hindered by pass-police to bring young child activists to international meetings because of the children's subaltern positions. They were supposed to stay outside and be hindered from becoming individuals with rights, and with rights to assembly on their own conditions (Butler 2015).

What a suggestion like the one in the SIDA land report misses, for example, is what it could mean to hear about one's rights, which, due to the national system, one does not yet have. Could it be an insight into the possibility of another life or another society? Could it be important for a political subjectivity to emerge? The concept of rights is often connected with, and criticised for, having a liberal bias, focusing on the individual and individuals' rights instead of demanding societal transformations. But when Grace heard about workers' rights, she became aware of a whole political conflict and the necessity to go and inform others in the group and take part in assembling people for change. There is, as Saba Mahmood underlines (2012), many ways to inhabit a subject position, even the one as utterly poor as a woman, as an illiterate bonded labourer and as a racialised Other. The discourse of rights as a transnational narrative, which articulates or connects with other understandings in multiple ways, makes it impossible to predict what sort of trajectory it will take, or its origin (cf. Chakrabarty, 2007). Workers' or women's rights could never be a single story, or have a single meaning. The concepts are part of on-going and quite unpredictable border-struggles. Something will happen with it when it is reiterated, when it emerges in different peoples' lives.

A transnational place, products and interruptions

Invited by the Swedish support organisation, Grace visited Sweden and Gothenburg in 2012 together with two other Pakistani women: the older, Shamim, from the Baluchistan city of Quetta, and Roksana, a young woman. Shamim worked as a nurse before she retired and became involved in the Organisation struggling against bonded labour. Roksana grew up in a family where her parents had been bonded labourers and her uncle had been, like Grace, a founding member of the anti-slavery organisation.

This time Grace and I met as two activists, and Grace was to speak at the international book fair in Gothenburg, together with Roksana. Shamim would translate their speeches. One of the founding members of the Swedish support organisation, Britt-Marie Klang, who has been involved in international work for change all her life, and has a strong postcolonial and critical consciousness, was hosting the three guests in her home. I remember that in the support organisation, we had a lot of confidence in Grace, but we were also worried. It was not possible to practise, to prepare issues, to plan for a panel. Grace had a terrible cough, she was tired, old, and stubborn, and could not remember what we tried to practise. Britt-Marie and I became self-critical: Why did we try to teach Grace how to speak to a European audience? Why did we press Grace into, what is for us, a familiar form of presentation – a panel, with someone asking and governing the 'conversation' and someone explaining and informing? We knew that she was a strong political voice back home. Why did we not trust her? Why did we not think it was possible to just listen to her? After a while we just asked her: "Can you not just talk, Grace? As you usually do, you tell them what is important".

With reference to the work of the Subaltern Studies Group, Spivak says that it is not about giving the subaltern a voice, "but to clear the space to allow it to speak" (Mukherjee 2016:69). It is an important remark, even if it re-establishes the hegemonic subject as the one who should clear up the space. But Spivak's point is that the problem is not the voice of the subaltern but the ignorance and discursive inability to listen to anyone 'outside' the hegemonic order, an ignorance we became an example of. However, what Grace did some days later was to blur the border between inside/outside this hegemony (cf. Trinh 2011). At this time Grace brought her red flag with a clenched fist up to the book fair stage and talked. Shamim tried her best to translate. Grace spoke about bonded labourers, their struggles and everyone understood that, but maybe even more important was the political performance. Grace talked, she raised her hands, clenched her fist, not one time but again and again. Her shawl fell to the side. I imagined, standing close to the stage, that her speech, or act, could change anyone. It was impossible not to be touched, be affected, be transformed. She also got big applause.

Afterwards I tried to understand what had happened. It had been a very affective moment. Maybe the sticky idea fixed to bodies of poor, illiterate women from Pakistan, so often understood in the West, but also in Pakistan, as a helpless and problematic mass, was interrupted for a moment (cf. Ahmed 2004). For sure, the Swedish support organisation had contributed by arranging a platform, from which to speak, which of course is a materiality of some importance. It hails or interpellates the speaker to speak and the listener to actually be silent and listen. However, Grace, who is politically experienced and politically educated after being an activist for such a long time, told another transcending and transforming story through her performance. By using recognisable transnational cultural artefacts and expressions from the discursive field of political struggle such as the red flag, the clenched fist, and her voice, she became a political subject transcending the position as a subaltern and thereby also the unifying dualism between the West and the rest, between the subordinated other and a political We. The artefacts, owned by all and none, possible to recognise and acknowledge as political signs of struggle, did something; they were, in that meaning, not simply used. They created connections and challenged colonial notions of other materialities such as a poor Pakistani woman with a body marked by hard work, wearing a shawl (cf. Anzaldúa 1987). The speech was held in a hall called 'The International Square', and the people in the audience were probably engaged in international solidarity work. They may also have had a desire to listen to an activist like Grace. Grace was perhaps not understood or recognised as a subaltern, a bonded labourer from a faraway country but as one of 'us', a modern activist. As a leader and activist she maybe became fetishised, gave a Western *us* some sort of revolutionary hope but did not actually challenge the notions about the mass or the faraway subaltern. Maybe Grace ceased to be a subaltern in that moment (Latour 2005; Trinh 2011). Mahmood writes that political projects are predicated upon affective, ethical and sensible capacities and that these projects necessitate a whole series of affective and sensible reorientations (2012:xiii). Grace's performance might have transcended the notion of the subaltern Other. It became a diffraction and, at least, a temporary mess.

Books and red materiality

I will now go back to Pakistan and more specifically to Sughran's office and to another transnational moment and entanglements full of different materialities such as books and money, ideological orientations, and visions. Sughran is in her thirties and lives in a small Pakistani town near the Thar Desert. She got her basic education as an adult. The first time I visited her and we had the opportunity to talk, she was both working as a 'women helper', employed by the government, and, as she says, as 'the boss' for some sewing and adult centres for women and girls, employed by the Organisation. She started our conversation with a question: "What do you want with the sewing centres?" She knew I was a researcher, that I had come in order to do an interview, but she also knew that I was a member of the Swedish support organisation. The question was asked, at least that was my interpretation, in a critical way. With that question, Sughran put me in a dubious subject position. For me, her question echoed a long tradition of people like me coming from the West: white, colonising, with a mission to fulfil. I mumbled something to the effect that *we* did not want anything; it was *they*, the Organisation in Pakistan, who had asked the Swedish support organisation to apply for money to run these centres. Sughran nodded. My answer was true but left out what I think both Sughran and I were very aware of. The transnational discourse about what is important to organise in order to make women's situation better is very strong. The Organisation as well as its supportive organisation in Sweden also knew what kind of project would attract money. Neither of these two organisations controlled or could influence the transnational discourses about the importance of vocational education, sewing machines and meeting places for women. We were, at least partly, subjected to them, reiterating and thereby materialising them.

But there were also, partly, other discursive reiterations that messed up the straightforward implementation of sewing centres. Sughran is a member of an international socialist organisation and had made a similar analysis of the situation for bonded labourers as Grace, and the red flag is also very present in Sughran's struggle. Before I met Sughran, I had already heard rumours about the library she had in her office. The interpreter, Najma Shahik, my research colleague from Sweden, Erika Alm, and I went to visit her. Her office was adjacent to a room where some girls attended a sewing machine course. Some of the sewing machines were, by the way, also paid for by a women's organisation in Europe. The small library, paid for entirely by one international organisation which was struggling for children's rights, and placed in Sughran's office and organised by her, consisted of two or three one-metre shelves. The library was meant for girls who had problems leaving their homes and was intended as a place to meet, where girls could both practise their reading skills and be 'safe' from rumours and harassment. These arguments are representative of dominant discourses about aid for women. However, the library contained books that may not have been in the mind of the donor. The books were written by Marx, Lenin and Mandela, and on Sugrahn's desk there was a copy of one of Rosa Luxemburg's books. Sughran picked it up and turned to us: "It is a book about change. Have you read it?" she asked. We shook our heads. But these books were of course familiar to us, and thereby, like the red flag, working as connecting products. They not only reminded us about the transnational space we inhabited. They were part of producing this transnational space as well and gave it alternative meanings and contexts (Latour 2005; Eriksson 2016). The international donation had in Sughran's hands merged with the transnational socialist organisation she was a very active member of. I suppose it is possible to say that the library might have taken another direction than what had been intended by the donor.

The critique against Western NGOs and how they interfere with what is described as 'other cultures' is very important, but could be developed further. The critique is often a very modern and linear story, denying, just like the donors themselves, possible border struggles, which I will call Sughran's initiative. Unsuccessful implementations of donors' will and money are usually limited by what is defined as corruption (cf. Bernal and Grewal 2014). The example of this small library shows that the money from donors connects with other materialities, ideologies and struggles, and new assemblages emerge. The assemblage with the office, the library and the different transnational organisations also enables other possible orientations to emerge or be stabilised. Political subjectivity and political space are not a one-way production; nor is the small library. Sughran messed up the discourse about what young women need and thereby made another orientation of the money possible. She is part of many local, translocal and transnational networks. She brings her socialist conviction and ideology into other less outspoken ideological rooms. Or, as she said on a female network meeting, arranged by the Organisation, in an attempt to empower her comrades:

We can change the system, we can do revolution!

A messiness of economic normativities

Sughrahn's socialist orientation and its frictional articulation with a donor's will to give aid to young women is just one example of how different economic discourses are reiterated (and sometimes merge with each other) in everyday life. An important starting point for me when discussing the role of the economy is that it is a discursive materiality, in line with Ernesto Laclau's and Chantal Mouffe's postmarxist perspective (1985). I find it impossible to try to understand the economy as a natural or fundamental force. It is inseparable from the on-going discursive production of it (Laclau and Mouffe 1985).

Let me go back to the annual book fair in Gothenburg in order to give more examples of how we are oriented by different economic discourses and ideologies in the activist struggle. During her speech, Grace, with her aim to abolish slavery and class hierarchies, criticised not only what she and others call a feudal system with landlords – the brick kiln owners, or the owners of the looms – but also her own government, and SIDA, who did not want to fund the Organisation's schools any more. She thereby criticised different and parallel economic systems that all together, in a messy way, conditioned the Organisation's work in Pakistan. She had to act in a multidirectional way. It was not enough to struggle against a global neo-liberal order, to take one example of a unifying economic story (cf. Rofel 2007; Rivera Cusicanqui 2012). We, in the small support organisation, also acted in accordance with different economic discourses. We criticised the economic order, the North/South divide, how Swedish companies used child labour in Pakistan, and how money from this child labour was part of the Swedish pension fund money. The struggle was about us, about our modern welfare, about our responsibility. While criticising this strong capitalist colonial discursive materiality, we were also governed by a neo-liberal transnational audit culture. At the book fair we, the support organisation, had a stand where we not only informed people passing by about where some of the money from our pension system came from and the existence of slavery in different parts of the world; we were also supposed to count the visitors and categorise them as women or men. The donors of the Swedish support organisation, SIDA, and its partner organisation, Forum Syd, required measurability. We had to struggle in a way that was countable (Biesta 2009). We were, then, both oriented by a neo-liberal discourse and by a radical critique against the capitalist system. The same goes for Sughran. At the same time she was talking about revolution, and struggled against the feudal system, she also needed to count the women who came to the sewing centre and give a report to the Organisation, who sent it to the support organisation in Sweden, who, in turn, sent it to SIDA. She also named herself both boss and socialist.

Sughran, as well as we in the support organisation, had to subject herself to the neo-liberal principle of measurability. I remember that we, in the support organisation, had a lot of discussions about this economic governing, constantly reminding ourselves of what the demands for evaluation did to our work, how it formed our applications and our practices, and how it forced us to do things that were measurable and possible to evaluate. This messy economic normativity (Brown 2015), which turned us into a certain kind of economic subject, oriented us and also the Organisation in Pakistan in many different directions (Biesta 2009). Anna Lowenhaupt Tsing writes that it has "become increasingly clear, all human cultures are shaped and transformed in long histories of regional-to-global networks of power, trade and meaning" (2005:3). Sughran's critical question when I first came to her office shows that we have different positions in the transnational sphere historically as well as in this situation, where I was closer to the money. But the critique also shows that there are many parallel economic transnational discourses that connect us, give us similar experiences of being governed, and we are governed in different directions. "We get", as Anzaldúa wrote, "multiple, often opposing messages" and "we develop a tolerance for differences" (1987:77–80). Neither of us are faithful to neo-liberal principles; they do not take over our lives or our activism. The different economic discourses remind us of the political and contingent quality of economic discourses, and the struggle for economic hegemony going on all around the world.

Messy education

I have already touched upon the question of education several times. Education is understood around the world as the solution to poverty and there are many donors who support educational projects (cf. Lindblad and Popkewitz 2004, Ball 2012). Others underline the need for education in order to become a political voice, to be able to take part, to be 'empowered'. The Organisations', the support organisation's, and many other NGOs' struggle for education is in line with this discourse. The Organisations want to, as they put it, "struggle against slavery through education". However, even if the discourse about the need for education is strong, and even if I personally agree strongly with the need for and right to good education, I have also criticised this discourse for a long time (Martinsson 2017). Among other things, I have argued that it makes it difficult to understand illiterate people as possible political subjects. They are supposed to be educated first, before being able to take part. They become a mass, in a typical subaltern position, an object on the outside for others to develop, to transform into subjects. But, as Grace has also reminded me, keeping someone outside education reconstructs a subaltern position in a powerful way (cf. Spivak 2012).

The struggle for education is also a struggle for recognition, and, as I will now try to show, this could also become a situation of transnational messiness. When Grace came to Sweden to inform us about the struggle against bonded labour, I understood after a while that she had a hope of her own, namely that the Swedish support organisation would support the Pakistani Organisation's schools again, a support that had once been of importance and was built on money from SIDA. The Swedish support organisation had applied for money and the schools had become the joint work of activists in Pakistan and in Sweden. Grace's very strong engagement in the schools could maybe be connected to the moment when someone else told her about the content in the pamphlet. She knew that a text, and the ability to gain knowledge about its content, could change one's life, and of course she had experienced illiteracy herself. But the support from SIDA was on a project basis and after ten years the Swedish authority withdrew the funding. Grace was told that it was impossible to get more money from the Swedish state, that it was hopeless to try to convince people otherwise, but, as we understood it, she was trying anyway. I asked her some years later: "Why can your own governments not pay for the schools, why can they not give the Pakistani children education? Why do you want *our* government to pay for another nation's schools?" She answered that Pakistani government schools were no good. She gave me examples. I agreed. I knew. I had not only heard many stories about it during my fieldwork; I had also read Pakistani academic critique of these schools (Hussain 2012; Siddiqui 2012). I knew. Many children did not have any schools to go to at all. I had met some of them as well. The goal of the Organisation, "to end slavery through education", is built on the idea that if the children could read and count it would not be possible to fool them into becoming debt slaves and bonded labourers. The stick, used for corporal punishment, was forbidden in these schools and it was important that the children learned to question and challenge paradigms of obedience, and they were trained to be confident. For Grace, as for the Organisation she once founded together with others, education was therefore a way to challenge the class hierarchy, to challenge the brick kiln owners' exploitation of workers, to challenge the power of the feudal leaders, locally as well as nationally.

Grace's struggle shows that the transnational, non-governmental organisations had produced a sort of orientation towards a transnational sphere or to faraway states rather than towards the Pakistani one. In that way, transnational NGOs are both part of the production of reluctant and ignorant citizens, not willing to recognise the state, which did not recognise them, and in reproducing colonial subjectivities, recognising faraway states as the true organisers of the world (Foucault 2008; Grewal 2005). Another way to understand it is that the political struggle is just moved from a national arena to a transnational one. If people like Grace are not recognised by their own state, they struggle to be recognised by someone else.

Grace's relationship to the Pakistani state is complex in many ways. She has been working politically since she understood that it was against the law to have bonded labourers. In that way the state has been of tremendous importance for her. The legislation had interpellated or talked to her in a way that was new for her, and said it would protect her against what she had been subjected to, and thereby transformed her subjectivity. But she and her people are still suffering; they cannot access their rights as pupils, citizens, women or as workers. The interpellation of the state is therefore contradictory. To ask for recognition by someone else, by a transnational imagined community, might be very understandable. In that sense Grace acts as a global citizen (Grewal 2005).

The educational look

Today some of the schools Grace struggles for try to survive without support from any faraway state. Some of them have closed. Instead, the Swedish state supports vocational training centres for adults, intended to contribute to making women especially aware of their rights and giving them places to meet. Grace and Sunita, who I will soon come back to, both have strong political goals connected to education beyond the notion that all that is needed is knowledge about work and to get a profession in order to support oneself. I remember when I first heard that the Organisation in Pakistan wanted support in order to arrange education for girls to open beauty parlours. I reacted with a sense of unease. Beauty parlours? At this time I somewhat sceptically imagined beauty parlours as places where young women would learn how to dress up for men, where they were supposed to learn how to be beautiful. And was that not a reiteration of the notion that women should get education in order to be good wives and mothers? The others in the support organisation agreed with me to some extent, but they also asked me: "Who are you to know what is best for them?" And I agreed. It was argued that it would create a meeting place for girls, where they could "come out to a safe place" and of course a beauty parlour could earn some money. And I agreed again. And of course information about their rights should be given. I agreed again. And maybe, it provided the possibility to have fun. Yes, of course, to actually have fun. If I do not agree before, I really agreed about this.

The Swedish gender researcher Ulrika Dahl (2014) has written about how femininity is understood in disparaging terms, also, or maybe especially, among feminists. I was reminded of this and it affected my view. Some years after the first confrontation with what I thought was a strange idea about education in the struggle for women's rights or against bonded labour, I asked the then 17-year-old Sunita, coming from a subaltern context, what she liked most about her work as a teacher, and she answered: "I mostly like to do hair styling as a beauty teacher". I had noticed how she loved to dress in beautiful dresses, how she changed between Western and Pakistani clothes when she once, as a representative for the Organisation, visited Sweden, and also between different Pakistani outfits, opening up different possible positions to identify with, becoming herself in different ways (cf. Dahl 2014). In her political speeches Sunita also made brilliant connections between her work in a beauty parlour and the struggle for rights, education and better conditions for young women. She continuously worked across different kinds of borders built on notions of gender, transformed from the poor position her family was once subjected to through clothes and make up. She showed me that the beauty parlour was also a messy place with political potentials.

Sunita also taught me something about the role of the family. A lesson that of course messed up my individualised worldview again. Like many of the activists I have met, she has become an activist, struggling for individual rights such as the right for education for girls, workers' rights and the right to divorce, in a context where the role of the family is very strong. She has received her education and also learned English at one of the Organisation's schools. She is eager to talk about the right to education, and women's rights. But it is not the NGOs generally, or the Organisation in particular, that she is most grateful for; it is her dad and family. I have reflected upon her and others' gratitude towards their families many times. The families, who so often are described as a problem not only by Western feminists but also by many of the women I have interviewed and followed, as well as by activists, Pakistani intellectuals, and researchers, are also often pointed out as a unity of importance for change. Sunita, as well as Grace (who is divorced), talked about their families as platforms for their struggle. Sunita talks about her strong family and especially her father, who always supported her, and gave her the possibility to receive education and work as a beauty parlour teacher. Grace talked about her supportive father and her supportive children. These stories, accompanied by the worldwide story about Malala Yousafzai (Yousafzai and Lamb 2013) and her father, point to the role of the father and of the family in the struggle for rights and for education. Many of the interviewees walked from door to door in their neighbourhoods accompanied by their father, in order to both invite women to different courses and convince them or their families of the importance of education for women. These stories say something about the limitations of struggle for change and the necessity of having the family with you. But, the father follows the young women's initiative, and the family becomes not only a conservative assemblage but also sometimes a community for change.

The desire for education, the hope connected with it, and the role of the family was also emphasised in an interview Britt-Marie Klang, an interpreter, and I once did with a young woman who studied at an adult centre organised by the Pakistani Organisations seeking to abolish slavery through education. She had struggled for education a lot after being married. She wanted so badly to go to school. She persuaded her husband to let her go, and after that he had to persuade his parents as well. In a society with a long history of patriarchal norms, and colonial as well as local and national leaders who have actively made education for women into a non-issue (cf. Rose 2006), this struggle by a this young woman must be understood as part of a transformative force. She understood herself as someone other than who she was meant to be. But the story has another twist as well. After telling us about her struggle for education, she turned to us and said, "they say I look educated" and we all nodded and said, "Yes, yes absolutely". And we meant it, she really 'looked' educated. So, what did we see? What did we recognise? How did we differentiate people from people? What I think we saw, and what I think she wanted us to see, was respectability; to be educated was to be respectable, to look nice, in order to be someone, to be one who could take part. To moralise about this in any way is ignorant. But it is important to see that, even if the ambition is to transform society, education also becomes an individual project to become someone, to leave the disrespected mass behind in order to become someone who is listened to, not ignored, and thereby respectable.

Conclusions

In this chapter I have focused especially on moments of changed directions, multiple messages, and a messiness of meanings and materialities. I have written about situations when something happened with a person's understanding of herself and of the society around her; when materiality, such as a directed donation, takes a new direction in the hands of an NGO employee who is also an activist; when an audience in the West was reached and might have been changed by a person coming from what is usually understood as a 'mass' in need of faraway help. The role of family as a politically contested community has been discussed. I have also written about discourses re-establishing privileged subjects and an objectified 'mass' and, in line with this, a notion of modern linearity and orderliness.

These moments and situations of transformations have been characterised by a lot of different messages and interpellations and a presence of different discourses, ideologies, norms and materialities. I have analysed these conditions as 'messy' and unavoidable. One example is the existence of parallel, but connected, economic discourses such as the colonial, feudal, capitalist/neo-liberal and socialist, and how the activists, myself and the Organisation as well as support organisations are part of this messiness. We move between these discourses that also govern us and make us into different subjects, letting them merge or keeping them apart. But this messiness, with reference to Anzaldúa (1987), is also a political possibility. This messiness shows that the economic order is not fundamental. The economic systems are constructions and there are other possibilities. Neo-liberal interventions are never just smoothly implemented, neither in a country like Sweden nor in Pakistan. It is one of several discourses, articulated in far from predictable ways together with, but also parallel to, other discourses and ambitions.

Even if my examples are mostly from Pakistan, it has been the transnational sphere I have been most interested in. I have wondered how transnational feminism can ever be possible? To focus on the messiness, the many parallel and contradictory discourses, that individuals, single organisations as well as nations are reiterating and transforming around the world, is also a way of challenging the notion of modern orderliness, of a single direction, one from North/West to South/East, from subject to object. It challenges a modern understanding of space and temporality, of homogenous identities and subjectivities, the notion that someone is first (West, middle class) and then leads others in how to organise their lives (cf. Massey 2005). When one disregards the dominant discourses and instead examines the space between them, a multitude of political emergences appear. However, the transnational situation risks recreating a colonial order. If the state does not recognise you as a citizen worthy of protection and rights, you might start to ignore it. The risk is that the colonial orientation reappears and people recognise faraway states as the true organisers of the world. As a result, they might lose their hope again.

Through ethnographic work it is possible to focus on the contingency and multidimensionality of the everyday life of politics, the banal unpredictability of the social, and thereby the many on-going afflicting as well as hopeful emergences of society. To theoretically embrace messiness is also a way of thinking beyond big narratives about a global community where colonialism seems naturalised, and the West is reconstructed as the origin of democracy. It is a way of challenging the notion of linear modernity, where the West takes the lead, as well as a way of challenging the emergence of the European subject. To challenge the notion of a linear modernity is, as so many decolonial feminist researchers have noted, an unavoidable condition for transnational feminism to emerge. By focusing on the messiness, it also becomes possible to challenge the ignorance of the knowledge production of others among Western people who want to make a difference, want to take part in development, want to change faraway societies, with the aspiration of having the solution to what is understood to be the problem.

Note

1 A very special and warm thank you to Grace Bibi, Sughran Khaskhelly and Sunita Devi.

References

Ahmed, S., (2004) *The cultural politics of emotion*. Edinburgh: Edinburgh University Press.

Anzaldúa, G., (1987) *Borderlands. La Frontera*. San Francisco: Spinsters.

Ball, S.J., (2012). *Global Education*. New York: Routledge.

Bernal, V., and Grewal, I., (2014) *Theorizing NGOs: States, feminisms, and neoliberalism*. Durham, NC: Duke University Press.

Biesta, G., (2009) *Good education in an age of measurement: Ethics, politics, democracy*. Boulder, CO: Paradigm Publisher.

Brah, A., (2003) Diaspora, border, and transnational identitites. *In*:Lewis, R. and Mills, S. (eds.) *Postcolonial theory: A reader*. New York: Routledge. pp. 613–634.

Brown, W., (2015) *Undoing the demos: Neoliberalism's stealth revolution*. Cambridge, MA: MIT Press.

Butler, J., (1990) *Gender trouble: Feminism and the subversion of identity*. London: Routledge.

Butler, J., (2015) *Notes toward a performative theory of assembling*. London: Harvard University Press.

Chakrabarty, D., (2007) *Provincializing Europe: Postcolonial thought and historical difference*. New ed. Princeton, NJ: Princeton University Press.

Dahl, U., (2014) *Skamgrepp: Femme-inistiska essäer* [Underhand: Femme-nistic essays]. Stockholm: Leopard förlag.

Eriksson, M., (2016) *Berättelser om Breivik: Affektiva läsningar av våld och terrorism* [*Narratives about Breivik*]. Göteborg: Makadam förlag.

Foucault, M., (2008) *The birth of biopolitics: Lectures at the Collége de France, 1978–1979*. Basingstoke: Palgrave Macmillan.

Goyder, H., Ali, S.R., Quasmi, M., and Haider, M.N., (2014) *Pakistan country report*. Stockholm: Sipu.

Green, M., (2002) Gramsci Cannot Speak: Presentations and Interpretations of Gramsci's Concept of the Subaltern. *Rethinking Marxism*. 14(3). pp. 1–24.

Greiner, C., and Sakdapolak, P., (2013) Translocality: Concepts, Applications and Emerging Research Perspectives. *Geography Compass*. 7(5). pp. 373–384.

Grewal, I., (2005) *Transnational America: Feminisms, diasporas, neoliberalism*. Durham, NC: Duke University.

Hussain, K., (2012) *Rethinking education: Critical discourses and society*. Islamabad: Narratives.

Laclau, E., and Mouffe, C., (1985) *Hegemony and socialist strategy*. London: Verso.

Latour, B., (2005) *Reassembling the social: An introduction to actor-network-theory*. Oxford: Oxford University Press.

Leve, L., (2014) Failed development and rural revolution in Nepal: Rethinking subaltern consciousness and women empowerment. *In*:Bernal, V., and Grewal, I., (eds.). *Theorizing NGOs: States, feminisms, and neoliberalism*. Durham, NC: Duke University Press. pp. 50–92.

Lindblad, S., and Popkewitz, T., (eds.) (2004) *Educational restructuring: International perspectives on traveling policies*. Greenwich, CN: Information Age Publishing.

Lundahl, M., (2014). Inledning [Introduction]. *In*: Spivak, G.C. (ed.). *Subalternisering och den globala utopin* [*Subalternisation and the utopia of the global*]. Hagerstown: Tankekraft förlag. pp. 11–25.

Mahmood, S., (2012) *Politics of piety: The Islamic revival and the feminist subject*. Princeton, NJ: Princeton University Press.

Martinsson, L., (2017) Messy norms and desire for education. *In*: Reimers, E., and Martinsson, L., (eds.). *Education and political subjectivities in neoliberal times and places: Emergences of norms and possibilities*. London: Routledge. pp. 31–49.

Martinsson, L., and Reimers, E., (2017) Introduction. *In*: Reimers, E., and Martinsson, L., (eds.). *Education and political subjectivities in neoliberal times and places: Emergences of norms and possibilities*. London: Routledge. pp. 1–13.

Massey, D.B., (2005) *For space*. London: SAGE.

Mouffe, C., (2013) Hegemony and new political subjects. *In*: Martin, J., (ed.). *Chantal Mouffe: Hegemony, radical democracy and the political*. London: Routledge. pp. 45–57.

Mukherjee, A., (2016) Border worlds. *In*: Braidotti, R., and Gilroy, P., (eds.). *Conflicting humanities*. New York: Bloomsbury Academic. pp. 61–75.

Paulson, S., (2016). *Critical intimacy: An interview with Gayatri Chakravorty Spivak*. https://lareviewofbooks.org/article/critical-intimacy-interview-gayatri-chakravorty-spivak/#!

Rivera Cusicanqui, S., (2012). Ch'ixinakax utxiwa: A Reflection on the Practices and Discourses of Decolonization. *The South Atlantic Quarterly*. 111(1). pp. 95–109.

Rofel, L., (2007) *Desiring China: Experiments in neoliberalis, sexuality, and public culture*. Durham, NC: Duke University Press.

Rose, S., (2006) *Gender, nation, state in Pakistan – Shifting body politics*. Lahore: Vanguards Books.

Shaheed, F., and Shaheed, A., (2011) *Great ancestors: Women claiming rights in Muslim contexts*. Karachi: Oxford University Press.

Siddiqui, S., (2012) *Education inequalities and freedom: A socio-political critique*. Islamabad: Narratives.

Spivak, G.C., (1988) Can the subaltern speak?*In*: Nelson, C. and Grossberg, L. (eds.). *Marxism and the interpretation of culture*. London: Macmillan. pp. 271–313.

Spivak, G.C., (2012) *An aesthetic education in the era of globalization*. London: Harvard University Press.

Trinh, M.-h. T., (2011) *Elsewhere, within here*. New York: Routledge.

Tsing, A.L., (2005) *Friction: An ethnography of global connection*. Princeton, NJ: Princeton University Press.

Yousafzai, M., and Lamb, C., (2013) *I am Malala: The girl who stood up for education and was shot by the Taliban*. London: Phoenix.

3

WOMEN RESISTING BORDER REGIMES

Two case studies from Eastern and Northern Europe

Mia Liinason and Olga Sasunkevich

Introduction

In this chapter, we address the possibilities of women's resistance to border regimes. We understand border regimes broadly – as a literal embodiment of the state control over its territorial integrity and national purity and as a symbolic construct that represents our existential need to differentiate between people and to ascribe them to certain groups. The cases we analyse in the chapter show how resistance to literal state borders and migration policies simultaneously enables women to oppose inequalities and hierarchies imposed on them by the powerful. Following Lugones (2003), we consider cross-border movement, whether geographic mobility across state borders or symbolic transgression of social and cultural boundaries, as empowering. Our focus is on border struggles (Mezzadra and Neilson 2013), or various tactics by which women challenge the differentiating power of borders and turn regulations of border regimes to their advantage.

The cases we examine are collected in the framework of two different research projects which are discussed in more detail in related sub-chapters. The scope and aim of the projects varied and they were implemented independently. Therefore, we use our own voices ('I') when we discuss the cases. The projects examine border experiences of women whose origin, age, educational background and social status as well as the aim of border crossings vary significantly. Olga Sasunkevich's research is about heterosexual middle-aged or elderly women from a small Belarusian town who use the border between Belarus and Lithuania to gain financially in the situation of economic marginalisation. Mia Liinason's case covers the experience of two educated women from Sweden and Ukraine with artistic ambitions who consider border crossings as a part of their professional development and integration into the global artistic community and who consciously challenge hierarchies and restrictions imposed by border regimes through their same-sex marriage. In spite of the differences in the positions the women from our cases occupy in their local communities, within the national states of their origin and on a global level, we also see commonalities in the ways they resist border challenges. We consider their border struggle as a response to various types of marginalisation (economic, social, political, judicial) that women encounter in their lives. The fact that women of different backgrounds are unanimous in questioning border persistence gives us hope that the injustice of border regimes and bordering practices can be challenged by a myriad of small and often unnoticeable but yet powerful actions, which we consider as practices of resistance.

Border theory and spatial meaning of resistance

Our theoretical standpoint is based on a twofold understanding of borders. On the one hand, the cases we discuss deal with literal territorial and political borders of the European Union (EU). On the other hand, we interpret border in a broader sense, as a metaphor of social processes which lead to othering and ordering (see van Houtum and van Naerssen 2001; van Houtum 2010). We consider border regimes as symbols of national states' sovereignty, which are at the same time practices of social differentiation and inequality production.

In the scholarly literature, a number of critical voices have been raised in relation to the EU border policy. Long before 'the refugee crisis' of 2015–2016, the EU's approaches towards asylum seekers and migrants had been criticised for their unfairness, the lack of transparency and a discriminatory attitude towards people from outside of the EU (e.g. Andreas and Snyder 2000; Grabbe 2000; Lemberg-Pedersen 2012, 2015; Zielonka 2003). New security regimes implemented by the EU created a new colonial European frontier that "unlike the traditional colonial border which existed in geographical space because of their enforcement by European territorial regime, [...] is geographically dispersed and instituted by means of various regulatory practices" (Andersen and Sandberg 2012: 4). These practices are designated as a 'paper wall' (Gawlewicz and Yndigegn 2012; Walters 2006) built up from bureaucracies and numerous administrative procedures which one has to undergo in order to be allowed to enter the EU. They are aimed at differentiating between the 'wanted' – those who contribute to the well-being and comfort of the 'gated community' of the EU (van Houtum and Pijpers 2007) – and the 'unwanted' who threaten the comfort and bring a burden. The differentiation between the 'wanted' and 'unwanted' occurs along various lines – from educational background and economic status to gender and sexuality.

Beyond the pragmatic meaning of border control, the differentiating function of borders is also existential. The border as a process, a practice of othering and ordering (van Houtum and van Naerssen 2001), provides individuals with a sense of collective self ('us' vs 'them'). Balibar defines this process as:

> ...the subjective interiorisation of the idea of the border – the way individuals represent their place in the world to themselves by tracing in their imaginations

> impenetrable borders between groups to which they belong or by subjectively appropriating borders assigned to them from on high, peacefully and otherwise.
>
> *(Balibar 2004: 8)*

Thus, bordering is an integral part of our self-identification and understanding of the position we held vis-à-vis multiple others who surround us.

In this chapter, we investigate how two functions of borders – the pragmatic and literal function of selective control and the existential function of symbolic differentiation – intersect. We assume that the latter is inherently inscribed into the former. In other words, the practices and procedures of border bureaucracy (e.g. application for visas or asylum) are at least implicitly based on the notion of a division into 'us' and 'them', the 'wanted' and the 'unwanted', the 'normal' and the 'deviant'. People who want to enter the EU have to comply with the idea of a normal decent citizen, the one "born in the 'normal' fabric of the so-called European culture and believed to be a product of an imagined and invented European and culturally homogeneous civilisation and enlightenment" (van Houtum and Pijpers 2007: 296). The 'wanted' of the European migration are those who meet the standards of normativity, whether economic, racial or sexual. The latter does not mean that LGBTQ-people are not accepted under these conditions. It rather means that they also have to correspond to certain ideas of homonormativity (Duggan 2003; Stryker 2008) in order to prove that they fit (Murray 2014).

Henk van Houtum (2010) rightfully considers borders as the embodiment of the Law. To wait at the border is to wait before the Law, according to his argument. Waiting before the Law requires docility and disciplining. In exchange, this waiting promises "final appreciation by the Other" through which the social Self is constructed (van Houtum 2010: 290). Although docility and self-disciplining have agentive potential (Mahmood 2001, 2005), in van Houtum's interpretation they represent subordination to the dominant order where individuals have little or no influence on borders. Bordering is a strategy, which, in de Certeau's terms, is the domain of the powerful (de Certeau 1988); it "reifies power, displaces others, and depersonalises, neutralises, fills and contains space" (van Houtum and van Naerssen 2001: 126).

Focusing on the experience of those who presumably wait outside the border for the acceptance by the Other, we, however, aspire to pay attention to border struggles, "those struggles that take shape around the ever more unstable line between 'inside' and 'outside', between inclusion and exclusion" (Mezzadra and Neilson 2013: 13). While bordering is a strategy, we are interested in tactics, i.e. everyday practices of manoeuvring within the space of the powerful (de Certeau 1988). We examine how 'unwanted' women of different ages, class and social status undermine the power of border regimes. We are interested not only in how people take part in the making of borders but also in how their bordering practices lead to political subjectivity (Mezzadra and Neilson 2013) and empowerment (Andersen and Sandberg 2012).

Being rooted in this processual interpretation of borders, domination and resistance are understood as spatial concepts. As the spatial is neither static nor passive, spatiality is always connected with time (Massey 2005). To visualise the spatiality of domination and resistance, María Lugones uses the metaphor of a map, drawn by those in positions of dominant power: "All the roads and places are marked as places you may, must, or cannot occupy. Your life is spatially mapped by power" (Lugones 2003: 8). Such a thought experiment, Lugones continues, enables one to notice the "tensions, the small deviations [...] within the spatiality of power" (2003: 9). At this point, she writes, we have reached the spot where we can start to talk about resistance. Within and against the spatiality of dominations, resistance can be exercised in different ways: travelling, walking, hanging out, trespassing or pilgrimages are examples mentioned by Lugones where oppression is noted and where there is movement against it. However, central to this understanding is that such resistance locates one "*inside* the *processes* of production of multiple realities" (Lugones 2003: 17). The shift to a practice of different constructions can only take place from within such processes and Lugones thus defines resistance as a response, as a "thoughtful, often complex, devious, insightful response, insightful to the very intricacies of the structure of what is being resisted" (2003: 29). In this chapter, we analyse the spatiality of domination by attending to the multiple modes of marginalisation or limitation that the women in our case studies were experiencing. As we will show, their active response to these forms of marginalisation – their resistance – takes different shapes, but all are located inside particular processes of production of multiple realities: bordering, manoeuvring, resisting. Their actions illuminate the spatiality of domination at the same time as they visualise tensions, deviations or transgressions from such modes of power.

In her theorisation about oppression and resistance, Lugones takes departure from de Certeau's (1988) distinction of strategy and tactic as two modes of everyday life practice. In similarity with Lugones, we have found it useful to include these notions in our analysis. However, while de Certeau understands strategy and tactic as separated from each other, we would like to highlight possible linkages between the two, seeing that tactics can also involve strategies, for example when tactical forms of resistance slip into modes of dominance or when strategical forces make use of tactical moves, to expand or retain dominance. As defined by de Certeau, strategy is "the calculus of force-relationships", the capability of those with power to change the spaces and practices they operate within (1988: xix; Round et al. 2010). As examples of places from where strategy is exercised, de Certeau mentions the state, the academy, or the economic market. Tactics, in turn, are "victories of the 'weak'" (de Certeau 1988: xix). The idea of the tactic describes the situation of those who do not have resources to change the structure, but who manipulate resources or events within the structure, adjusting to structural constraints, or utilise openings in the logics of domination and turn these into an advantage. "The place of a tactic", de Certeau argues, "belongs to the other" (Ibid). As a result, tactics are mobile forms of resistance that operate on a field and under circumstances not of their own making.

One concern that occupied us during the work on this chapter is the limit of tactics as resistance. While tactics, as we will demonstrate, visualise modes of domination and can create a space in-between structures, during our work on this chapter we struggled with two questions linked to the scope and depth of this form of resistance. Our first concern dealt with the question of whether tactics can actually change structures. This question is not, in our view, related to the fragmented or diffuse character of tactics. After all, tactics are an insightful, alert or devious response to domination, and follow the dispersed character of such modes of power which we understand as one of the strengths of tactics. Rather, it is the exchange between domination (strategy) and resistance (tactic) that concerns us, since that could imply that resistance cannot move beyond the forms of life and sociality that dominant powers construct/control. That would present a scenario where strategy in the long run determines the outcome. However, thinking about strategies and tactics as two distinct practices of everyday life involves understanding that strategy needs to respond to tactics, as much as tactics respond to strategies. That implies that strategies have to adjust to tactics, as they are being transformed from within – although this may be a slow and unpredictable process of transformation.

Our second concern was related to the question of solidarity: what do tactics do to solidarity? When a tactic manipulates or takes advantage of openings in the logic of strategy, it uses existing conceptual, material, or institutional limitations to reshape the "meaning of the possible" (Lugones 2003: 226). While in our work we often found such tactics important and inspiring, it seemed to us that, if the actions exercised lacked an awareness of solidarity, they could risk strengthening certain relations of power since tactics are exercised in tacit collusion with certain dominant powers (Liinason 2018). Without aiming to strive for purity or firm positionings of oppositionality (Puar 2008), it appears to us as if this question ultimately depends on the tactics exercised and the modes of domination resisted; thus, it is an empirical question that needs to be explored more fully.

Departing from those theoretical standpoints, we analyse in the following two case studies how women, who in different ways are 'unwanted', challenge the power of border regimes by manipulating resources or taking advantage of certain openings in the logics of these regimes. The first case study explores the resistance of women engaged in informal cross-border trade on the border between Belarus and Lithuania. The second case study analyses the resistance of two women, one from Ukraine and the other from Sweden, involved in an intimate relationship across geographic and symbolic borders.

Informal cross-border economy as gendered resistance to multiple modes of marginalisation

In the focus of this case is the resistance of women engaged in informal cross-border trade (ICBT) on the border between Belarus and Lithuania. The border between these two former Soviet republics is a relatively recent phenomenon. Throughout history, the region where the Belarus-Lithuania border lies belonged to various state entities. The region was divided only in 1940 when Lithuania was annexed by the USSR and the border between two Soviet republics – Belorussian SSR and Lithuanian SSR – was established. After World War II, the border functioned as an administrative boundary within the Soviet Union. It was completely permeable and did not have a significant impact on the daily life of borderlanders. The border acquired its national status only in the early 1990s when Lithuania proclaimed independence from the Soviet Union in 1990 and the USSR ceased its existence in 1991. In 2004 after Lithuania became a member of the EU, the Belarus-Lithuania border received the status of the external border of the EU. In 2007 it also became one of the Schengen borders in Eastern Europe.

In my ethnographic study conducted in this region in 2010–2012, I focused on female experience of ICBT, "a form of arbitrage […], understood as the exploitation of differences in prices and exchange rates over time and space via circulation activities" (Williams and Baláž 2002: 323). My data include fieldwork diaries and 14 semi-structured interviews with female traders of various ages (25–78). Most of the informants originate from a small town on the Belarusian side of the border. Half of them are widowed, divorced or single, with or without children. Some of them have university or college education; others finished only secondary school. Trade is not the single source of income for any of my respondents. The money earned from trading practices often supplements the official salary or the state pension. Women are largely concentrated in small-scale smuggling and trading. They bring from Belarus to Lithuania cigarettes, alcohol and medicine and from Lithuania to Belarus clothes, household chemistry and groceries.

Women most often use public transportation for their trade-related trips to Lithuania. My first encounters with female traders happened in 2006 when I became a Masters student in gender studies at the European Humanities University, the Belarusian University in Lithuanian exile. Travelling on a regular basis between my native city of Minsk, the Belarusian capital, and Vilnius, the capital of Lithuania, I observed the economic activities of loud adventurous women in their 40s–60s speaking a mixture of Russian and Belarusian with sprinkles of Polish words. As with many other passengers travelling along this route, I initially intended to distance myself from these women as if their behaviour and the purpose of travel were perceived as an inappropriate experience of cross-border mobility. The easiest way to draw a line between traders and other passengers was to refuse assisting women in their entrepreneurial activities. When traders approached passengers asking them to help carry goods across the border in order to avoid customs inspection, many declined to do so. Some people (including myself) found good excuses, saying that they/we carried goods ourselves. Others expressed their difference more openly, either demonstratively refusing to communicate with women or even shaming them for being involved in illicit trading.

However, my deeper immersion into gender theory made me reconsider this activity from the feminist standpoint. Although I understand the importance of class and age differences in our experience, I also see some parallels between the mobility of traders and my own, academic, mobility. While the latter may seem to be the experience of the more privileged, I notice striking commonalities in our experiences, including the fact that we do not take our mobility for granted. We know that it is determined by the existing border regime. We also know that in order to obtain the privilege of mobility we first have to obtain visas, i.e. to subordinate ourselves to the political order where mobility is not an unquestionable right but a hierarchised unequal experience. I also feel that we stay on the move for similar reasons, that our mobility is our resource to achieve a better life, even though our understanding of 'good life' may differ. At the same time, I also share traders' understanding of mobility which reveals moral and physical demands that constant cross-border movement requires from women. The ambiguous character of cross-border mobility of informal traders is pointed out by Mirjana Morokvasic who argues:

> mobility as a strategy can be empowering, a resource, a tool for social innovation and agency and an important dimension of social capital – if under the migrants' own control. However, mobility may reflect increased dependencies, proliferation of precarious jobs and, as in the case of trafficking in women, lack of mobility and freedom.
>
> *(Morokvasic 2004: 7)*

Yet, in this chapter I want to focus on the resistant potential of mobility and cross-border trade for women. Mobility and cross-border trade are interconnected in two ways here. First, they predetermine each other. On the one hand, cross-border trade is impossible without cross-border mobility; on the other hand, access to mobility often initiates trading practices. The second interconnection is rather conceptual. Both cross-border mobility and cross-border trade can be understood as resistance from within the structure, "a space of possibilities" (Morokvasic 2004: 9), "a weapon of the weak" (Scott 1985) to challenge the power hierarchies.

I make this assumption combining two texts. The first – theoretical – is Lugones' book *Pilgrimages/Peregrinajes* (2003) where she uses spatial metaphors of pilgrimage, trespassing, travelling, walking, hanging out to underline a logic of resistance in the situation where it remains unexplored or invisible. Following Turner's understanding of pilgrimages, Lugones considers the movement of people as an important experience "that loosens the hold of institutional, structural descriptions in the creation of liminal spaces" (Lugones 2003: 6). Thus, in a broad sense she sees movement/mobility as an important way to "go in-between structures", "to be without structure and thus without structural construction" (Lugones 2003: 61). Another piece of research is the empirical study of domestic food production in Ukraine, where the authors (Round et al. 2010) consider the myriad of informal economic activities existing in post-socialist Eastern Europe as "spaces of resistance and coping tactics" in response to different types of marginalisation (Round et al. 2010: 1198). To recognise the active – resistant position of 'the weak', both of the texts depart from de Certeau's (1988) distinction of strategies and tactics as two modes of daily life practices.

Approaching ICBT and mobility as coping tactics in response to marginalisation, I suggest considering informal economic practices in a broad sense as "complex cultural and socioeconomic phenomena" (Smith 2010: 47, cited in Sasunkevich 2014). Thus, women involved in ICBT resist multiple types of marginalisation, not only the economic one. Drawing on my fieldwork, I distinguish three types of marginalisation that women challenge through their trading practices and their "*know-how-to-move*"(Tarrius 1992, cited in Morokvasic 2004: 14): 1) economic, i.e. the national and transnational economic order; 2) political, in particular, control over cross-border mobility and unequal access to mobility by people of different nationalities; and 3) social – ideas about women's belonging and societal responsibilities and about a 'proper place' for women.

The idea that informal economy resists economic marginalisation lies on the surface. Being involved in ICBT, women resist multiple economic pressures. Informal trade helps them cope with the low incomes they earn from their primary sources such as wage employment or a state pension. Cross-border trade is also a way to avoid economic deprivation caused by gender segregation and the gender wage gap which characterises the labour market in Belarus. Buying or selling semi-legally goods brought from Belarus to Lithuania or vice versa, women openly oppose the global economic order where the interests of states or large corporations are prioritised. They avoid paying import taxes, which many of them consider as an unjust burden on people whose salaries are insufficient. In Belarus, they also resist a rigid and overpriced system of state-run groceries which dominates the consumption sphere of the small town they live in. Bringing cheaper alcohol and tobacco from Belarus to EU residents, women challenge the EU fiscal policy on these goods. Cross-border traders are the agents of the global transnational network of illegal cigarette commerce. Cigarettes brought from Belarus to neighbouring Poland, Lithuania and Latvia travel across the EU and reach as far as the UK and the countries of Scandinavia. In Sweden, for example, they are distributed through migrant networks. Thus, traders indeed take part in creating and facilitating a space in-between the structures. This is the space of moving objects (cigarettes) and subjects (migrants) that represents an invisible alternative reality of circulating commodities and people and that challenges the existing power structures and hierarchies.

Traders resist the state and political order in yet another way. When states or supra-state actors such as the EU impose stricter border controls, women find their way to cope with this marginalising practice and to stay on-the-move as long as possible. In the early 1990s, when Belarus and Lithuania were still in the process of establishing a border and visa regime in the formerly borderless region, women claimed their right to visit the neighbouring country through illegal border crossings outside newly emerged border posts. Although many of them knew that the border could not be crossed the same way as during the Soviet times any more, they insistently continued using old paths. With time, the border became less porous. Now women, most of whom are Belarusian citizens, trick Schengen-based rules in order to preserve their mobility rights. For example, they obtain visas for cultural or professional purposes such as tourism, pilgrimages to the Catholic holy places in Poland or Lithuania, or for sport competitions in France or Belgium but then use them mostly for trading practices.

Finally, women's mobility and informal economic practices subvert the existing societal norms which determine women's place and position within the patriarchal structure. On the one hand, in order to start trade women "seize on opportunities" (de Certeau 1988: xix) available to them within the patriarchal society. Their knowledge of how and in which goods to trade is based on their responsibility to take care of household and family consumption prescribed to them by the patriarchal order and ideology of gender-based division of labour (Sasunkevich 2015). On the other hand, women clearly transgress the boundaries imposed on them by the patriarchal culture. They challenge the patriarchal idea of a man as a breadwinner. Many traders are more successful in finding additional sources of financial support or taking financial care of children than their male partners and husbands. While men rather give up finding a proper source of income if it does not correspond to their idea of manhood (see also Andreeva 2003; Kiblitskaya 2000), women do not hesitate to start or at least to consider starting even the most deteriorating activities. As one of my respondents, 46-year-old Anna (divorced, with a son) states:

> I have a child now and for the sake of my child, if he needs anything, I don't care, I will clean toilets, or, I beg your pardon, I will prostitute but I have to provide for my son!

Trading experience makes women self-confident and self-sufficient. It helps them acknowledge their capability to take care of their families or to find a way out of precarious conditions (Sasunkevich 2015). The cross-border mobility of traders also becomes an important socialising experience for women. It substitutes a workplace as a more traditional and acceptable space of socialisation available to women in small towns in the Belarusian provinces. Retired women in the region often experience social marginalisation due to the deficit of possibilities to sustain their social life outside workplace, household and family responsibilities. Joint cross-border trips create for them a space to resist this marginalisation as well as to challenge the notion of the appropriate place which the Belarusian society reserves for elderly women. The experience of collective trips between Belarus and Lithuania is warmly represented in women's narratives as a cheerful adventurous time spent together with other local women. Such a perception of cross-border mobility circulates across interviews with women of various ages. In their own stories of trading experience, women are not simply carriers of the patriarchal tradition who behave in accordance with societal expectations. They are active subjects who openly or invisibly undermine the norms imposed on women. During their trips they enjoy drinking cheap alcohol together, eating strong-smelling food and loudly discussing their daily life affairs. Their behaviour often annoys non-local people who travel between Minsk and Vilnius. Thus, they clearly transcend the boundary of what is understood as appropriate behaviour for women and cross-border travellers, symbolising in this sense the rebellion against various types of structural constructions. In this sense, cross-border trade becomes a space which, on the one hand, is clearly determined by structural limitations but on the other hand, provides resources to go beyond these limitations and to widen the structural boundaries if only for a short moment of border crossing.

Resisting border regimes through same-sex marriage

This case study focuses on women who resist border regimes at the crossroads of nationhood, femininity and sexuality. The interview material presents the narrative of two women engaged in an intimate relationship across geographic and symbolic borders.[1] The case study itself is located in and travels across national borders, as the narrative of the women is situated in both Ukraine and Sweden, and touches upon the notions of state control, femininity, sexuality and migration in a Ukrainian and a Swedish context. The women's narrative about their marriage illuminates resistance against multiple modes of marginalisation, resulting from variegated processes of domination.

The narrative analysed was uncovered during fieldwork with feminist grassroots activists in Sweden (2012–2014). During this fieldwork, together with a co-researcher,[2] I gathered material guided by the wider aim to study the visions, practices and strategies in contemporary feminist activism in Sweden. We conducted ethnographic fieldwork over a 24-month period, which included participant observation during activist events, meetings, workshops, festivals and other sites as well as in-depth interviews and focus group interviews with members of the organisations. Research participants were mainly young women between the age of 20 and 30 of varied sexual orientations (hetero-, lesbian/gay/bi-, poly- or a-sexual). They were of diverse ethnic/national backgrounds. At the time of research, all were living their everyday life in a Swedish context. There was an even distribution between white women and women of colour, and a small number of research participants identified as transwomen. All research participants were based in one of the three largest Swedish cities – Malmö, Gothenburg or Stockholm. During the time of research, many research participants, although far from all, were or had previously studied at the university. Following their activities and listening to their reflections around feminism and resistance filled me with a deep respect for their struggle. The fieldwork awakened some tensions, as my presence in the groups, being a white, native-born woman and a feminist researcher, was viewed with suspicion most notably by members of colour or migrant women. Much due to the fact that my co-researcher was a migrant Latina woman, it was still possible for me to build trust with these research participants who conceptualised me as a white dissident. Being a woman and a feminist, I was also seen as an ally in the struggle. These multi-layered insider/outsider positions fractured my perspectives during the fieldwork and analysis. At times, feelings of empathy and respect for their struggle strongly influenced my thinking about their activism. Other times, I was torn between competing identifications, most evidently in the case of research participants' critique of feminist academics. Such complexities both conditioned and enabled our participation in the groups, a circumstance that I and my co-researcher later attempted to grasp through analysis.[3]

During the collection and analysis of the material, the notion of borders (geographical, social, material, epistemological) often appeared at the centre of the activities carried out in the groups. This could be an explicit engagement with territorial borders, such as, for example, a musical written and performed by one group engaged in asylum rights, titled 'No Border'. But it could also be engagement with symbolic and material borders, such as the claiming of power in white spaces by women of colour, as illustrated by the slogan of one group engaged in anti-racism and anti-sexism, 'We take power in white spaces'. In my ambition to understand this engagement with borders in contemporary feminist activism, decolonial theory and theorisations from border studies were useful. However, this demanded a rethinking of existing understandings of feminist struggle in this context. During the time of fieldwork, in popular debate and feminist scholarship, Swedish feminism was seen to have encountered certain challenges. In these descriptions, contemporary feminism in Sweden was portrayed as fragmented due to identity politics; as riddled by tensions between gender equality and diversity politics due to increased migration; and as weakened by internal conflicts due to the recent popularity of transfeminist activism (Witt Brattström 2011; Siim and Borchorst 2010; Lindeborg 2014). Yet, during the fieldwork, feminist grassroots activists critically engaged with these descriptions of feminism and with the dominant conceptions of womanhood, race, ethnicity, sexuality, gender and national belonging that such media- and scholarly portrayals had been producing. In my attempts to understand how these grassroots feminists developed a critique of mainstream understandings of feminism, and how their resistance reshaped the feminist agenda in this context, I found inspiration in scholarship that theorised borders as multifaceted phenomena, marking a limit as well as a point of encounter, affecting both sides of the border. In the words of Walter Mignolo and Madina Tlostanova:

> [...] the very concept of 'border' implies the existence of people, languages, religions, and knowledge on both sides, linked through relations established by the coloniality of power (i.e. structured by the imperial and colonial differences).
> *(Mignolo and Tlostanova 2006: 208)*

While Swedish feminism is often celebrated for being at the forefront globally (Martinsson et al. 2016), I found that feminist grassroots activists located in the Swedish context opposed this claim. They not only exercised a protest against this very narrative, which in their view resulted in the processes of inclusion and exclusion from the nation state, but they also developed mobile and shifting tactics to resist the multiple forms of marginalisation that were shaped as a result of this phenomenon (de Certeau 1988). In this chapter, I draw on one case study from this wider material to examine the ways in which women exercised such resistance, as they took advantage of certain modes of power to expand the "meaning of the possible" (Lugones 2003: 231).

The narrative analysed in this case study tells the story of two women, Jade and Mika, who met for the first time during a cultural exchange of curators and artists between Ukraine and Sweden. The next time the two women met, Mika proposed to Jade and she said yes. Our conversations about their marriage took place a few days before and shortly after their wedding ceremony in the City Hall of Malmö. Mika and Jade are both artists, and they conceptualise their marriage as both a personal and an artistic project. Yet, they explain, the artistic part of their marriage is not just for the art space; it is for people everywhere.

At the core of my analysis of this marriage as a resistant tactic in response to marginalisation is an understanding of marriage as "one of several ways to regulate intimate relationships" (Andersson 2011: 18). Marriage does not only concern relations of intimacy in a narrow sense. Rather, intimate relationships are linked with wider social, economic and political phenomena. Feminist scholarship has produced in-depth critiques of marriage as an institution (Rubin 1975; Wittig [1981] 2003; Rich 1986; Duggan 2003; Puar 2007). However, in this analysis I want to approach marriage as a tactic of both survival and protest in response to marginalisation. Thus, women who marry can do this in resistance against variegated forms of marginalisation, such as economic, social or judicial. I identify three kinds of marginalisation that the women involved resisted: 1) hierarchical, i.e. gender hierarchies and hierarchically differentiating discourses about migrants; 2) political, i.e. the aspirations of states and other authorities such as the church to control the borders and the population of the nation/the community; and 3) social, i.e. expectations about essential or authentic forms of sexuality. The narrative of Mika and Jade visualises the mundane processes through which borders between 'us' and 'them'; the 'wanted' and 'unwanted'; the 'normal' and 'deviant' have been facilitated and sustained. Simultaneously, their tactical response exercised resistance both against the authority of the nation state and against the production of hierarchical differentiations, as they utilised certain openings in the processes of domination to challenge the authority of the state over its territories and its population and to blur the borders between 'inclusion' and 'exclusion', the 'normal' and 'deviant'.

In Ukrainian and Swedish contexts, the marriage between Jade and Mika resists different kinds of social hierarchies. In Ukraine, Mika explains, the position of women has been strongly affected by a neo-traditional shift, so that women nowadays are expected to be "good staff for the men". Simultaneously, she mentions, sexist advertisement has increased and the art space is deeply sexist. She describes that women who study at the university are viewed upon with suspicion by male professors. Mika herself studies architecture and she explains how a male professor approached her one day and said, "You are a woman. [...] you are here at the university only to find a good man [...] who can pay you money just to be a beautiful woman". In relation to her architectural studies, Mika continues, she meets "a lot of rich women". Now and then, these women tell her, "In our society, you can become rich. You should behave in a more feminine way with our rich guys, then, they will pay you money". In our conversation, Mika describes her anger and aggressiveness towards such women who "agree to be a gift to men". When she learned that in Sweden marriage between lesbian women was legally approved, she was strongly affected and thought that she could change something. Meeting Jade made her feel a close connection with another person, in a way that she had never felt before and so she decided to propose to her.

Although it is legal to get married as a same-sex couple in Sweden, Jade, in turn, points at other problems that shape hierarchical differentiations in Sweden. In relation to their marriage, Jade explains, the first question Swedish people ask her is – "Is it because you want to give her a visa?" Jade finds this suspicion towards the other a huge problem in Swedish society and she asks, "What are you defending yourself against?" She explains that these commentaries seem to view migrants like a "virus that is coming here to use our system of welfare". By deciding to marry, Jade and Mika resisted these multiple social hierarchies, refusing to consent to the structural constraints in their respective contexts. Although the marriage concerns specific subjective dimensions between the two women involved, their marriage also intersects with wider political, social and structural dynamics. In Ukraine, their marriage is a way to avoid sexist assumptions, and in Sweden, it challenges the superiority expressed by Swedes taking a position of moral authority in relation to migrants. They resist the heteronormativity in Ukrainian discourse while simultaneously resisting the feel-good homonationalism in Sweden by protesting against the idea of migrants as 'parasites' who should be 'thankful' for Swedish rights and welfare.

Their marriage also resists aspirations of the states to control the national borders and the population of the nation. In our conversation, Mika describes a memory from a previous cross-border experience. She had been awarded a scholarship and moved to Switzerland to work on an exhibition. She also had an invitation from a big company but despite these advantages she was not allowed to stay in Switzerland because the authorities did not believe her. The authorities told her, Mika explains:

> You are not married, you have no flat, you have no bank account, you are 24, and first of all, you come from Ukraine and in our canton there are a lot of prostitutes from Ukraine and Bulgaria. You have all papers, wonderful invitations, but we don't believe you because from your countries women come to Switzerland like artists and now we have a big Ukrainian and Russian mafia who trafficked women who pretend to be artists. […] You should leave Switzerland in three days. If not, you'll be deported.

The marginalisation experienced by Mika was the result of strict border controls based on the idea of division between 'wanted' and 'unwanted' migrants. To become a 'wanted' migrant, people need to fulfil the expectations of normativity. In the case of Mika and Jade, they took advantage of these expectations by utilising "the new homonormativity" (Duggan 2003: 50) in Sweden and marrying each other to resist such processes of marginalisation. As a result of their marriage, Mika is now a 'wanted' migrant and would be able to work in Switzerland, for example, without running the risk of being deported. Yet, Mika and Jade also have plans to resist the aspirations of the Ukrainian state to control its population. "When I come back to Ukraine", Mika describes, "I will be free". In Ukraine, her same-sex marriage is illegal, which means that in Ukraine Mika could still marry (a man). If she travels to other European countries, or to Canada or the USA, her marriage with Jade will be legally recognised. To challenge such expectations of states to control the population, they planned that Jade should apply for a residence permit in Ukraine:

> It's a long and difficult process and they will ask her, "Why should we give you a residence permit?" She says, "I have a wife here". They say, "What wife? It's not legal." [...] It would be interesting to make this provocation. The last point [we want to do] is to write [a complaint] to the European [court], that the Ukrainian government discriminates us and that they won't give us residence permit because gay marriage in our law doesn't exist.

Jade adds that before they start with these provocations, they are going to meet a priest and talk with her about their wedding. They want to have a ceremony in a church and the priest they have already been in contact with is very reassuring. Jade and Mika told the priest that they were artists and were working on the marriage "on different levels". "It's always the question", Jade adds, "if it is real or not. Who decides if it's fake or not?" By such provocations Mika and Jade tease out different layers in the attempts by state or church authorities to regulate its population/community through divisions between the 'wanted' and 'unwanted' or the 'normal' and 'deviant'. Their marriage has enabled them to create a space in-between these layers from which they can visualise and challenge attempts to control territorial and social borders as they take advantage of the marriage as a legal institution, which enables them to resist expectations of normativity in diverse locations.

Finally, their marriage resisted expectations of 'essential' or 'authentic' forms of sexuality. In order to travel to Sweden for her wedding, Mika had to apply for a tourist visa. During the interview at the Swedish Embassy in Ukraine, the staff members asked her, "You met this girl just twice in your life, how can you love her? You live in different countries". Mika describes that she said to the staff members that that was not their business: "If you ask me about our sex – you know a lot of people are asexual and in our relationship sex is not more important for us". Then, she explains, they looked at her and said, "Okay, we want a picture of the two of you making love". In the Swedish context, marriage is still presented as an ideal way of life but in contrast to the previous emphasis on the nuclear family, the idea of two-some togetherness has today come to uphold a hegemonic position (Adeniji 2008). In this context, 'authentic' sexuality is seen to facilitate love and support stable forms of togetherness. This notion of love, exercised through 'authentic' forms of sexuality, entered the discourse at the same time as the recognition of the rights of same-sex couples began to take hold. In the

Swedish gender-neutral marriage act of 2009, marriage is described as both a manifestation of love and a way to satisfy legal and economic safety (Andersson 2011). While in the case of Mika and Jade, such expectations of 'authentic' sexuality were emphasised by staff members at the Swedish embassy, they could take advantage of the opportunities these expectations opened for them, as Mika and Jade did not agree on the idea of 'authentic' forms of sexuality but wanted to provoke and challenge such ideas.

Receiving her tourist visa, Mika could travel to Sweden for her wedding. Yet, in our conversation, they refused to disclose any information about their sexual practices. In response to our question about this, Jade explained that their rationale behind that was not to hide information, but to "reveal which institution that crosses the borders of integrity [...] I choose if I want to tell you who I sleep with". Mika and Jade describe that they encountered critique on this point also from feminist activists. A friend of Mika from Moscow, a feminist and a lesbian woman, published an article about their project, explaining that "I don't like this project [...] because she [Mika] is not a lesbian. She is heterosexual and wants to support us. [...] For her, it's not dangerous". Mika disagrees with this point, and explains the many ways in which this project actually is very dangerous for her, as she has a "real lesbian marriage": she could lose her job as a teacher for young children; she could "lose everything". While Mika and Jade destabilise the discourse on the 'authentic' forms of sexuality in Sweden by resisting compliance with these expectations and by refusing to disclose information about their sex life, in Ukraine they resist the assumption of the 'essential' forms of sexuality by undermining the discourse. In Mika's case, she explains, the primary point of this project – the marriage – was not to receive the visa but to instigate discussion and discomfort, to make people nervous by the uncertainty: is she really a lesbian? The ambiguity of this position has protected her ability to continue exercising resistance since, she explains, "if you say that you are a gay or a lesbian [in Ukraine], some people begin to silence you, don't speak with you".

By taking advantage of the marriage function to control intimate relationships, Mika and Jade do not passively use this regulation or submit to hetero/homonormative or homonational discourses of femininity, migration or sexuality, but they act as subjects who in complex and provocative ways try to expand the limits of legal and social norms. Precisely because such legal and social norms in different countries function to support marriage as an institution in different ways, they can utilise their marriage to challenge the attempts of the states to control their territory and population, to protest against hierarchical differentiations in terms of gender relations and citizenship status (migration), and to resist normative understandings of sexuality. The legal recognition of the marriage enables them to provoke and challenge different ways in which border regimes are exercised in different places. In Sweden, their marriage visualises and resists the notions of moral authority and hierarchical differentiations between 'us' and 'them'. Their refusal to disclose information about their sexual practice challenges the ideas of 'authentic' sexuality. Simultaneously, in Ukraine, their marriage resists gender hierarchies and sexism, and undermines discourses of 'essential' sexuality. That their marriage is only recognised in certain countries visualises the arbitrariness of border regimes, an arbitrariness they later are planning to utilise to provoke state authorities and citizens in Ukraine and to challenge the sovereignty of the nation state, if they decide to write a complaint to the EU. In this way, Mika and Jade's marriage utilises the spaces between legal and social norms in different national contexts to create a space in-between the structures from which they could visualise and resist contextually situated border regimes. Finally, their marriage is also a way to establish relationships and create coalitions across national borders, which they understand as the only possible way to achieve change in solidarity with others. In the words of Jade, "We are together with each other as one human being with another human being, not as a government with another government that both have their own strategic interests".

Conclusion: Border regimes and varieties of resistance

Drawing on two case studies, in this chapter we have examined the resistant potential of tactics developed in struggles around territorial, political and social borders. Paying attention to the everyday practices of manoeuvring within the space of the powerful, our analysis took a different approach than scholarship that focuses on women's lack of mobility and freedom within processes of domination. Distinguishing variegated ways in which differently situated women took advantage of certain modes of power, we have demonstrated how the women utilised the opportunities given to them within the dominant structure to challenge marginalisation and expand the limits of the possible. Our first case study showed how the women's cross-border trading practices had developed a tactical resistance to economic, political and social marginalisation. We highlighted how their trading practices enabled them to find a way out of precarious conditions, challenge unequal access to mobility and transcend the boundaries of the notions of a proper place and appropriate behaviour for women. Our second case study revealed how same-sex marriage across geographical and symbolic borders allowed women to challenge hierarchical, political and social forms of marginalisation. We demonstrated how the marriage resisted hierarchically differentiating discourses about nationhood, femininity and sexuality and how it enabled the women to transgress the attempts of the nation-states to control their population and territory. Both of the case studies illuminated particular dimensions of the variegated ways in which women's manoeuvring across different borders created a space in-between the structure from which they could resist marginalisation and challenge the norms that determined women's position within the structure. These dimensions, we discussed, were connected to the spatiality of resistance, in which resistance took shape as a response within and against processes of domination. In this mode of resistance, women are not simply carriers of normative expectations or traditions, but active subjects who provocatively undermine the norms imposed on them. The notion of resistance as tactics enabled us to grasp how the structural limitations that determine women's mobility and relationships, such as territorial borders, patriarchal traditions, sexism or heteronormativity, provided resources for women to move beyond these limitations and transgress diverse forms of border regimes.

While resistance against the attempts of states to control the objects and subjects that enter the territorial border had a central position in both our case studies, the women in these cases also visualised and challenged different kinds of borders. In the first case study, the women resisted the expectations of the proper place and behaviour for women within the patriarchal structure. In the second case study, the women resisted normative understandings of femininity, sexuality and intimate relationships. It appears that border regimes, and resistance against them, are linked with particular forms of belonging in terms of class, race, ethnicity, gender and sexuality. This has to do with the fact that borders are attempts to literally and symbolically demarcate and administer lines between 'us' and 'them', the 'inside' and 'outside'. Thus, actors with other forms of belonging than the women we followed during our fieldwork would likely have encountered and resisted another set of border regimes. In our view, this does not weaken the implications of our analysis. Instead, we would argue that this insight provides a serious challenge to all attempts to naturalise borders of any kind – territorial, political or social. Yet, since tactical forms of resistance utilise certain dominant powers as resources to transcend structural limitations, this insight finally brings into view the significance and powerful force of a variety of ways through which border regimes are resisted, undermined and transgressed.

Notes

1 The interview with the two women was conducted on two different occasions. On both occasions, both women were present. The interview was conducted in English.
2 Marta Cuesta, associate professor at Halmstad University College.
3 For an in-depth analysis of tensions and contradictions during fieldwork, see Liinason and Cuesta (2014).

References

Adeniji, A., (2008) *Inte den typ som gifter sig? Feministiska samtal om äktenskapsmotstånd* [*Not the Marrying Kind? Feminist Conversations on Resistance against Marriage*]. Göteborg, Stockholm: Makadam.

Andersen, D.J., and Sandberg, M., (2012) Introduction. *In*: Andersen, D.J., Klatt, M. and Sandberg, M. (eds.). *The Border Multiple: The Practicing of Borders between Public Policy and Everyday Life in a Re-scaling Europe*. Farnham, Burlington: Ashgate. pp. 1–18.

Andersson, C., (2011) *Hundra år av tvåsamhet: Äktenskapet i svenska statliga utredningar 1909–2009* [*Hundred Years of Togetherness: Marriage in Swedish State Official Investigations 1909–2009*]. Uppsala: Uppsala universitet.

Andreas, P., and Snyder, T., (eds.). (2000). *The Wall around the West: State Borders and Immigration Controls in North America and Europe*. Oxford: Rowman and Littlefield.

Andreeva, T., (2003) Chelnochnyj biznes kak strategiya domohozyaistva: Analiz rezultatov empiricheskogo issledovaniya [Shuttle business as a household strategy: the analysis of empirical data]. *In*: Popkova, L., and Tartakovskaja, I., (eds.). *Gendernye otnosheniya v sovremennoi Rossii: issledovaniya 1990-ch godov* [*Gender Relations in Contemporary Russia: Studies of the 1990s*]. Samara: Samarskii Universitet. pp. 121–142.

Balibar, E., (2004) *We, the People of Europe? Reflections on Transnational Citizenship. Princeton.* Princeton: Princeton University Press.

Certeau de, M., (1988) *The Practice of Everyday Life*. Berkeley: University of California Press.

Duggan, L., (2003) *The Twilight of Equality? Neoliberalism, Cultural Politics and the Attack on Democracy*. Boston: Beacon Press.

Gawlewicz, A., and Yndigegn, C., (2012) The (in)visible wall of fortress Europe? Elite migrating youth perceiving the sensitive Polish-Ukrainian border. *In*: Andersen, D.J., Klatt, M., and Sandberg, M., (eds.). *The Border Multiple: The Practicing of Borders between Public Policy and Everyday Life in a Re-scaling Europe*. Farnham, Burlington: Ashgate. pp. 179–199.

Grabbe, H., (2000) The Sharp Edges of Europe: Extending Schengen Eastwards. *International Affairs* 76(3). pp. 519–536.

Houtum van, H., (2010) Waiting Before the Law: Kafka on the Border. *Social and Legal Studies*. 19(3). pp. 285–297.

Houtum van, H., and van Naerssen, T., (2001) Bordering, Ordering and Othering. *Tijdschrift voor economische en sociale geografie*. 93(2). pp. 125–136.

Houtum van, H., and Pijpers, R., (2007) The European Union as a Gated Community: The Two-faced Border and Immigration Regime of the EU. *Antipode*. 39(2). pp. 291–309.

Kiblitskaya, M., (2000) Russia's female breadwinners: The changing subjective experience. *In*:Ashwin, S., *Gender, State and Society in Soviet and Post-Soviet Russia*. London; New York: Routledge. pp. 55–70.

Lemberg-Pedersen, M. (2012). Forcing flows of migrants: European externalization and border-induced displacement. *In*:Andersen, D.J., Klatt, M., and Sandberg, M., (2012). *The Border Multiple: The Practicing of Borders between Public Policy and Everyday Life in a Re-scaling Europe*. Farnham, Burlington: Ashgate. pp. 179–200.

Lemberg-Pedersen, M., (2015) Losing the right to have rights: EU externalization of border control. *In*: Andersen, E.A., and Lassen, E.M., (eds.). *Europe and the Americas: Transatlantic Approaches to Human Rights*. Leiden: Brill Academic Publishers, Incorporated. pp. 393–417.

Liinason, M., (2018) *Equality Struggles: Women's Movements, Neoliberal Markets and State Political Agendas in Scandinavia*. London; New York: Routledge.

Liinason, M., and CuestaM., (2014) Subjective emotions, political implications: Thinking through tensions and contradictions in feminist knowledge production. *ex aequo – Portuguese Journal of Women's Studies*. 29. pp. 23–38.

Lindeborg, Å., (2014) Det ska fan vara politiskt korrekt [It should be politically correct, goddammit], *Aftonbladet Kultur*, 7 November.

Lugones, M. (2003). *Pilgrimages/Peregrinajes: Theorizing Coalition against Multiple Oppressions*. New York: Rowman and Littlefield.

Martinsson, L., GriffinG., and Giritli Nygren, K., (2016) Introduction: Challenging the myth of gender equality in Sweden. *In*:Martinsson, L., Griffin, G., and Giritli Nygren, K., (eds.). *Challenging the Myth of Gender Equality in Sweden*. Bristol: Policy Press. pp. 1–22.

Mahmood, S., (2001) Feminist Theory, Embodiment, and the Docile Agency: Some Reflections on the Egyptian Islamic Revival. *Cultural Anthropology*. 16(2). pp. 202–236.

Mahmood, S., (2005) *Politics of Piety: The Islamic Revival and the Feminist Subject*. Princeton; Oxford: Princeton University Press.

Massey, D., (2005) *For Space*. London: Sage.

Mezzadra, S., and Neilson, B., (2013) *Border as Method, or, the Multiplication of Labor*. Durham; London: Duke University Press.

Mignolo, W., and TlostanovaM., (2006) Theorizing from the Borders: Shifting to Geo- and Body-politics of Knowledge. *European Journal of Social Theory*. 9(2). pp. 205–221.

Morokvasic, M. (2004) 'Settled in Mobility': Engendering Post-Wall Migration in Europe. *Feminist Review*. 77. pp. 7–25.

Murray, D.A.B., (2014) Real Queer: 'Authentic' LGBT Refugee Claimants and Homonationalism in the Canadian Refugee System. *Anthropologica*. 56(1). pp. 21–32.

Puar, J., (2007) *Terrorist Assemblages: Homonationalism in Queer Times*. Durham: Duke University Press.

Puar, J., (2008) Q & A with Jasbir Puar. *darkmatter 3: Postcolonial sexuality*. www.darkmatter101.org/site/2008/05/02/qa-with-jasbir-puar/ (Accessed: 6 September 2017).

Rich, A., (1986) *Blood, Bread and Poetry: Selected Prose 1979–1985*. New York: Norton.

Round, J., Williams, C., and Rodgers, P., (2010) The Role of Domestic Food Production in Everyday Life in Post-Soviet Ukraine. *Annals of the Association of American Geographers*. 100(5). pp. 1197–1211.

Rubin, G., (1975) The traffic in women: Notes on the political economy of sex. *In*:Reiter, R.R., (ed.). *Toward an Anthropology of Women*. New York; London: Monthly Review Press. pp. 157–210.

Sasunkevich, O., (2014) 'Business as casual': Shuttle trade on the Belarus-Lithuania border. *In*:Morris, J., and Polese, A., (eds.). *The Informal Post-Socialist Economy: Embedded Practices and Livelihoods*. London: Routledge. pp. 135–151.

Sasunkevich, O., (2015) *Informal Trade, Gender and the Border Experience: From Political Borders to Social Boundaries*. Farnham, Burlington: Ashgate.

Scott, J.C., (1985) *Weapons of the Weak: Everyday Forms of Peasant Resistance*. New Haven; London: Yale University Press.

Siim, B., and BorchorstA., (2010) The multicultural challenge to the Danish welfare state: Tensions between gender equality and diversity. *In*:Fink, J., and Lundqvist, Å., (eds.). *Changing Relations of Welfare*. Farnham; Burlington: Ashgate. pp. 133–154.

Smith, A., (2010) Informal work in the diverse economies of 'post-socialist' Europe. *In*: Williams, C.C., and Joassart, P., (2010) *Informal Economy in Developed Nations*. London; New York: Routledge. pp. 47–65.

Stryker, S., (2008) Transgender History, Homonormativity, and Disciplinarity. *Radical History Review*. 100. pp. 144–157.

Tarrius, A., (1992) *Les fourmis d'Europe: Migrants riches, migrants pauvres et nouvelles villes internationals* [*The Ants of Europe: Rich migrants, Poor Migrants and New International Cities*]. Paris: L'Harmattan.

Walters, W., (2006) Rethinking Borders Beyond the State. *Comparative European Politics*. 4(2–3). pp. 141–159.

Williams, A.A., and Baláž, V., (2002) International Petty Trading: Changing Practices in Trans-Carpathian Ukraine. *International Journal of Urban and Regional Research*. 26(2). pp. 323–342.

Witt Brattström, E., (2011) När systerskapet var en politisk handling [When sisterhood was a political act]. *Dagens Nyheter*. 8 March.

Wittig, M., ([1981] 2003) One is not born a woman. *In*:Martín Alcoff, L., and Eduardo, M., ([1981] 2003). *Identities: Race, Class, Gender, and Nationality*. Malden: Blackwell. pp. 158–162.

Zielonka, J., (2003) *Europe Unbound: Enlarging and Reshaping the Boundaries of the European Union*. London: Routledge.

4

IN, AGAINST (AND BEYOND?) THE STATE[1]

Women's rights, global gender equality regime, and feminist counterpublics in 21st-century Turkey

Selin Çağatay

Introduction

The scholarship on the feminism-state relationship in Turkey in the 2000s focused on how feminists negotiated the terms of gender politics through participating in the state-civil society-transnational governance framework mediated by the global gender equality regime. Turkey's candidacy for European Union (EU) membership created a political landscape in which feminists, translating their local demands into a universalist language of rights, could counter the Justice and Development Party's (hereafter AKP) conservative gender politics that increasingly hinged on the Islamism-secularism societal divide. Many scholars of women's and gender studies examined feminists' inclusion in policy-making processes as proof of Turkey's democratisation, excluding feminist politics in counterpublics from their analysis of the feminism-state relationship (e.g. Kardam 2005; Ertürk 2006; Fisher Onar and Paker 2012; Aldıkaçtı Marshall 2013).[2] Yet the window of opportunity available to feminists at the institutional level closed as a consequence of developments in the 2010s. These developments included challenges to the global gender equality regime by neoliberalism and the rise of illiberal, authoritarian regimes (Razavi and Jenichen 2010; Razavi 2016), the weakening of Turkey's EU membership prospects (Rumelili 2011; Icoz 2016), and AKP's redefinition of women's rights in Islamist, anti-feminist terms (Yazıcı 2012; Dedeoğlu 2013). Thus from the perspective of mainstream gender and politics scholarship, feminist politics in Turkey seems to be in decline (e.g. Negrón-Gonzales 2016). However, excluded and marginalised by the state, feminist politics thrives in the counterpublic sphere as a crucial constituent of the democratic social opposition, and remains a powerful actor in gender politics. This calls for a critical reconsideration of the state-civil society-transnational governance as the dominant framework within which to analyse feminists' engagement in the politics of gender.

In this chapter, I offer a nuanced perspective on the feminism-state relationship in Turkey by bringing feminist counterpublics into the discussion alongside the state-civil society-transnational governance framework. Following Nancy Fraser's definition of counterpublics as "discursive arenas where members of subordinated social groups invent and circulate counterdiscourses to formulate oppositional interpretations of their identities, interests, and needs" (Fraser 1992, p.123; see also Felski 1989), my aim is to show that limiting the analysis of feminists' gender politics to the dominant state-civil society-transnational governance framework does not allow for a comprehensive understanding of the multiplicity of sites and agendas of feminist struggles and of shifting power configurations and alliances between feminists and other actors of gender politics. A major shortcoming of this framework is that it draws on a liberal conceptualisation of state-civil society relations where civil society works as a democratic force counterbalancing patriarchal state power. As such, it disregards the power struggles among civil society groups, including feminisms, which are asymmetrically positioned vis-à-vis the state and have various strategies to pursue gender politics based on their differential political belongings. In Turkey, feminist struggles concern both, issues that pertain to the global gender equality agenda like gender-based violence, civil rights, women's economic empowerment and political participation, and those that are rather excluded in the state-civil society-transnational governance triangle such as women's involvement in peacemaking, struggles against neoliberalism and for the rights of domestic workers, sex workers, queer and refugee women. Feminists pursue politics not only in donor-funded NGOs and various mechanisms of transnational governance but also in informal collectives, web-based groups, and non-institutionalised platforms and campaigns that seek broader alliances among women. Different forms of feminisms are hierarchically positioned in relation to each other and the state, and only by integrating these multiple sites and issues in our analysis can we assess the feminism-state relationship more comprehensively.

The perspective I offer on the Turkish case links to the recent debates in critical feminist scholarship on the relationship between feminism and neoliberalism, which flared up following the 2008 financial crisis when some prominent feminist scholars argued that feminism got co-opted by neoliberalism (Eisenstein 2009; Fraser 2009; McRobbie 2009). Nancy Fraser (2009) for example asserted that neoliberalisation has turned feminism into a variant of identity politics, which deepened the class divisions between women by putting too much emphasis on the critique of culture and too little on political economy (p.108). Other feminist scholars, however, criticised Fraser's and similar assessments for universalising the experience of the U.S. hegemonic feminism – a specific form of feminism which did not represent the feminist movement globally as a whole – and for neglecting the original, antisystemic forms of resistance in the global South, including the lower strata in the global North (e.g. Aslan and Gambetti 2011; Eschle and Maiguashca 2014). I contribute to this debate by problematising, based on the example of Turkey, the relationship between dominant feminisms that engage in the state-civil society-transnational governance tripartite cooperation and non-dominant feminisms that occupy counterpublics as their main site of political struggle. Dominant and non-dominant feminisms coexist with each other in a given context, and the contingency of their position vis-à-vis state power makes it difficult to classify them strictly into "co-opted" and "progressive" forms of feminism, respectively. Feminism is a fragmented, multi-layered movement, and analyses that build on both dominant and counterpublic feminisms would lead to more grounded evaluations of the impact of feminist politics.

In the following, I first propose a methodological approach to situate dominant and non-dominant feminisms in relation to the state, transnational governance and to each other across the global North and South. Then, I provide a brief historical account of the formation of dominant and non-dominant feminisms in Turkey until the 2000s. In the subsequent sections, I discuss the various ways in which dominant and non-dominant feminists pursued gender politics, responding to Turkey's Europeanisation and Islamisation in the 2000s and their marginalisation and exclusion by the state in the 2010s. I thereby show the changing character of feminists' access to state power, their strategic use of the mechanisms of transnational governance, and the ambivalence of the line of demarcation and the possibilities of a strategic alliance between dominant and non-dominant feminisms.

The analysis I present builds on a variety of data, namely print and online; formal and informal material produced by feminist and women's organisations and platforms; and news sources on feminist, state and transnational governance discourses and practices. This data was collected for over more than a decade at two interconnected sites: the first is my academic research on the history of feminist and women's activisms in Turkey, with a focus on the relationship between different actors of gender politics (Çağatay 2017). The second is my participation in feminist counterpublics, in a number of organisations and platforms, as a socialist feminist activist. My analysis employs a combination of methods including netnography, participant observation, historical analysis, textual analysis, and discourse analysis.

Feminisms and the state across the global North-South divide: A methodological discussion

In the last four decades, the feminism-state relationship has been mediated by a global "gender equality regime" (Kardam 2005), one that is progressively built on the UN International Women's Year (1975), the Convention on the Elimination of All Forms of Discrimination against Women (CEDAW, 1979) and UN conferences at Nairobi (1985), Vienna (1993), Cairo (1994) and Beijing (1995). Following the fourth UN World Conference on Women (1995), the Beijing Declaration and Platform for Action jumpstarted the mainstreaming of women's rights as human rights by adopting it in its entire agenda. It equipped different groups of feminists with a common framework to address women's oppression, to set women's rights and empowerment as national and transnational priorities, and to communicate their agendas to each other and build solidarity (Bunch and Frost 2000; Grewal 2005; Ewig and Ferree 2013). The global gender equality regime's proposed agenda strengthened feminists' hand before the state internationally (Bunch and Frost 2000) and gave them an opportunity to unite women of different political belongings under a common language of rights in their local contexts. States across the global North and South adopted gender agendas in line with the global gender equality regime, sometimes because they were keen on gender-egalitarian policy-making, other times because it served as a badge of international prestige. The regulative power of transnational governance structures served in the North, no less than in the South, as an opportunity for women's groups to participate in decision making because they transcended the hierarchical structures of the state that gave women little room (Sauer and Wöhl 2011, p.109).

In mainstream gender and politics literature, the hegemonic influence of the global gender equality regime in gender politics has been the limitation of the analysis of the feminism-state relationship to feminists' participation in the state-civil society-transnational governance framework (e.g. Kantola 2006; Krook and Childs 2010; McBride and Mazur 2010). This is problematic because it attributes universality to dominant forms of feminism that are positioned in the institutional field of politics. It leaves outside of the discussion the many ways in which the feminism-state relationship occurs and silences the dynamics between feminist counterpublics and the global gender equality regime.

The lens of dominant and non-dominant feminisms often overlaps with the North-South divide, but this divide refers to more than geographical location. Processes of globalisation characterised by "de-gendering and re-gendering based on the requirements of the global restructuring of the nation state and together with it the gender regimes previously fenced by the nation state" (Sauer and Wöhl 2011, p.110) created similar forms of participation in gender politics across the globe that favoured certain feminist agendas over others in each context, making a North-South divide based purely on geographical location difficult to maintain. Like Raewyn Connell suggests in her book *Southern Theory* (2009), the North-South divide does not imply a clearly defined category of states and societies but emphasises the relations of "authority, exclusion and inclusion, hegemony, partnership, sponsorship – between intellectuals and institutions in the metropole and those in the world periphery" (Connell 2009, p.ix). Thus, the North-South divide can be read as dominant vs. non-dominant feminisms – two forms characterised by their proximity to state power and global hegemonic discourses. Seen this way, dominant/Northern and non-dominant/Southern feminisms coexist on local, national, regional and transnational levels.

One method to differentiate between dominant/Northern and non-dominant/Southern feminisms, which I employ in this chapter, is by looking at their agendas. These agendas differ in the extent to which they represent the interests of the dominant class, ethnicity, religion and sexuality in their historically specific contexts. In many contexts, dominant feminisms tend to represent the interests of dominant groups through their singular focus on gender, while for non-dominant feminisms gender alone does not account for women's oppression (see Mohanty 1991). The global gender equality regime with its gender-only agenda favours dominant feminisms, and encourages Southern feminists to subsume their intersectional demands under this agenda as a prerequisite to participate in decision-making processes within the state-civil society-transnational governance framework. Many women in the global South, in return, challenge feminism for reproducing the interests of women who belong to the dominant class, ethnicity, religion, and sexuality, and thus they often refuse the label "feminism." A discussion on dominant and non-dominant feminisms, therefore, has to concede the multiplicity of feminisms that are potentially incompatible and in conflict with each other on local, national, regional and transnational levels. It should draw on an inclusive definition of feminism that accommodates women's differential agendas on the intersecting categories of gender, class, ethnicity, religion, and sexuality (Moghadam 2005; Ferree and Tripp 2006). This multiplicity of feminisms marks the field of gender activism by domination, heteronomy, exclusion and injustice (Sauer 2011, p.295). At the same time, depending on political opportunity structures, dominant and non-dominant feminisms can form strategic alliances, raise common demands, and engage in agenda building from below.

The recognition of the multiplicity of hierarchically positioned feminisms allows us to move beyond the simplistic autonomy vs. co-optation approach when analysing the feminism-state relationship. Instead of a liberal understanding of the state and civil society as two separate entities interacting with each other, a Gramscian conceptualisation that entails a symbiotic relationship between the two, where civil society belongs to the broader notion of statehood (Katz 2009; Sauer 2011), helps to grasp the various ways in which feminists relate to the state. In this conceptualisation the state is seen as embedded in the public sphere (Schudson 1994), which is understood as a "multiplicity of dialectically related public spheres rather than a single, encompassing arena of discourse" (Asen and Brouwer 2001, p.6; see also Benhabib 1992; Fraser 1992; Habermas 1992). In multiple public spheres, actors of gender politics have differential access to state power. These actors include not only feminists and institutions of transnational governance but also religious, conservative, masculinist as well as democratic, gender-egalitarian political parties, social movements and civil society organisations that compete over state power and the definition of women's rights. The state is not only where women's interests are represented but also where they are constituted; since the groups that are able to articulate their interests at the level of the state and hegemonise their claims are historically specific and therefore partial and temporary, the content and scope of the interaction between the state and other actors of gender politics is dynamic and conjunctural (Pringle and Watson 1992). Thus, dominant and non-dominant feminisms are not fixed categories with pre-defined agendas; inclusion and exclusion in these categories depend on which social groups have access to state power in a given historical context. A careful analysis of the feminism-state relationship that pays attention to historically specific contexts and the multiplicity of public spheres as well as of the actors of gender politics shall neither condemn feminists' collaboration with, nor celebrate their independence from, the state.

If feminists have no unitary experience with the state, what are the terms of their collaboration with it? How do these terms shape dominant and non-dominant feminist projects, and the relationship between different groups of feminists? Commenting on political opportunity structures, Ewig and Ferree (2013) state that "[f]eminist organizing strategies shift between autonomy and embeddedness, emphasizing autonomy when gender concerns are ignored or trivialized by other movements and embeddedness when their participation is welcomed" (p.451). Political opportunity structures at global, regional, national and local levels influence the appeal and effectiveness of feminists' autonomous strategies or embeddedness (Ibid., p.443). Looking at the feminism-state relationship through the lens of dominant/Northern and non-dominant/Southern feminisms, we can say that feminists have differential access to political opportunity structures based on their agendas that reflect class, ethnic, religious and sexual belongings *and* their level of engagement with the global gender equality regime. Differences in feminists' access to political opportunity structures often influence whether they organise in small-scale, grassroots or well-established, institutionalised organisations (Naples 2004, p.276), and characterise their relationship with the state. As Sauer's (2011) analysis of women's organisations in the EU countries shows, dominant feminisms are those that have the infrastructures, resources, and strategic frames to interact with state institutions (p.295). That is to say, feminists who successfully employ the mechanisms of transnational governance, and whose class, ethnic, religious and sexual interests overlap with those of the groups that hold state power, are likely to find it a meaningful strategy to cooperate with the state in their struggle for gender equality. Those feminists for whom political opportunity structures do not allow them to raise their agendas within the state-civil society-transnational governance framework, as well as those who simply adopt an anti-state (but not necessarily an anti-transnational governance) stance, establish feminist counterpublics.

Marginalisation and exclusion by or refusal to collaborate with the state, however, does not deprive counterpublic feminists of a relationship with the state. This is because, first, feminists who occupy counterpublic spheres often address the state with their demands, with or without the mediation of the global gender equality regime. Second, states engage with counterpublics, be it by keeping them under surveillance, deliberating with them or extending a branch to them (Asen and Brouwer 2001, p.18). Third, from a historical perspective, dominant and non-dominant positions are not absolute; changes in state power result in feminists' mobility between these two positions. Hegemonic forms of feminism at a given time might have belonged in the past or belong in the future in the counterpublic sphere. Finally, there's often an organic relationship between dominant and non-dominant feminisms because some feminists occupy multiple locations in the broad field of feminist activism. Seen this way, feminist counterpublics are potentially as constitutive of the feminism-state relationship as dominant feminisms.

Turkey's gender equality agenda and the formation of dominant and non-dominant feminisms (1980s–1990s)

In Turkey in the 1980s, a small but influential group of women who identified as "feminists" mobilised in the counterpublic sphere. Politicising issues that were previously confined to the private sphere, they challenged the state by exposing the patriarchal legal framework it maintained despite the official discourse that gender equality had been attained through the Kemalist reforms in the early-Republican era (1923–1935). From the 1990s onwards, as feminist activism grew, women of different political belongings questioned their position in gender relations, and many of them adopted feminism alongside their political identities as Kemalist, socialist, Islamist, and Kurdish. The global gender equality regime has always had an influence over the formation of different agendas within women's activism and the ways in which women engaged with the state. Feminists followed Turkey's commitment to CEDAW (1985) closely and organised campaigns for its enforcement. The formation of a women's policy agency in 1990 (General Directorate of Women's Status and Problems) allowed an inflow of funding from the institutions of transnational governance and provided feminists with a "framework within which to penetrate and influence the state apparatus" (Ertürk 2006, p.99).

The 1990s saw the mushrooming of new organisations influenced by the global gender equality agenda and an accelerating recognition of women's cause formulated as "women's rights are human rights" (Arat 2001). "Women's rights" was not only a catchphrase for feminist demands but also a suitable framing for recruiting into gender politics women who hesitated to identify as feminist. In this period, women's activism diversified parallel to the emergence of social movements that drew their strength from identity politics. Throughout the 1990s, thousands of women joined the ranks of women's rights activism in NGOs as providers or recipients of training on literacy, health, violence and income-generating activities within a "development from below" paradigm (Diner and Toktaş 2010). Islamist women politicised the headscarf ban which excluded them from public education and civil service. They supported democratic values in the context of universal human rights and drew on feminist ideas – without identifying themselves as feminists (Aslan-Akman 2011). Kemalist women were the first proponents of the women's human rights framework in gender politics, but their primary agenda was to struggle against the rise of political Islam and the politicisation of the headscarf (Çağatay 2017). Kurdish women, although their rights-based consciousness was due to the armed conflict between the Kurdistan Workers' Party (PKK) and the Turkish army (Gökalp 2010, p.562), found the human rights framework equally useful and developed a perspective within which they addressed the intersection of their ethnic and gender-based oppression.

It was a conscious decision of feminists who operated in the state-civil society-transnational governance framework to endorse a discourse of rights because reference to transnational frameworks gave them a certain impartiality before the state in a political landscape marked by political polarisations based on laicism-Islamism and

Turkish-Kurdish nationalisms. As women's rights activism evolved into a particular – dominant – brand of feminism, activists pushed the Turkish state for gender-egalitarian policies and legislation. Their successful adoption of the global gender equality agenda brought significant legal gains for women but also demarcated dominant from non-dominant feminisms. At the central state level, the "universality" of women's rights meant that these rights were undifferentiated by class, religion and ethnicity. In practice, this favoured Kemalist women's organisations in policy-making processes and pushed Islamist and Kurdish women's organisations into the counterpublic sphere. At the level of grassroots activism, state support went mostly to Kemalist women's organisations that perceived "women's rights" as an antidote to women's instrumentalisation in Islamist and Kurdish nationalist discourses (Esim and Cindoğlu 1999). The state's entanglement with civil society designated which groups of feminists, and to what extent, would be allowed access to state power.

Throughout this time, feminists who pursued politics in counterpublic spheres developed a powerful critique of patriarchy. Counterpublic feminists were not a homogeneous group; just like women's rights activists, they belonged to different political cultures and had conflicting perspectives on gender politics. Broadly speaking, what differentiated feminists in counterpublics from those in the state-civil society-transnational governance framework was their take on the headscarf issue, the Kurdish question and the status of women's labour. Counterpublic feminists generally supported covered women's struggle to participate in public life. They also politicised the double discrimination Kurdish women faced based on their gender and ethnic belongings, and criticised the assimilationist politics of the Turkish state. Socialist, materialist, and labour feminists discussed how gender relations shaped women's position in the relations of production and reproduction. Based on their stance on these three issues, counterpublic feminists were neither willing nor welcomed to cooperate with the state.

Notwithstanding the difference in their stance towards the state, dominant and counterpublic feminists did not exist in isolation from each other. First of all, there were many women who engaged in gender politics in counterpublics while simultaneously doing women's rights activism. Second, the relationship between counterpublic feminists and women's rights activists took the form of a strategic alliance when it came to feminist campaigns for gender-egalitarian legislation. As I show in greater detail in the following sections, the line of demarcation between dominant and non-dominant feminisms was contingent on the state-civil society relations, and the power struggle between different groups of feminists did not necessarily preclude the possibility of their strategic alliance and joint action. In the meantime, the role of transnational governance in gender politics linked the state and civil society in unique ways that made feminists' autonomy from state power questionable; feminists who were critical towards the state and its policies received funding from donor agencies and relied on the support of local state structures as they established institutions that targeted various aspects of gender inequality.

2000s' conjuncture for gender politics: Europeanisation and Islamisation

Europeanisation and Islamisation, the two projects that marked the Turkish political sphere in the 2000s, influenced decisively the ways in which feminists engaged with the state. Turkey's candidacy for membership in the EU (1999) enhanced the state-civil society-transnational governance framework in gender politics. The pre-EU accession reforms included those regarding cultural and economic rights of minorities, which ensured religious and ethnic identities a legal framework within which to formulate demands in terms of human rights. The state's official gender agenda changed to meet the EU criteria by incorporating the notion of gender equality in key legal texts such as the Constitution (2001, 2004, 2010), Civil Law (2001), Penal Law (2004) and Labour Law (2003), improving women's legal status significantly.

During its first two terms in government (2002–2011), AKP incorporated Turkey's EU prospect in its Islamisation project. Europeanisation was instrumental for AKP's neoliberal restructuring of public policies since the EU accession process was perceived by political actors on various levels as bearing the power to make an Islamist party embrace the norms of liberal democracy and thereby democratise Turkey's political system (Atasoy 2009; Bedirhanoğlu and Yalman 2009). Drawing on the EU framework, AKP cut down the power of the Kemalist military and softened state control over the public practice and visibility of Sunni Islamic belonging. At the same time, the rise of a new Islamic middle class, the expansion of Islamist civil society, the step-by-step liberalisation of the headscarf ban and the recognition of Kurdish claims to cultural rights were presented by the party as the democratisation of the Kemalist state (Atasoy 2009, p.241; Kandiyoti 2012). AKP's growing hegemony over state and society thereby translated social antagonisms based on gender, class and ethnicity into a Kemalism vs. Islamism/anti-Kemalism binary.

As for its gender politics, AKP recognised gender equality in its programme and referred to CEDAW as the correct means to approach the EU accession process. For an Islamist party that promoted a conservative interpretation of gender relations, adhering to the global gender equality regime looked paradoxical, but as Kandiyoti (2010) suggests, this has been a widespread tactic of the governments in the post-9/11 Middle East region. Compliance with gender reforms instead of implementing genuine democratic representation helped governments to present themselves as more democratic, and the disintegration of gender justice and social justice in the global neoliberal agenda made gender reforms unthreatening for neoliberal states (Kandiyoti 2010, p.171). AKP too emphasised the democratic potential of women's rights in its critique of covered women's exclusion from the public sphere, but this went hand in hand with policies that designated the family institution as the site where the care needs of children, the elderly and disabled were met. In fact, EU-oriented reforms did not contradict with AKP's goal of "strengthening the family institution" that lay at the heart of its gender politics. Steps taken towards gender-neutral citizenship (Kılıç 2008) pushed women into informal, low-paid, flexible, insecure jobs, which meant that only those urban, educated, upper-class women who could outsource housework and care work could benefit from the EU-related gender reforms.

At the same time, Europeanisation strengthened feminists' ground from which to engage in gender politics because its legal framework required the state to further include the civil society in decision-making processes. In the 2000s, a greater number of women struggled for gender equality while the fragmentation of women's rights activism based on identity politics deepened. Islamist women in their struggle for participating in public life with their headscarf shifted their emphasis from freedom of thought and faith to individual rights and freedoms. Kurdish women politicised their exclusion from the public sphere and demanded rights to counter the assimilationist policies of the state. As Islamist and Kurdish nationalist movements became legitimate actors in Turkish politics, Kemalist women adhered further to the "universality" of women's rights as opposed to the "particularistic" demands raised by Islamist and Kurdish women.

Europeanisation also intensified the NGOisation of women's activism and provided women's organisations with an unprecedented amount of money via EU-supported projects as well as foundations and think tanks in and embassies of EU member states. Yet, the EU framework encompassed gender equality primarily in its employment and social policy aspects, and emphasised "development" as an indispensable dimension of gender equality. In this framework, women's empowerment was understood as women's entrepreneurship in order to alleviate their low labour force participation (Landig 2011). The accentuation of women's entrepreneurship resulted in new NGOs that brought together women not only with donor agencies and the state but also with big business, emptying the meaning of empowerment in relation to neoliberalism. The limitation of women's empowerment in a developmentalist perspective fed into AKP's instrumentalisation of gender equality without endangering its gender politics. Shortly after it came to power, the party proved to include feminists in decision-making processes only to a limited extent; feminists' policy proposals during the EU-oriented reform period went largely ignored. This brought them closer to counterpublic feminists in terms of their proximity to state power.

Gender politics in issue-based platforms

Sidelined by the state, feminists who occupied the institutional sphere of politics drew on the mechanisms of transnational governance more rigorously and more autonomously. Already experienced from 1990s' activism, they formed issue-based platforms to influence policy-making processes. During the EU-oriented reform period, these platforms functioned similarly to what Lang (2014) refers to as "women's advocacy networks" in the EU context where "different constellations of feminist actors from inside and outside EU institutions joined forces to achieve policy goals" (p.266). Feminists united women's rights activists from feminist, Kemalist, Kurdish, Islamist women's organisations to build a civil societal front, and allied with bureaucrats and MPs from political parties that supported their cause.

Issue-based platforms like the Civil Law Platform, the Turkish Penal Law Women's Platform, the Constitutional Platform of Women and the European Women's Lobby–Turkish Coordination raised public awareness about the EU-oriented gender reforms and lobbied to participate in policy-making. This strategy worked so long as the Turkish state elite maintained their pro-EU stance (Aldıkaçtı Marshall 2013). The EU-oriented reform period also provided a ground for feminists to hold on to CEDAW-related processes more visibly. The CEDAW Civil Society Executive Committee, a platform established in 2003, prepared shadow reports to the UN CEDAW Committee. Feminists' demands were communicated to the state through these reports which openly stated the state's violations of CEDAW. In the context of Europeanisation and Islamisation, feminists' adherence to the global gender equality regime was a response to the changes in state power as well as a necessary choice to keep influencing state policies.

What made feminists' intervention in gender politics through issue-based platforms effective was their reliance on the "rhetorical and mobilising power" of the language of rights (Molyneux and Razavi 2002, p.12). This strategy put pressure on bureaucrats and MPs, who saw feminism as a Western import against the values of Turkish society but embraced the "universality" of human rights in their own political programmes. It also provided women of different political belongings with a normative framework in which political tensions could be eased (Ertürk 2006). Kemalist, Islamist and Kurdish women's organisations that participated in issue-based platforms had differential agendas that were in conflict with each other, and their approach to feminism was far from uniform. Yet, Kemalist women had translated laicism, Islamist women the headscarf issue, and Kurdish women their culture-based demands into the language of women's human rights since the 1990s. An overarching language of rights counterbalanced the absence of a shared feminist stance in issue-based platforms and facilitated the development of democratic forms of dialogue and coalition building between different groups of women.

At a time when AKP governments drew on the discourses of Europeanisation and democratisation, a women's front united for rights struggle albeit their political diversity had a greater potential in negotiating the terms of gender politics with the state. This was not only because, similar to the 1990s, "women's human rights" were the legitimate imperative of the global gender equality regime to which the Turkish state adhered or because historically "woman rights" were part and parcel of Turkish modernisation. It was also because the strategy to unite women under the rubric of "women's rights," rather than that of "feminism," helped generate popular support for gender equality. "Feminism" on the societal level was still associated with the (imperialist) West and thereby was delegitimised. "Women's rights," on the other hand, became a popular theme of corporate social responsibility projects that attracted the private sector into partnerships with women's organisations in promoting women's empowerment. Implications of the notion of women's empowerment were ambiguous, but its promotion helped the principle of gender equality to become an acknowledged element of Turkey's democratisation, which gave feminists leverage in negotiating with the state. In this sense, feminists' "co-optation by neoliberalism" worked as a problematic but effective tool that helped them remain in the state-civil society-strategic governance framework.

Despite its strategic use, organising in issue-based platforms placed limitations on the dominant feminist agenda. Platforms were established based on the premise that women had common interests, yet in practice the differential interests sought by Kemalist, Islamist and Kurdish women's rights organisations made these structures operate by constant struggle and negotiation. Regardless of whether they identified as feminist or not, women's differential political belongings shaped their analysis of patriarchy in ways that were incompatible with each other. For example, on the issue of violence against women, Islamist women had a pro-family stance and did not support solutions centred around the idea of women's independence from the family. Or, Kurdish women's demand to include armed-conflict related violence in the notion of violence against women was met with resistance (Fisher Onar and Paker 2012). Women's low labour force participation was acknowledged as a problem, but the elimination of the gender division of labour in public and private spheres did not become a common goal of all parties. More contested issues such as militarism and its relation to sexual violence, heteronormativity, rights of domestic workers and sex workers, problems of migrant and refugee women, did not make it to the agenda in issue-based platforms. The absence of a common analysis of patriarchy as a system of oppression also made "men" invisible as perpetrators of women's subordination and appropriators of their unpaid labour. At the same time, a women's rights activism that did not emphasise the social antagonism between men and women was the only brand of feminism that could, through the mediation of the global gender equality regime, reach the state, especially when it was run by a party with a neoliberal-conservative political programme and with no intention to serve women's strategic, long-term gender interests.

Feminist counterpublics

Leaving the analysis at this point could lead to the conclusion that feminism was co-opted by the state-civil society-transnational governance framework, that it lost its radical kernel by being absorbed into identity politics. But counterpublic feminists addressed the state in the demands they raised and responded to their exclusion and/or marginalisation by the state in various ways. They also engaged with the global gender equality regime, be it by receiving funds or by criticising its dominance in gender politics. During the EU-oriented reform period, similar to the EU context where feminist efforts were channelled towards institutional advocacy (Lang 2014, p.269), street activism and other contentious forms of feminism remained low profile. However, alongside the activism in issue-based platforms, a powerful critique of neoliberal patriarchy grew in feminist counterpublics and gained visibility in the second half of the 2000s. Organised mostly in autonomous, informal, non-hierarchical, horizontal, small-scale, and local structures, counterpublic feminists addressed those issues that were excluded or only partially addressed in the state-civil society-transnational governance framework.

Three interrelated issues were especially problematised in feminist counterpublics: NGOisation and, in relation to it, the global gender equality regime; Kurdish conflict, peace, and the relationship between Turkish and Kurdish feminists; neoliberalism and women's entrapment between paid and unpaid labour. Since the 1990s, NGOisation had not only shaped women's rights activism but also influenced feminist activism in the counterpublic sphere. Activists criticised NGOisation for launching a type of "virtual feminism" which, from a developmentalist perspective, prioritised the number of "underdeveloped women" it reached over posing a coherent challenge to patriarchy (Sirman 2006). One of feminists' main concerns was that NGOisation reinstated class differences between women. Many NGOs functioned like informal microcredit organisations where an initial capital was raised to help individual or groups of women sell their products and invest the earnings in further production. This provided an immediate means to women's empowerment but also translated social problems of lower-class women such as poverty and unemployment into individual matters that could be dealt with through projects (Çoban 2008). Class differences between women were further reproduced because foreign funds were accessible to women's organisations in urban areas, and even then, the English language requirement in writing grant applications excluded many grassroots organisations from the process (Işat 2009). These criticisms often came from the very organisations that operated thanks to foreign funding, showing that donor-funded organisations could not be automatically classified as handmaidens of neoliberal patriarchy (Alvarez 2014).

Another dimension of NGOisation that counterpublic feminists problematised was its intertwining of neoliberalism with Turkish nationalism. Helping lower-class women to become self-reliant, self-confident, disciplined individuals, traits that were compatible with neoliberal thinking, reproduced middle-class values of NGO volunteers such as "representing" and "guiding" the people and thereby supporting the state as responsible citizens (Ipek 2006). A more compelling challenge to the entanglement between Turkish nationalism and dominant feminism came from Kurdish feminists who criticised Turkish feminists for alienating Kurdish women with their arbitrary application of universal principles (Deniz 2005). Kurdish feminists especially denounced the Multi-Purpose Community Centres in Kurdistan, a significant example of state-civil society-transnational governance cooperation, for being the embodiment of state feminism that aimed at the assimilation of Kurds by promoting birth control methods under the guise of "health education" (Kutluata 2002).

Feminists in counterpublics generally acknowledged the positive aspects of the global gender equality regime, such as its contribution to the visibility of feminist politics, but criticised it for prioritising women's individual struggle over their collective struggle for liberation. In the second half of the 2000s, socialist feminists developed this critique into a holistic agenda against capitalist patriarchy. Established in 2008, the Socialist Feminist Collective addressed AKP's neoliberal-conservative gender politics in its campaigns, publications and street demonstrations. Similar to autonomous feminists in Latin America (see Alvarez 2014), socialist feminists in Turkey refrained from receiving funds from donor agencies, emphasising their independence from the state, capital and men (SFK 2008). In a number of campaigns, the Collective demanded not only the state to provide free, universal and qualified care services to eliminate women's disadvantaged position in paid labour but also men to take an equal share of responsibilities in housework and care work at home. As the consequences of AKP's neoliberal labour policies became visible and even stricter labour regulations appeared due to the 2008 global financial crisis, the issue of women's paid and unpaid labour has led to various feminist mobilisations in the counterpublic sphere.

Feminist counterpublics have not been immune to the political tensions that marked the field of women's rights activism. Yet, instead of taking women's belonging to male-dominant political projects for granted, counterpublic feminists challenged women's division along the lines of identity politics by creating space for dialogue and joint action. *Amargi* Women's Cooperative was one example of this challenge that drew on the notions of diversity feminism and transversal politics (Özakın 2012). Socialist feminists perceived women's differential political belongings as varieties of patriarchal capitalism and sought the similarities between them, and employed the notion of "women as a political collective subject" as compensation for the negative consequences of identity politics in feminist activism (Acar Savran 2009). These efforts were fruitful, especially in Turkish and Kurdish feminists' struggle for the peaceful resolution of the Kurdish conflict. Initially, it was NGOisation and the global gender equality regime that brought Kurdish and Turkish feminists together in issue-based platforms. Then, women from different political backgrounds founded the Women's Initiative for Peace (2009) in the counterpublic sphere. The Initiative regularly organised conferences and released reports on the peace process and women's involvement in it from a feminist perspective. Encounters between Islamist and secular women in feminist counterpublics was less frequent due to Islamisation, which shifted Islamist women's position in civil society from the margins to the centre, but there were attempts at dialogue; in 2008, hundreds of feminist and women's rights activists became signatories to the manifesto "We are Looking Out for Each Other" against the ban of the headscarf in higher education, which sought the collective struggle of women, covered or not, for liberation from gender-based oppression.

Feminist counterpublics accommodated agendas that challenged, from various angles, dominant feminisms' cooperation with the state. Still, the hegemonic influence of transnational governance over feminist activism as a whole made the separation of dominant and non-dominant feminisms analytically meaningful but dubious in practice. Many feminist activists, including those who simultaneously identified as Kemalist, Islamist or Kurdish, pursued politics in both feminist counterpublics and the state-civil society-transnational governance framework. These feminists took their experiences from issue-based platforms to counterpublics and launched issue-based initiatives that brought counterpublic feminists and women's rights activists together. The alliance between the two groups ranged from organising forums and conferences to street demonstrations and running campaigns on various topics. Authentic demands were produced at this juncture, circulated to the public, translated into the language of rights and communicated to the state. It was this alliance that made it possible for women's rights activists to join feminist counterpublics in the conjuncture of post-2010 developments.

The 2010s: women's rights against feminism

From the 1980s on, in spite of conservative politicians and the Islamisation of the political sphere, the state had taken steps towards improving women's legal status. This Turkish version of state feminism destabilised parallel to AKP's "authoritarian turn" (Öktem and Akkoyunlu 2016). In 2010, the then Prime Minister Tayyip Erdoğan declared that he didn't believe in gender equality but only in equal opportunities. Following Erdoğan's statement, AKP took more decisive steps towards institutionalising their version of gender politics. In 2011, the State Ministry of Women and Social Affairs was replaced with the new Ministry of Family and Social Policy. Policies of the new ministry illustrated that "a seemingly promising if mainstreaming inclusion of gender and even feminist perspectives into state discourse and policy early in the first decade of the 2000s has transformed or perhaps matured into a state-sponsored familialism in the 2010s" (Kurtuluş Korkman 2016, p.112). More recent policies regarding women openly violated the laicism principle and posed a threat to women's legal gains (Kuyucu 2016). In the face of these developments, feminists' decades-long strategy of drawing on the universal rights regime to put pressure on the state came to a dead end, showing how context-dependent and fragile the already indirect cooperation between dominant feminisms and the state was. A new era began, where the notion of women's rights is defined by non-feminist actors and in opposition to feminism.

The post-2011 changes in Turkey's gender politics are part of a broader tendency to disregard the imperatives of the global gender equality regime for the sake of populist and authoritarian discourses. Across the global North and South, the rise of neoliberalism and conservatism goes hand in hand with a politics of gender whose implications are similar to those in Turkey: insecure jobs and low wages under the slogan "flexibility for women," emphasis on the family and tradition, pro-natalist policies, and utter anti-feminism. Since the 2000s, the global gender equality regime's regulative power weakened under the "growing influence of illiberal, religious and conservative forces worldwide which became increasingly effective in the battleground over women's rights" (Ewig and Ferree 2013, p.443). Global developments, together with Turkey's loss of the prospect of EU membership, which was the driving force behind the reforms of the 2000s, encouraged AKP to build a new gender regime in line with its Islamisation project. The new state discourse claims that the notion of "gender equity" is superior to the Western, universalist notion of gender equality and more compatible with Turkish-Islamic culture. Feminists as proponents of gender equality are thereby discredited for not belonging to "our civilization, our belief, our religion" (*Diken*,17 February 2015).

At the same time, the notion of women's rights – now detached from gender equality – continue to be monopolised by the state and used as a marker of modernity and democracy. AKP governments still rely on the language of rights and take pride in, for example, making Turkey the first signatory to the Council of Europe Convention on preventing and combating violence against women and domestic violence (Istanbul Convention, 2014). Yet, the state now invests in government-organised non-governmental organisations (GONGOs) to promote its gender politics in the field of civil society. A women's activism that builds its agenda on gender inequality under the brand name "gender justice," led by women with an organic relationship to AKP, is rising. For example, the Women and Democracy Association (KADEM, foundation, 2013) claims that the most oppressive gender practices in history have been seen in the West and promotes the idea that Islamic norms regarding social rights and responsibilities transcend the universal notion of equality (*Hürriyet*, 30 March 2015). While adopting an anti-feminist discourse, organisations like KADEM use the local and global strategies developed by feminist activists over decades such as celebrating the International Women's Day or organising events on the International Day for the Elimination of Violence against Women. Backed by the state ideologically as well as financially, Islamist women's GONGOs collaborate in high-budget projects with state institutions and, as the new partners of the state-civil society-transnational governance framework, participate in processes such as GREVIO or Beijing 20+. This major shift in gender politics shows how the state-favoured definition of women's rights plays a key role in the power struggles within the women's movement and in the making of the relationship between dominant and non-dominant feminisms.

Feminism as an opposition front?

In response to AKP's neoliberal-conservative gender politics and the state monopolisation of women's rights, feminist counterpublics in the 2010s grew bigger and stronger. Feminists who so far pursued politics within the state-civil society-transnational governance framework were relocated in counterpublics. Combined with the canalisation of state resources to Islamist women's GONGOs, the global gender equality regime and NGOisation lost momentum in feminist activism. Inegalitarian, anti-secular and sexist claims by high-ranking AKP members made women from different generations, and political belongings, identify with feminism with greater ease. In the 2010s thousands of women joined the ranks of feminist politics. Many of them, especially young women, chose not to organise in NGOs; as Turkey's gender politics was more and more defined by AKP's anti-democratic political project, women sought non-institutionalised ways of pursuing feminist politics.

Just like AKP's exclusion of feminists from gender politics is part of a global trend towards more authoritarian political regimes, the growth of feminist counterpublics in Turkey is part of a process of change in the form and content of feminism worldwide. Bernal and Grewal argue that among women's NGOs "there is increasing awareness of many pitfalls and of the critiques levelled at NGOs as having been co-opted by powerful interests, including states, donors, corporations, and elites of various kinds" (2014, p.301; see also Cornwall and Molyneux 2008, pp.2–3). As street activism and the visibility of feminists increase, there's also a move "beyond NGOisation" (Alvarez 2014), where some organisations explicitly position themselves against neoliberalism even if they maintain the NGO form of organising. Similar to what Helms (2014) calls the "movementization of NGOs" in the post-war Bosnian context, thousands of activists recruited through NGOisation now work in the counterpublic sphere to render the notion of gender equality a crucial element of democratic society. In many parts of the world new forms of activism, especially social media activism, contribute to the growth of feminist counterpublics. Online activism creates a crucial counterpublic where excluded groups can challenge authoritarian regimes in ways that are more difficult to suppress than street activism (Nordenson 2017).

The expansion of feminist counterpublics in the Turkish context accelerated the politicisation of the already existing issues and added new ones to the feminist agenda. Labour feminists established new platforms that tackled specific dimensions of gender and labour such as employment policies (Women's Labour Platform, 2013) or child care provision (Créche is a Right Platform, 2013). Through issue-based platforms, feminists launched vigorous campaigns on violence against women and on sexual and reproductive health rights. Kurdish feminists' critique of dominant feminisms matured into "Jineoloji," the "science of women," which builds on Kurdish women's collective struggle for liberation (Özgür Kadın Akademisi 2015). Lesbian and bisexual feminists formed the Lesbian Bisexual Feminists Group in 2015. Other feminists politicised sex workers' rights and refugee women's rights in various organisations. Islamist women became more concerned with issues related to gender oppression and violence against women, and their visibility in feminist counterpublics increased. The use of the internet in feminist activism nurtured the further consolidation of a critical feminist culture, with numerous Facebook and Twitter accounts as well as websites.

Feminists' exclusion and marginalisation by the state fed into feminist counterpublics, changed its composition, and increased the visibility as well as the legitimacy of feminist critique. AKP's attacks on women's legal gains resulted in a bigger opposition to its gender politics and made feminism a significant element of the greater social opposition as more and more women joined protests and campaigns organised by feminists. In 2012, thousands of women took the streets and organised web-based campaigns when AKP attempted to ban abortion, forcing the party to step back. In 2013, women joined the Gezi-inspired protests raising feminist demands alongside demands for greater rights and freedoms. In 2015, the murder of the young university student Özgecan Aslan after an attempted rape led to nation-wide protests and greater public awareness of public sexual assault and femicide. In 2016, AKP's attempt to decriminalise child abuse was pushed back thanks to feminists' mobilisation in the counterpublic sphere. At the same time, feminists kept building alliances between women across the political spectrum in issue-based platforms. Since 2015, termination of the peace process between PKK and the Turkish state, state violence in Kurdistan, and – particularly – state oppression towards Kurdish feminist organisations and members of the Parliament, triggered a stronger opposition against ethnic discrimination in feminist counterpublics. Hitherto unwilling to engage with this issue, Kemalist women's organisations became signatories to joint petitions by Turkish and Kurdish feminists demanding peace. Islamist women supported feminists' peace campaigns and some of them became active in the Women's Initiative for Peace. Feminists who transitioned to counterpublics from the state-civil society-transnational governance framework also continued embracing the global gender equality regime, this time with a greater willingness to encompass in their agenda issues that they previously excluded. As the difference between dominant and non-dominant feminisms in relation to their proximity to state power diminished, greater alliances across different feminisms became possible. Feminist activism remained an essential constituent of Turkey's gender politics by pursuing agendas despite the state, going beyond the state.

Conclusion

In her discussion on feminist politics, feminist philosopher Françoise Collin (2016) suggests that women's collective struggle for gender equality is an irreversible gain, but this collectivity is experienced in a fragmented way, in the form of contentious disagreements. Emphasising the importance of the simultaneity of feminist endeavours for substantive equality and the transformation of patriarchy, she argues that feminism cannot be reduced to its strategies of "seeping" into political structures but at the same time it cannot abandon these strategies (Collin and Kaufer 2016, pp.98; 203). A common tendency in mainstream and critical feminist scholarship on gender and politics has been to focus exclusively on either dominant or non-dominant forms of feminism for these forms were perceived by scholars as more effective in "policy-making" or "challenging patriarchal gender relations," respectively. The result was partial accounts of feminist politics in general and the feminism-state relationship in particular. In this chapter I have offered a nuanced perspective by examining the Turkish case through the lens of dominant/Northern and non-dominant/Southern feminisms, that is, by incorporating feminist counterpublics into the analysis of the feminism-state relationship and its mediation by the global gender equality regime. My examination has shown that, when feminist counterpublics are included in the analysis, it is difficult to argue that feminists excluded from their agendas issues related to political economy, elitism, ethnic discrimination, heteronormativity, border regimes and other topics marginalised by states and the mechanisms of transnational governance. A more fruitful inquiry is to look at the dynamics by which certain feminisms occupy dominant positions while others reside in counterpublics, to trace the changes in these dynamics and see their impact on how feminists negotiate and strategise their politics in relation to each other and to various centres of power. Such an inquiry has the potential to destabilise simplistic arguments around feminisms' co-optation by neoliberalism and other hegemonic discourses and structures. The current state of the feminism-state relationship in Turkey runs parallel to the global developments marked by the rise of regimes that identify against gender equality and attack some very basic rights of women, which create common agendas for feminists across the dominant/Northern and non-dominant/Southern divide, as massive demonstrations in 2016 and 2017 in Argentina, Poland, Ireland, the U.S. and many other countries have shown. In this new phase of a global-scale struggle to define the terms of gender relations, feminists are likely to be seeking, as they do in Turkey, the possibilities of strategic alliances between dominant and non-dominant feminisms. In response to this, critical feminist scholarship will need to develop non-teleological approaches that allow researchers to grasp the complex relationship between feminisms and the political contexts in which they operate.

Acknowledgements

I would like to thank Ewa Mączyńska, Ece Kocabıçak, Görkem Akgöz, and the editors of this book for their valuable comments and suggestions on the earlier versions of this chapter.

Notes

1 I borrow the title from the anti-capitalist feminist collective Feminist Fightback (Feminist Fightback, 25 October 2010).
2 Some notable exceptions are Arat 2004; Fougner and Kurtoğlu 2011; Özmen Yılmaz 2015; Potuoğlu-Cook 2015.

References

Acar Savran, G., (2009) Feministler, Kadınlar ve Politik Özne Olmak [Feminists, Women, and Becoming a Political Subject]. *Feminist Politika*. 2. pp. 36–37.

Aldıkaçtı Marshall, G., (2013) *Shaping Gender Policy in Turkey: Grassroots Women Activists, the European Union, and the Turkish State*. New York: SUNY Press.

Alvarez, V., (2014) Beyond NGOization? Reflections from Latin America. *In*: Bernal, V., and Grewal, I. (eds.). *Theorizing NGOs: States, Feminisms, and Neoliberalism*. Durham: Duke University Press. pp. 285–300.

Arat, Y., (2001) Women's Rights as Human Rights: The Turkish Case. *Human Rights Review*. 3(1). pp. 27–34.

Arat, Y., (2004) Rethinking the Political: A Feminist Journal in Turkey, Pazartesi. *Women's Studies International Forum*. 27. pp. 281–292.

Asen, R., and Brouwer, D.C., (2001) Introduction: Reconfigurations in the Public Sphere. *In*: Asen, R., and Brouwer, D.C., (eds.). *Counterpublics and the State*. Albany: State University of New York Press. pp. 1–34.

Aslan, Ö., and Gambetti, Z., (2011) Provincializing Fraser's History: Feminism and Neoliberalism Revisited. *History of the Present*. 1(1). pp. 130–147.

Aslan-Akman, C., (2011) Challenging Religious and Secularist Patriarchy: Islamist Women's New Activism in Turkey. *Journal of Levantine Studies*. 1(2). pp. 103–124.

Atasoy, Y., (2009) *Islam's Marriage with Neo-Liberalism: State Transformation in Turkey*. New York: Palgrave Macmillan.

Bedirhanoğlu, P., and Yalman, G.L., (2009) State, Class and the Discourse: Reflections on the Neoliberal Transformations in Turkey. *In*: Saad-Filho, A., and Yalman, G.L., (eds.). *Economic Transitions to Neoliberalism in Middle-Income Countries: Policy Dilemmas, Crises, Mass Resistance*. New York: Routledge. pp. 107–127.

Benhabib, S., (1992) Models of Public Space: Hannah Arendt, the Liberal Tradition, and Jürgen Habermas. *In*: Calhoun, C., (ed.). *Habermas and the Public Sphere*. Cambridge, MA and London: MIT Press. pp. 73–98.

Bernal, V., and Grewal, I., (2014) Feminisms and the NGO Form. *In*: Bernal, V., and Grewal, I., (eds.). *Theorizing NGOs: States, Feminisms, and Neoliberalism*. Durham, NC: Duke University Press. pp. 301–310.

Bunch, C., and Frost, S., (2000) Women's Human Rights: An Introduction. *In*: Kramarae, C., and Spender, D. (eds), *Routledge International Encyclopedia of Women: Global Women's Issues and Knowledge*. Vol. 4. New York: Routledge.

Çağatay, S., (2017) *The Politics of Gender and the Making of Kemalist Feminist Activism in Contemporary Turkey (1946–2011)*. PhD thesis, Dept. of Gender Studies, Central European University.

Çoban, A., (2008) Feminizmden Kadın Hareketine ve STK'ya [From Feminism to the Women's Movement and NGOs]. *Amargi*. 10. pp. 29–30.

Collin, F., and Kaufer, I., (2016) *Feminist Güzergah [Feminist Route*; Original title in French: *Parcours féministe*]. Istanbul: Dipnot Yayınları.

Connell, R., (2009) *Southern Theory: The Global Dynamics of Knowledge in Social Science*. Cambridge and Malden, MA: Polity Press.

Cornwall, A., and Molyneux, M., (2008) *The Politics of Rights: Dilemmas for Feminist Praxis*. New York and London: Routledge.

Dedeoğlu, S., (2013) Veiled Europeanisation of Welfare State in Turkey: Gender and Social Policy in the 2000s. *Women's Studies International Forum*. 41(1). pp. 7–13.

Deniz, D., (2005) *No title*. Paper presented at the 8th Congress of Women's Shelters and Solidarity Centers: Diyarbakır.

Diken, (2015) Erdoğan'dan Feministlere: Ya Senin Bizim Dinimizle Medeniyetimizle Ilgin Yok Ki [Erdoğan to Feminists: You Have Nothing to do with Our Religion and Civilization]. *Diken*. 17 February.www.diken.com.tr/erdogandan-feministlere-ya-senin-bizim-dinimizle-medeniyetimizle-ilgin-yok-ki/. (Accessed: 12 July 2017)

Diner, Ç., and Toktaş, Ş., (2010) Waves of Feminism in Turkey: Kemalist, Islamist and Kurdish Women's Movements in an Era of Globalization. *Journal of Balkan and Near Eastern Studies*. 12(1). pp. 41–57.

Eisenstein, H., (2009) *Feminism Seduced: How Global Elites Use Women's Labor and Ideas to Exploit the World*. Boulder: Paradigm Publishers.

Ertürk, Y., (2006) Turkey's Modern Paradoxes: Identity Politics, Women's Agency, and Universal Rights. *In*: Ferree, M.M., and Tripp, A.M. (eds.). *Global Feminism: Transnational Women's Activism, Organizing, and Human Rights*. New York: New York University Press. pp. 79–109.

Eschle, C., and Maiguashca, B., (2014) Reclaiming Feminist Futures: Co-Opted and Progressive Politics in a Neo-Liberal Age. *Political Studies*. 62(3). pp. 634–651.

Esim, S., and Cindoğlu, D., (1999) Women's Organizations in 1990s Turkey: Predicaments and Prospects. *Middle Eastern Studies*. 35(1). pp. 178–188.

Ewig, C., and Ferree, M.M., (2013) Feminist Organizing: What's Old, What's New? History, Trends, and Issues. *In*: Waylen, G., Celis, K., Kantola, J., and Weldon, S.L., (eds.). *The Oxford Handbook of Gender and Politics*. New York: Oxford University Press. pp. 437–461.

Felski, R., (1989) *Beyond Feminist Aesthetics: Feminist Literature and Social Change*. Cambridge, MA: Harvard University Press.

Feminist Fightback, (2010) In, Against (and Beyond?) the State. *Feminist Fightback*. 25 October.www.feministfightback.org.uk/in-against-and-beyond-the-state/. (Accessed: 10 July 2017)

Ferree, M., and TrippA.M., (eds.). (2006) *Global Feminism: Transnational Women's Activism, Organizing, and Human Rights*. New York:New York University Press.

Fisher Onar, N., and Paker, H., (2012) Towards Cosmopolitan Citizenship? Women's Rights in Divided Turkey. *Theory and Society*. 41(4). pp. 375–394.

Fougner, T., and Kurtoğlu, A., (2011) Transnational Labour Solidarity and Social Movement Unionism: Insights from and beyond a Women Workers' Strike in Turkey. *British Journal of Industrial Relations*. 49 (Supplement). pp. 353–375.

Fraser, N., (1992) Rethinking the Public Sphere: A Contribution to the Critique of Actually Existing Democracy. *In*: Calhoun, C. (ed.). *Habermas and the Public Sphere*. Cambridge, MA and London: MIT Press. pp. 109–142.

Fraser, N., (2009) Feminism, Capitalism and the Cunning of History. *New Left Review*. 56. pp. 97–119.

Gökalp, D., (2010) A Gendered Analysis of Violence, Justice and Citizenship: Kurdish Women Facing War and Displacement in Turkey. *Women's Studies International Forum*. 33. pp. 561–569.

Grewal, I., (2005) *Transnational America: Feminisms, Diasporas, Neoliberalisms*. Durham, NC: Duke University Press.

Habermas, J., (1992) Further Reflections on the Public Sphere. *In*: Calhoun, C., (ed.). *Habermas and the Public Sphere*. Cambridge, MA and London: MIT Press. pp. 421–461.

Helms, E., (2014) The Movementization of NGOs? Women's Organizing in Postwar Bosnia-Herzegovina. *In*: Bernal, V., and Grewal, I. (eds.). *Theorizing NGOs: States, Feminisms, and Neoliberalism*. Durham, NC: Duke University Press. pp. 21–49.

Hürriyet, (2015) KADEM Başkan Yardımcısı Sümeyye Erdoğan: Dünya Tarihinde Kadını Ezen Uygulamaları En Çok Batı'da Görürsünüz [KADEM Vice President Sümeyye Erdoğan: The Most Oppressive Practices Against Women in World History are Seen in the West]. *Hürriyet*. 30 March.www.hurriyet.com.tr/kadem-baskan-yardimcisi-sumeyye-erdogan-dunya-tarihinde-kadini-ezen-uygulamalari-en-cok-batida-gorursunuz-28591556. (Accessed:12 July 2017)

Icoz, G., (2016) The Interconnectedness of the Past, the Present and the Future: Where Turkey–EU Relations Have Been, and Where They Are Heading. *Journal of Contemporary European Studies*. 24(4). pp. 494–508.

Ipek, Y., (2006) 'Görevimiz Gönüllülük': 1990'lar, Gönüllü Kuruluşlar, Gönüllü Vatandaşlar ['Mission Voluntarism': 1990s, Voluntary Organizations, Voluntary Citizens]. *Amargi*. 3. pp. 17–21.

Işat, C., (2009) *Fon Kuruluşları Üzerine Bir Araştırma [A Research on Funding Agencies]*. Istanbul: SOGEP.

Kandiyoti, D., (2010) Gender and Women's Studies in Turkey: A Moment for Reflection? *New Perspectives on Turkey*. 43. pp. 165–176.

Kandiyoti, D., (2012) The Travails of the Secular: Puzzle and Paradox in Turkey. *Economy and Society*. 41(4). pp. 513–531.

Kantola, J., (ed.). (2006) *Feminists Theorize the State*. New York: Palgrave Macmillan.

Kardam, N., (2005) *Turkey's Engagement with Global Women's Human Rights*. Aldershot, UK and Burlington: Ashgate.

Katz, H., (2009) Civil Society Theory: Gramsci. *In*: Anheier, H.K., and Toepler, S., (eds.). *International Encyclopedia of Civil Society*. New York: Springer. pp. 408–412.

Kılıç, A., (2008) The Gender Dimension of Social Policy Reform in Turkey: Towards Equal Citizenship? *Social Policy and Administration*. 42(5). pp. 487–503.

Krook, M.L., and Childs, S., (eds.). (2010) *Women, Gender, and Politics: A Reader.* Oxford and New York: Oxford University Press.

Kurtuluş Korkman, Z., (2016) Politics of Intimacy in Turkey: A Distraction from 'Real' Politics? *Journal of Middle East Women's Studies.* 12(1). pp. 112–121.

Kutluata, Z., (2002) Feminist Kürt Kadın Dergilerinde Doğum Kontrol Tartışmaları [Discussions on Contraception in Kurdish Feminist Women's Magazines]. *Toplum Bilim.* 15. pp. 35–39.

Kuyucu, N., (2016) Kadının Adı Yok [Woman has no Name]. *Praksis.* 41(2). pp. 419–442.

Landig, J.M., (2011) Bringing Women to the Table: European Union Funding for Women's Empowerment Projects in Turkey. *Women's Studies International Forum.* 34. pp. 206–219.

Lang, S., (2014) Women's Advocacy Networks: The European Union, Women's NGOs, and the Velvet Triangle. *In*: Bernal, V., and Grewal, I. (eds.). *Theorizing NGOs: States, Feminisms, and Neoliberalism.* Durham: Duke University Press. pp. 266–284.

McBride, D.E., and Mazur, A.G., (2010) *The Politics of State Feminism: Innovation in Comparative Research.* Philadelphia: Temple University Press.

McRobbie, A., (2009) *The Aftermath of Feminism: Gender, Culture and Social Change.* London: SAGE.

Moghadam, V.M., (2005) *Globalizing Women: Transnational Feminist Networks.* Baltimore and London: Johns Hopkins University Press.

Mohanty, C.T., (1991) Cartographies of Struggle: Third World Women and the Politics of Feminism. *In*: Mohanty, C.T., Russo, A., and Torres, L., (eds.). *Third World Women and the Politics of Feminism.* Bloomington, IN: Indiana University Press. pp. 1–47.

Molyneux, M., and Razavi, S., (eds.). (2002) *Gender Justice, Development, and Rights.* Oxford: Oxford University Press.

Naples, N.A., (2004) The Challanges and Possibilities of Transnational Feminist Praxis. *In*: Naples, N.A., and Desai, M., (eds.). *Women's Activism and Globalization: Linking Local Struggles and Global Politics.* New York: Routledge. pp. 267–282.

Negrón-Gonzales, M., (2016) The Feminist Movement during the AKP Era in Turkey: Challenges and Opportunities. *Middle Eastern Studies.* 52(2). pp. 198–214.

Nordenson, J., (2017) *Online Activism in the Middle East: Political Power and Authoritarian Governments from Egypt to Kuwait.* London: I.B. Tauris.

Öktem, K., and Akkoyunlu, K., (2016) Exit from Democracy: Illiberal Governance in Turkey and Beyond. *Journal of Southeast European and Black Sea Studies.* 16(4). pp. 469–480.

Özakın, Ü., (2012) *Accommodating Diversity within Feminism in Turkey: The Amargi Women's Cooperative, 2001–2011.* MA thesis, Institute of Social Sciences, Middle East Technical University.

Özgür Kadın Akademisi, (2015) *Jineoloji Tartışmaları [Discussions on Jineology].* Diyarbakır: Aram Yayınevi.

Özmen Yılmaz, D., (2015) Socialist Feminist Alternatives to Neoliberalism in Turkey. In: Pradella, L., and Marois, T., (eds.). *Polarizing Development: Alternatives to Neoliberalism and the Crisis.* London: Pluto Press. pp. 237–247.

Potuoğlu-Cook, Ö., (2015) Hope with Qualms: A Feminist Analysis of the 2013 Gezi Protests. *Feminist Review.* 109(1). pp. 96–123.

Pringle, R., and Watson, S., (1992) 'Women's Interests' and the Post-Structuralist State. In: Barrett, M., and Phillips, A., *Destabilizing Theory: Contemporary Feminist Debates.* Cambridge: Polity Press. pp. 53–73.

Razavi, S., (2016) The 2030 Agenda: Challenges of Implementation to Attain Gender Equality and Women's Rights. *Gender and Development.* 24(1). pp. 25–41.

Razavi, S., and Jenichen, A., (2010) The Unhappy Marriage of Religion and Politics: Problems and Pitfalls for Gender Equality. *Third World Quarterly.* 31(6). pp. 833–850.

Rumelili, B., (2011) Turkey: Identity, Foreign Policy, and Socialization in a Post-Enlargement Europe. *Journal of European Integration*. 33(2). pp. 235–249.

Sauer, B., (2011) Bringing the State Back In: Civil Society, Women's Movements, and the State. In: Hagemann, K., Michel, S., and Budde, G.F., (eds.). *Civil Society and Gender Justice: Historical and Comparative Perspectives*. New York and Oxford: Berghahn Books. pp. 285–301.

Sauer, B., and Wöhl, S., (2011) Feminist Perspectives on the Internationalization of The State. *Antipode*. 43(1). pp. 108–128.

Schudson, M., (1994) The Public Sphere and Its Problems: Bringing the State (Back) In. *Notre Dame Journal of Law, Ethics, and Public Policy*. 8(2). pp. 529–546.

SFK, (2008) As We Set Off. *Sosyalist Feminist Kolektif* [*Socialist Feminist Collective*]. www.sosyalistfeministkolektif.org/english/as-we-set-off/. (Accessed 12 July 2017)

Sirman, N., (2006) Proje Toplumunun Sanal Kadınları [Virtual Women of the Project Society]. *Amargi*. 3. p. 22.

Yazıcı, B., (2012) The Return to the Family: Welfare, State, and Politics of the Family in Turkey. *Anthropological Quarterly*. 85(1). pp. 103–140.

5

IS THE SOCIAL DEMOCRACY GONE?

Performing feminisms in times of right-wing populism

Tiina Rosenberg

> Not everything that is faced can be changed,
> but nothing can be changed until it is faced.
>
> – *James Baldwin*

Introduction

As its characters wander the endless paths of the Thirty Years' War in Europe, Bertolt Brecht's play *Mother Courage and her children* portrays the hopelessness of armed conflict. Brecht, however, also shows that despite their obvious lack of hope, people never relinquish the faith that eventually life will give them a second chance. In the play, the dumb Kattrin is the only one who dares to let go of hopelessness. The most helpless one of all, she prevents a massacre through her drumming. This incongruous, desperate action proves a successful strategy. Perhaps hope is precisely that one stops investing in hopelessness (Brecht [1940] 1991; Backström 2017: 47).

Brecht's Kattrin comes to mind as one observes how today's Europe is being pressured by nationalism, conservatism, and right-wing populism. The question feminists face in times of post-factual democracy is what can be done in the way of public protests and non-violent resistance when the revolution now hits us from the conservative and right-wing populist side. Post-factual (also called post-truth) politics denotes a political culture in which debate is largely framed by appeals to emotions disconnected from the details of policy, and by the repeated assertion of talking points whose factual rebuttals are ignored.

This chapter discusses feminist protests as performances in a political context where the vacuum that European social democracies have left behind has been filled by right-wing populism and their conservative supporters. The situation has accelerated since the 2016 election of Donald Trump as US president. It is difficult for a global media audience to accustom themselves to a US president whose performance is based on tweets that he delivers before he thinks, or even worse, tweeting *what* he thinks on the spur of the moment, with typos, exclamation marks, angry all-capital letters, and incomplete sentences. This political situation places liberals and the left in an alien, disadvantageous position, while conservatives and right-wing populists appropriate the language of rebellion with renewed protests against feminism, liberalism, and social democracy.

What remains is a feminist 'we' who want to defend freedoms and rights won after years of struggle. However, this 'we' is a very heterogeneous and fragmented one. While there is no recipe for feminist activism, it is instructive to look upon various forms of feminist protest that have generated hope through interventions in anxious times. The question is not whether anything can be done, but *what* can be done and *how* to do it in a way that is effective, responsible, and ethical (Taylor 2016: 168). A number of feminist *artivists* (artist-activists) are like Brecht's Kattrin with her drum, trying to get their messages of hope across with unique means in the face of awful situations. As Diana Taylor asks, "If public response had no power, why would governments bother to criminalise protests and demonstrations?" (2016: 168).

A note on performance and performativity

Performance has become a popular notion used in a variety of contexts, such as theatre, anthropology, visual arts, business, politics, and science. "Performance," Diana Taylor writes, "is a wide-ranging and difficult practice to define and holds many, at times conflicting, meanings and possibilities." It moves across many fields and shifts between "as if" and "is," between pretend and new constructions of the "real" (2016: 6).

One of the challenges of using a performance vocabulary in a political context has been the contested relationship between theatricality and performativity that emanates from mixed metaphors and genealogies. What is "just theatre" and what is "truly performative" that results in real change? "The reduction of performativity to performance would be a mistake," Judith Butler states in *Critically Queer*, explicitly distinguishing performativity from performance (1993: 234). However, performativity for her is not an act but a reiteration or citation, while performance is the site wherein performativity materialises in concentrated form (1993: 46–47). According to Diana Taylor, performance is not limited to mimetic repetition. It includes the possibility of change, critique, and creativity within frameworks of repetition. Performance practices have their own structures, conventions, and styles that clearly separate them from other social practices in daily life (2016: 15).

Performativity's location inside a tradition of speech act theory is indifferent, and in some cases hostile, to all things theatrical. Shannon Jackson has observed that the relationship between theatricality and performativity for theatre scholars is a cause for defensiveness in relating to theatrical performance acts and practices of role-playing, illusion, false appearance, masquerade, façade, and impersonation (2003: 209). Theatricality has been condemned by philosophers from Plato to J. L. Austin. Such opposition illustrates the dichotomy between appearance and reality. A series of antinomies are operative here: real versus false, genuine versus fake, intrinsic versus extrinsic, original versus imitative, true versus counterfeit, honest versus dishonest, sincere versus devious, accurate versus distorted, revealed versus disguised, face versus mask, serious versus playful, and essential versus artificial (Davis and Postlewait 2003: 4). All things theatrical seem to be on the negative cusp of the polarity.

Performativity, however, remains a concept with multiple meanings. As an adjective, it comes close to theatricality in indicating that *performative* behaviour is somehow similar – in form, intent, and effect – to theatre. Its adjectival form also urges scholars to consider events and behaviours as performance. As a noun, the term performative is an utterance or speech act that has real-life consequences. At first glance these two equally useful understandings of performativity may seem to conflict with each other: one indicates something done to show, while the other indicates something done for real. The concept of performativity is a significant one because of its ability to hold both meanings simultaneously (Bial and Brady 2016: 203).

The right-wing populist turn in Europe

In terms of performance, the right-wing populism prevalent in European politics today may be characterised by a division of society into two groups of political players. On the one hand, there is the establishment, which populists presume consists of a 'corrupt elite'. On the other are the people who articulate 'truth' while continuing to be oppressed by society. This conflict-oriented vision of society is based on the democratic ideal of a popular will. When the will of the people is in control, the people are sovereign – a democratic notion derived from Rousseau. As Cas Mudde points out, populism is the reaction to a moral breakdown by 'authentic' people who rise up to challenge a corrupt elite (2016, 2017).

Since the right-wing populist will of the people is homogeneous, a variety of wills cannot exist. Thus, populism often fits well with a nationalist ideology that sees its people as of one mind. Both right-wing populist and neo-fascist parties cultivate troubling fantasies about an unambiguous, unified national culture and history. These conjectures of 'pure' nations, unsullied by immigrants, are a part of the mythical imagination that echoes Europe's darkest past and seeks to resurrect nationalism as a model for the future in many European countries (Müller 2016). René Cuperus (2003) has described right-wing populism in Europe as a revolt against the so-called second modernity, based on individualism, the abandonment of traditions, cosmopolitanism, neoliberal capitalism, and the global network society. Such populism rebels against social democratic ruling political classes for their failure to control globalisation, financial markets, and the technocratic logic that drives the European Union. Right-wing populism is thus seen as the revenge of the working class in post-socialist and post-social democratic societies in which neoliberal downsizing of the welfare state has taken place.

In a world of rapid change, where traditions, identities, and social security are no longer priorities, right-wing populism is a romantic, irrational, emotional rebellion against what is seen as inhumane governance controlling both the market and the state. Cuperus finds that where socialism and Christianity no longer slow down the globalisation process, populism fills the empty space. This makes right-wing populism a dangerous, xenophobic reaction to poorly managed large-scale migration policies (Cuperus 2003; Mudde 2007, 2010, 2016, 2017; Müller 2016).

However, the right-wing populist turn would not have been possible without the conservative revolution that flourished between World Wars I and II, and in part inspired German Nazism. According to the conservative philosophers Edgar Julius Jung, Carl Schmitt, and Oswald Spengler, liberalism's notion of freedom and individualism presumed the same kind of equality as socialism. The conservative revolutionaries saw this equality and democracy as the 'masses' (by which they meant the lower classes) dominating and oppressing classes with higher standing in society, and so they advocated a return to a 'natural' hierarchy.

The first post-World War II right-wing wave occurred in the 1960s in Europe and the US. In the latter, it was triggered by the abolition of racial segregation. The backlash was characterised by the well-known 1963 statement by Alabama Governor George Wallace, "Segregation now, segregation tomorrow, segregation forever!" As Europe was losing its colonies, Great Britain experienced an influx of immigration, French nationalists licked their wounds after the war in Algeria, and several northern European countries, including Germany and Sweden, received large numbers of labour migrants attracted by their industries. At this stage, Europe suffered from a major recession that resulted in high unemployment and for which migrants were scapegoated (Aalberg et al. 2017).

The philosophy of today's European right-wing populism is based on the idea that there are distinct 'pure' cultures that should be safeguarded so they can survive in a global context. According to this view, multiculturalism brings about a degeneration that will ultimately lead white civilisation to collapse if the West does not keep out undesirable 'elements'. When this philosophy is combined with the right-wing populist claim that immigration poses a threat to a country's economy, it attracts many voters. However, the cultural threat to Europe is significantly greater than the threat to its economy. This means that right-wing populist parties do not have to worry about losing voters over failed economic predictions as long as xenophobia and racism persist (Aalberg et al. 2017).

Performing post-social democracy in Sweden

Sweden, *the* social democracy par excellence, has also been subject to so-called capitalist realism, the belief that no alternative to capitalism exists. There have been many theories about why the left has lost political ground. This is especially true regarding structural changes in the traditional manufacturing sector following the emergence of a growing middle class. However, Terry Eagleton views it differently, writing that it is unlikely most leftists changed their views of the system between the 1970s and 1980s simply because there were fewer textile industries. What prompted them to abandon Marxism was a conviction that the regime they faced was simply too powerful to shatter. They saw capitalism for what it was, but were disillusioned about the possibility of changing it in any significant way. The lack of belief in an alternative was decisive for many former socialists. As the labour movement became fragmented and the political left was repressed, all prospects for the future seemed to have disappeared (Eagleton 2011).

Powerlessness and political impotence have been the dominant characteristics of the post-social democratic condition. The social democrats moved more and more to the right in the 1990s and the 2000s. The explicit repudiation of socialism by Göran Persson (former chairman of the Social Democratic Party in Sweden) confirmed what had already become obvious. The party had lost both its political heritage and identity. Since the fall of the Berlin Wall in 1989, Swedish social democrats have embarked upon a Third Way, inspired by Tony Blair's programme for New Labour. Rather than defending democratic socialism, the social democrats chose a neoliberal path that led directly to the post-social democratic condition prevailing today, making it easy for the conservatives to sharpen their rhetoric and promulgate their own version of Swedish history. Thus, a new narrative of the Swedish welfare state was born. Meanwhile, countermeasures have yet to be advanced by the social democrats. The crucial question remains: how was it possible that this major ideological shift was not better articulated and forcefully criticised by contemporary social democrats in Sweden?

As right-wing populists reduce politics to scapegoating an 'enemy', proclaiming that certain people do not belong in Europe because their values are inimical to European culture, the prospects for political solidarity are grim. The aim of progressive leftist feminist politics is the same as it always has been, namely, to explain and define the need for social justice for the entire population; to create solidarity in the economic sphere; and to cultivate a society in which people are respectful of one another. This has not been the case for the new capitalist culture, according to Richard Sennett. A viable alternative to the current late capitalistic social order is to return to the concept of 'the common', which can be contrasted with the privatisation of state property under capitalism. The common is neither unified nor uniform, but a sharing of resources and the fruits of human labour in a society based on solidarity (Sennett 2007: 10).

Identity politics

In recent decades, several left-wing theorists and intellectuals have debated how political movements (feminism included) have become increasingly preoccupied with their own questions, including that of their identity, and have drifted away from seeking solutions to global social problems. Eagleton argues that the transition from traditional modes of production to a post-industrial society based on consumerism, communication, information technology, the service industry, a deregulated employment market, and a weakened labour movement has meant that old class loyalties have declined, while focus has shifted to identities based on location, gender, sexuality, and race (Eagleton 2011: 15).

Eagleton is not alone in his critique of identity politics for turning away from the 'important' issues. There are those, particularly on the left, who believe that the common struggle has been shattered by a variety of social movements that are self-concerned and lack any unifying political vision. Nevertheless, identity politics are not primarily about 'other' policies concerning women, children, and minorities, who seem to have disappeared from male-dominated political agendas. Rather, feminist issues and anti-racist concerns are not about identity, but about citizens who lack access to shared democratic influence and power.

In the Nordic countries, right-wing populist parties have had great success in promoting their racist Nordic identity politics and encouraging activism. In addition, they co-opt pseudo-feminist and gay-friendly arguments in their Islamophobic political rhetoric, proclaiming that Christian, white, and 'truly' Nordic culture has been sacrificed to social democracy and multiculturalism. Such negative identity politics have lately resonated with a segment of the population, illustrating how rhetoric can be redirected and misused. Identity politics can no longer be embraced as was done a few centuries ago. Political action is not only a choice between different options existing in a pre-defined order, but an intervention: it redefines existing societal rules and channels them in a more democratic and inclusive direction. Although the economy remains the foundation and most crucial factor, the symbolic order is where the decisive battle is taking place. To strive for collective liberation today is to stand in opposition to the trend for everything – even digital space – to become privatised (Cornwell and Molyneux 2006: 1175–1191).

However, as Nancy Fraser has pointed out, the critique of identity politics has a valid point to make. Liberal feminist policy places women's liberation within the framework of the capitalist system of entrepreneurship, making it the ultimate form of self-realisation (2009: 1–11). It sees the presence of women in high social positions as the main goal of feminism. The lack of a broader social analysis that shares political insight and an ethos of solidarity has given way to a neoliberal, consumerist, imperialistic non-politics that embraces feminism without deepening the critical analysis of capitalism or developing political action for society in greater breadth.

Thanking social democracy

While social democracy guaranteed a social infrastructure, and worked for social equity, it was also built around specific political personalities. A new interest in Olof Palme (1927–1986), probably the best-known Swedish politician of all time, emerged in the mid-2000s in the form of biographies, films, and performances. In these books, productions, and works of art, a younger generation of scholars and artists raised questions about the downsizing of the social democratic project and the fading dream of a model welfare society as they reached adulthood. However, it was not only nostalgia for Palme, but at the same time a public mourning for the lost vision of a social democratic nation. The assassination of Palme in 1986 was a watershed in contemporary Swedish history. The brutal murder, the confused police investigation that followed, the various conspiracy theories that appeared in the media, and the capture of an unlikely suspect who was later released, created a national trauma that never entirely healed. The event shattered the confidence of the entire country.

Palme's controversial cult status, like his entry into politics, was turbulent and full of scandal, a fact that has generated numerous artistic interpretations. He might well have been a character in a novel, and so it is not surprising that his image is again before us in theatres and cinemas. Palme was an empathetic intellectual, but also arrogant and provocative. He had star quality and, as Wayne Koestenbaum notes, while the cult of modern icons tends to be stupefying, mystifying, or stimulating, it can also release a longing for a different life and a different kind of society (1995: 8).

Lo Kauppi, a feminist performer, has expressed her gratitude for being raised in a social democratic Sweden. Her performance *Bergsprängardottern som exploderade* [The Rock-Blaster's Daughter Who Exploded, 2003] delivered a naked, powerful, and candid account of her life and class origins, conveying to her audience both social reportage and the energy to keep going. She grew up in a working-class family of addicts who used to argue about who was the sickest. Years of drug abuse and other social problems followed. "I'm incredibly grateful that I grew up in Olof Palme's Sweden. It does not matter what the conservatives say. I would never have survived in a more competitive society" (Rosenberg 2016: 190). Kauppi credits Sweden's social democratic society for sustaining her life.

Palme's notion of democratic socialism and the systematic social criticism he embodied is emphasised by Swedish journalist Göran Greider. Those who drill down into Olof Palme's political action agenda discover a radical heritage that the official historical record has often repressed, the Marxist left has rarely understood, and conservatives would rather not hear about – because his cause was a democratically governed and well-regulated socialism. Those who try to make Olof Palme out to be a lofty statesman do not want to deal with the legacy of democratic socialism because it remains deeply controversial, even for social democracy itself, which has long celebrated the internationalist Palme more than the democratic socialist (Greider 2011: 136–137).

Greider underlines Palme's ideological position at a time when he is most remembered as a statesman. Instead of highlighting a remarkable individual, Greider shows democratic socialism to be the basis of Palme's vision of social democracy. The former chairman of the social democratic party, Göran Persson, officially abandoned socialism on Swedish Public Television in 2006. He explained that the word socialism implied false associations with fools who were "communists and national socialists." He therefore declared that 'socialism' was a political term he had no use for. Persson's statement was a deathblow to Palme's vision of democratic socialism, and the question of whether the social democrats continued to be social(ist) democrats at all. Palme would have said they should be proud to revive their legacy of social reforms and the struggle for democracy rather than letting go of their politics.

Performing popularised feminisms

While social democratic and socialist parties have grown weaker throughout Europe, the vacuum they have left behind has not been filled by right-wing populism alone. On the contrary, protests in Europe and the US have become stronger. Where neither social democracy nor democratic socialism seem to appeal to Western voters – with the exception of Bernie Sanders and Jeremy Corbyn – feminist interventions in many popularised versions do. Just as Kattrin with her drum was a whistle blower in Brecht's play, there are international celebrities drumming for feminism in various pop-cultural and pop-political contexts. Feminist activism is all about timing and context. Many surprising examples of co-optations and cultural misappropriation of feminist ideas exist today, including public celebrity addresses and pop-political performances. One such performance took place in September 2014 when the world's highest-paid models, Gisele Bündchen and Cara Delevingne, shouted through megaphones that were encased in lavish leather padding as they exchanged their heavily branded Chanel handbags for banners during the finale of the most anticipated show of Paris Fashion Week. They "strutted down the catwalk brandishing placards demanding women's rights, in a faux protest that was simultaneously hailed as a breakthrough for a new wave of feminism and decried as consumerist claptrap" (Topping 2014).

Another celebrity address was delivered in 2014 by Emma Watson, known worldwide as Hermione in the Harry Potter films. She not only launched the HeForShe campaign, but was also cover girl of *ELLE*'s Feminism Issue and of *Vogue*, with the superimposed headline "Voice of a Generation". *ELLE*'s editor-in-chief, Lorraine Candy, noted how proud she was to see decision-making politicians, actors, musicians, and directors wearing the Fawcett Society's iconic "This is What a Feminist Looks Like" T-shirt.

> It is such a shame that Prime Minister David Cameron was one of the very few who said no to our request (we did ask five times, just to be sure). For me his refusal is disappointing, as it feels so out of step with the worldwide and high-profile support for HeForShe."
>
> *(Candy 2014: 83–84)*

Although the fashion demonstration designed by Karl Lagerfeld might not have had any deeper meaning in itself, it responded to something in the *Zeitgeist*. Natasha Walter, author of *Living Dolls: The Return of Sexism* and founder of Women for Refugee Women, called the mock protest "quite amusing," but warned that using feminism as a trope could backfire.

> It is great to see more young women engaging with feminist ideas all the way from talking about them on social media to actually getting active, but real change requires huge social, economic and political shifts. If people start

> thinking that feminism is suddenly fashionable, then the danger is that the next moment they will say it has fallen *out* of fashion. There is a cynicism here – Lagerfeld is recognising that feminism has an energy now, but is just using that to flog expensive clothes.
>
> *(Walter 2011, cited in Topping 2014)*

Walter also noted that the women carrying feminist placards (one declared its bearer to be "Feminist but feminine," while another stated "Ladies first") were mainly white, uniformly beautiful, and thin – an image that did little to dispel the idea "that we have somehow failed if we don't live up to that idea of beauty" (2011).

Andi Zeisler picks up this thread from here and writes, in her introduction to *We Were Feminists Once: From Riot Grrl to Cover Girl, the Buying and Selling of a Political Movement*, "There's a mainstream, celebrity, consumer embrace of feminism that positions it as a cool, fun, accessible identity that anyone can adopt" (2016: ix). She calls this transformation a decontextualised and depoliticised marketplace feminism that has also gone by other names. It is probably feminism's most popular iteration ever. Zeisler emphasises that nothing could be more incorrect than assuming that this widespread embrace of "feminism" is a symptom of progress, a sign that the word has finally been decanted of its stigma. The problem, she fears, is that the feminist revolution has become privatised and neoliberalised. Feminists today are all about the right to make individual choices that may be totally estranged from the original objectives of feminism, which once meant collective action to change whole systems. Zeisler wishes to put an end to feel-good feminism (2016: 249–258; Senior 2016).

Writing and talking about homophobia, family leave policies, sexism, wage gaps, and many other things feminists talk about, immediately dampens any dinner conversation. Sara Ahmed's oeuvre and blog "feminist killjoys" both promote that symbolic figure as a world-making project. Ahmed is keen to remind readers all over the world not to avoid difficult issues. In *Living as a feminist,* she asks:

> What do you hear when you hear the word *feminism*? It is a word that fills me with hope, with energy. It brings to mind loud acts of refusal and rebellion as well as the quiet ways we might have of not holding on to things that diminish us. It brings to mind women who have stood up, spoken back, risked lives, homes, relationships in the struggle for more bearable worlds.
>
> *(Ahmed 2017: 1)*

Living a feminist life means trying to create more equal relationships with others, and finding ways to support those who are inadequately supported by social systems. Living as a feminist means holding everything open to question. "The question of how to live a feminist life is alive as a question as well as being a life question," writes Ahmed (2017: 2).

Pop-politics and celebrity addresses

There have been many examples of noteworthy feminist performances over the years. Celebrity speeches and contemporary pop-feminism reach large audiences while more underground feminist action groups seldom make newspaper headlines. Performers have long been criticised, marginalised, ostracised, and punished because of their suspect craft and skills, and those who resemble them are tarnished by the mimetic brush. In addition, a performer's identity and social behaviour have often been viewed as threats to the order and standards of the community because of their capacity to make mimesis credible (Davis and Postlewait 2003: 5).

Women, particularly those who go on stage, are simultaneously seen as devious and shallow. In a world of artificiality, they are assumed to lack moral rectitude, yet they do reveal (if at times in an overabundant manner) a talent for sexual display and duplicity. This anti-theatrical attitude, when applied to femininity, usually carries an additional prejudice against the sexual identities and activities of women. In the sets of antinomies, the realm of the theatrical is the inauthentic (Davis and Postlewait 2003: 17).

Regarding the repetition of acts, Judith Butler writes that "the task is not whether to repeat, but *how* to repeat, or indeed, to repeat and, through a radical proliferation of gender, to displace the very gender norms that enable the repetitions itself" (1990: 148, italics by the author). This raises the towering question of *how* to protest and resist. As Roland Barthes states, theatricality is in the many signs and codes of performance, because "the theatre alone, of all the figurative arts (cinema, painting) presents the bodies and not their representation" (1995: 83). Once again, timing and context are everything.

The body on stage is at once contingent and essential, something that became manifest at the 2016 Swedish music awards gala (*Grammisgalan*) when the Afro-Swedish vocalist Seynabo Sey, who was named best pop singer of 2016, performed her final song, "Hard Time," while 130 Afro-Swedish women came on stage and formed a semi-circle behind her. They stood still as a manifestation of black presence in a world of white supremacy and racism, making their performance part of a wider vision of political struggle, bringing the presence of racialised people to as wide an audience as possible. They reminded the audience in a Brechtian sense that (popular) culture cannot escape its political context. As Brecht asked rhetorically in the *Svendborg Poems* of 1938, "In the dark times, will there also be singing? Yes, there will be singing. About the dark times" ([1938], 1997: 505).

This performance of the Afro-Swedish girls and women standing still "in formation" was planned before Beyoncé performed her 2016 single "Formation," envoicing ongoing social inequalities bound up with racism and sexism. Neither Seynabo Sey's nor Beyoncé's performances were choreographed to please a white audience; instead, they were expressions of Afro-Swedish and African-American culture, presenting traditions from the civil rights era, through the Black is beautiful movement and the Black Panthers, to today's Black Lives Matter, an organisation that also exists in Sweden. Together with her "army" of women dancers, Beyoncé dominated the performance space. The dancers all wore black leather jackets and Black Panther berets, and they arranged themselves in symbolic formations that included an "X" in homage to Malcolm X. The same year was also the anniversary of the Black Panther movement, founded in Oakland, California, in 1966.

In 2014, Beyoncé performed before a viewing audience of 8.3 million people at the MTV Video Music Awards (VMA). She stood in front of a backdrop inscribed with words taken from Nigerian author Chimamanda Ngozi Adichie's (2015) *We should all be feminists*, a text that all 16-year-old Swedish students have been given a copy of in the hope of inspiring a new generation to engage in discussions about gender equality and feminism. This was not the first-time Beyoncé or her sister Solange Piaget Knowles took a political stand against racism and sexism (Zeisler 2016: 111–140).

A boldly effective performance strategy is to intervene while the world is watching. One of the most high-profile anti-Trump speeches was delivered by Meryl Streep at the Golden Globes gala in January 2017. Her address has been regarded as a masterpiece of the genre. Although she later talked at length with no difficulty, she created a great sense of authenticity just by dropping her voice, taking up a written note, and claiming to have to "read from it," which she (as the actor she is) then did not. Her speech act can be considered a high point of self-staged performance. Was she manipulating her audience? One presumes she meant what she said, although it could also have been acted; that is, an impure performative-like act.

Reading Streep's Golden Globe speech is completely different to watching her deliver it. The written text pales before her performance. The *performance* was critical: how her voice choked up, how a tear was wiped away with the back of her hand giving the impression that her contained rage overflowed its bounds. It was an intense, live moment of performed authenticity. The video format and the emotional outreach were ideally suited for social media. Nevertheless, she left open the question of how to reach the Trump supporters and make them shift their thinking (Ullgren 2017: 4).

A veteran actor like Meryl Streep understands how to make use of theatricality. For a performance to be effective, it must be perceived as authentic. Ironically, Donald Trump's lack of linguistic sophistication was a major factor in his electoral campaign's success. His unchecked aggression had a genuine feel. No one sensed themselves as intellectually inferior when he spoke. He has a habit of talking on and on, rambling so incoherently that there are people who find his performance of "authenticity" riveting. Perhaps this was why he was so irritated with Meryl Streep and called her "overrated" at the Golden Globes. She had the courage to take up the struggle against him on his own terrain, namely, in the media and with a performance of political authenticity (Ullgren 2017: 4).

Multi-solidarity

The point of departure when considering performance as political address and a form of activism is its capacity to evoke empathy, that is, to give the audience the feeling of standing in someone else's shoes. Telling stories, and more recently feminist stories, is how people have understood themselves, their place in the community, and the wider world. If political empathy enables us to share the feelings and experiences of others, solidarity becomes a principal attribute of that empathy. Moreover, empathy can foster individualisation or a group-specific collectivisation of emotion, although it may not necessarily extend to broader social issues. It is in the recognition of the other's needs that politics begins.

Judith Butler discusses the dynamics of public assembly as plural forms of performative action. She broadens her theory of performativity beyond speech acts to include embodied ways of coming together, including forms of long-distance solidarity. This would imply a new understanding of appearance in the public space that is essential to politics. By advocating a form of radical solidarity in opposition to political and economic forces, a sense of "the people" emerges in a unique way (Butler 2015).

In gathering for protests and demonstrations, feminists cannot focus solely on gender, just as the left cannot give their attention only to social class relations. While contemporary leftist politics that deal with commonalities do not require uniformity in their political ranks, they must stress multi-solidarity. Democratic interventions should agree with the Declaration of Human Rights, which acknowledges that all sovereign power is vested in the people. But who are the people? One difficulty at the core of democracy is that although power may derive from the people, it is not the exclusive possession of any individual or interest group.

In the face of complex contemporary political analysis, both the left and right have been hard pressed to re-establish a unified social body. Meanwhile, unions and parties cling to adhere to traditions from the past, although the power that once vivified the left no longer exists. But once that space is taken over by something that could be called "the people", their diversity terrifies the institutionalised Left. Thus, protesters from the 1980s AIDS activists to contemporary undocumented migrants are perceived as eccentric and menacing by the traditional left because it finds it hard to comprehend coalition-based multi-solidarity. One would think that being involved in the anti-racist struggle would make it easier for a person to have a feminist perspective on racism, to raise one's voice against homophobia, and to see the inequity that persists between rich and poor. But despite of all the years of neoliberalism, the word "I" continues to be heard everywhere – even in contexts where people should know better. For the neoliberal, personal success is everything, independent of gender, sexuality, race, or social class. This is a trend that has continued for a very long time (Rosenberg 2006).

To perceive oneself as part of an anonymous public does not appeal to many in an age so concerned with individualism. Still, there are hopeful, ongoing dialogues between various social movements and new negotiating positions have arisen. Swedish journalist Anna-Klara Bratt observes that protesters today are accustomed to speak of class, gender, ethnicity, and sexuality, either individually or all together. She writes that there are feminist actvists, political academics, and union veterans; some are even all in one with a global outlook. "Many of the pink protesters take the socialist cause to the Pride Parade," Bratt writes, "the sexual revolution to socialist demonstrations, class perspective in feminist circles, and keep the whole package hot in the universities. Added to it is that it usually does not happen without resistance" (Bratt 2008: 2, translation by the author).

Intersectionality

Multi-solidarity is based on the notion of intersectionality. It means that various forms of marginalisation and discrimination rarely occur alone. As a theoretical term, intersectionality is both a unifying (from the Latin *inter*, 'between, linking') and a divisive (Latin *sectio*, 'cut') term. To examine inequality in the vast field of race-related, class-based, and sexuality-oriented feminist practices requires a knowledge of what is specific to those actions, rather than simply using an intersectional approach as the "and-so-on-perspective." In an additive approach of this kind, several aspects of a phenomenon may be listed without going into a deeper analysis of any one. Feminist activists and scholars have expressed concern that women would once again be marginalised if all conceivable categories were mixed. Nevertheless, it is also a feminist axiom that social and cultural phenomena rarely function autonomously but always in interaction with each other.

If the word intersectionality seems awkward when applied to real politics, it can be translated into the more understandable everyday political concept of multi-solidarity. Thus, even for those who feel most at home in one of the social movements, other perspectives must be brought in. Intersectionality as a concept first appeared in the literature of anti-racist feminism. Kimberlé Crenshaw's classic essay on intersectionality, "Mapping the margins: Intersectionality, identity politics, and violence against women of colour" (1991), brings the discussion back to racialised structures and the discrimination they cause. In North America, intersectionality has become a signifier for race, while in Europe the debate has taken another direction in which the focus on racial discrimination is not always as distinct.

The complexities of the fight against colonialism and racism set the stage for the notion of post-colonial and critical race studies. Those women who were drawn to the anti-racist movement and black feminism in the early days are therefore central to the emergence of intersectionality. Classic texts such as Gloria Hull et al.'s *All the women are white, all the blacks are men, but some of us are brave* (1982) and Angela Davis's *Women, race, and class* (1983), with their explicit intersectional perspectives, were some of the first challenges to hegemonic white feminism. Because of these protests and the unrelenting efforts that lay behind them, class, gender, race, and sexuality have begun to be brought together on a theoretical and historic level, rather than being pursued as isolated phenomena. While there have always been scholars, theorists, and activists who have analysed multiple aspects simultaneously, they have been exceptions. The reason intersectionality has been resisted within feminist theory and politics is that its perspective engenders many complicated and often disturbing questions that unavoidably need to be addressed.

Thus, it is no coincidence that those voices advocating post-colonial and critical race studies have been central in introducing the concept of intersectionality. In a Swedish context, white feminism has been tied implicitly and explicitly to the formulation of the Swedish nation, thereby constructing Swedishness as a white privileged position (de los Reyes and Mulinari 2005). White feminist discourses are characterised not only by what is said, but also by what remains unexpressed. With regard to gender equality, Sweden's national brand, so to speak, is based on the achievements of a group of women who are predominantly white, middle class, and heterosexual.

What do these victories entail in relation to other groups of women who are excluded from such benefits? The intersectional approach has developed in opposition to the prevailing normative and hegemonic positions. Its critical edge has not only been aimed towards society and scholarship, but has also resulted in an internal feminist critique that demonstrates how different power axes interact and construct one another. However, it is never sufficient to simply add different power asymmetries to one another. For this reason, white feminism in Sweden and elsewhere must differentiate its analytical concepts to understand how various power regimes interact and enhance one another (de los Reyes and Mulinari 2005: 83).

Practising solidarity

Neither scholars nor others can grasp a global reality in all of its complexity. Nevertheless, one tries to make sense of the fragments and, above all, of those voices that would otherwise be silenced and the stories that would be ignored. The task is to listen attentively and respectfully, and try to situate and analyse these stories in a larger social and political context. Dialogic politics aim to bring about social change, even if only on a small scale. In politically coherent communities a mutual desire for change might enable consensus in the group. However, identity political insight would be needed, given the problems that arise when an intellectual (who is often white, male, straight, and middle class) takes on a subordinate group. The belief that dialogue can solve all problems is naïve, since the situation of many people is too desperate, due to poverty, war, or hunger, for any dialogue to even begin. Wherever people come together, power relations are activated and the social injustice that follows undermines people's ability to live freely and independently. "Free" relations are fundamentally problematic because all human beings are interdependent. It is lamentable that we continue to promulgate sexist, racist, and homophobic structures, even though intellectually we may see through them and attempt to dismantle them verbally and theoretically.

In discussing norms, Judith Butler makes an analytical distinction between social norms as opposed to rules and laws. Like queer theorists Lauren Berlant and Michael Warner, Butler describes the processes by which norms are turned into something "ordinary and inconspicuous."

> A norm is not the same as a rule, and it is not the same as a law. A norm operates within social practices as the implicit standard of normalization

> Although, a norm may be analytically separable from the practices in which it is embedded, it may also prove to be recalcitrant to any effort to decontextualize its operation. Norms may or may not be explicit, and when they operate as the normalizing principle in social practice, they usually remain implicit, difficult to read, discernible most clearly and dramatically in the effects they produce.
>
> *(Butler 2004: 41)*

This is a part of Butler's overall discussion of social comprehension. She explains that a norm differs from a symbolic position. Heteronormative preconceptions are embedded in traditions, institutionalised rules, and procedures. They manifest themselves in the social consequences of rules and procedures when they are widely accepted and obeyed. In the spirit of Michel Foucault, Butler notes that both compliance and resistance take place within the norm. Therefore, norms should be perceived as active doing, whether by restricting or liberating.

Although intersectionality can open up many rewarding perspectives, its potential can be undermined, resulting in its transformation into a conventional social technique. de los Reyes and Mulinari are critical of an intersectional analysis based on political identity because this would only reinforce essentialist tendencies in feminism and weaken the theoretical and political power of intersectionality:

> We believe the revolutionary power of intersectionality lies primarily in the development of a theoretical perspective that links power and inequality to the individual's potential to act as a subject within the framework of society's structures, institutional practices and prevailing ideologies. This also entails a critical stance toward the potential of knowledge production to institutionalize and naturalize a non-egalitarian social order. The political content of both knowledge production and academic practices is consequently a key element of our understanding of intersectionality.
>
> *(de los Reyes and Mulinari, 2005: 16, translation by the author)*

The anti-essentialist interpretation of intersectionality and identity is a fruitful one. Even if identity is a social construction, it is no less real or necessary in the prevailing political and social reality. As Chandra Talpade Mohanty points out, there appears to be only two viable approaches to identity: either one allows excluding and self-promoting ideas of identity to go unchallenged, or one accepts an unstable identity concept in which one's own (racial, class-based, sexual, national) identity is merely regarded as a strategy. Mohanty maintains that instead of seeing the concept of identity as a source of knowledge and a possible basis for progressive mobilisation, in this perspective it would be regarded as either naïve or irrelevant (2003: 1–13). However, both theory and practice also depend on solidarity. Which side a person is on will decide the outcome of the battle.

In a feminist context, multi-solidarity forces us to cooperate with each other across borders, rather than act at the expense of one another. The priority of class struggle was invoked by the early labour movement as a pretext for not addressing women's specific demands for action. It was stated then that class and gender struggle could not be fought simultaneously and that class struggle must always take precedence over the women's struggle. Multi-solidarity encourages us to refine our analysis with multiple parallel perspectives. One form of discrimination recognises others and conveys such thoughts and concerns to a larger social movement in which political questions are raised and negotiated. Freedom requires interpersonal solidarity, ethics, meaningful work, cultural richness, and shared prosperity. People can only be free together, not separately (Rosenberg 2016: 185–206).

It is all about address

Making use of one's fame to take a political stand is one way of acting in solidarity and addressing inequalities. Popular culture and the popularisation of ideas are important because they reach more people than traditional high culture or alternative avant-garde art forms. This is not to mention direct political actions that may attract attention through social media. Popular culture also seems to be several steps ahead of traditional art forms. Jack Halberstam maintains that this is how we communicate today (2012: ix-x). Swedish artist Zinat Pirzadeh claims that when she performs "Hangover in a burka" or as a talking fabric vagina, she reaches far more people than she would as a politician.

"Without address, there is no survival," as Judith Butler has stated (Ahmed 2014: 4). Being addressed means that the stories performed have to make sense to the audience. The more pleasurable those stories are, the better. A single show or protest performance might not change the whole system, but it might alter people's attitudes. A finely crafted performance has the potential of being in tune with audiences, evoking empathy, and making people feel closer to their actual lives.

What might be empowering in a feminist context does not necessarily function as such under more mainstream circumstances. Feminist activists should look beyond commercial settings because these tend to neutralise criticism rather than being transformed by it. Social movements that are drawn to neither authoritarianism nor violence can empower people to turn toward empathy and solidarity, and in so doing make life hopeful again. It is encouraging to see artists using their fame and public space to speak out against injustice, but a world of entertainment cannot make up for the inequality brought about by structural discrimination. Life without joy would be dismal. Political hope promises us a future in which all can share the goods of the earth.

References

Aalberg, T., Esser, F., Reinemann, C., and Stromback, J., (eds.). (2017) *Populist political communication in Europe*. London: Routledge.

Adichie, C.N., (2015) *We should all be feminists*. New York: Anchor Books.

Ahmed, S., (2017) *Living as a feminist*. Durham, NC: Duke University Press.

Ahmed, S., (2014) *Willful subjects*. Durham, NC: Duke University Press.
Backström, J., (2017). Sluta hoppas! [Stop hoping!]. *Ny Tid* 1. pp. 46–47.
Barthes, R., (1995) *Roland Barthes by Roland Barthes*. London: MacMillan/Papermac.
Bial, H., and Brady, S., (2016) *The performance studies reader*. Third Edition. London and New York: Routledge.
Brecht, B., ([1940], 1991) *Mother Courage and her children*. New York: Grove Press.
Brecht, B., ([1938] 1997) *Poems 1913–1956*. London: Routledge.
Bratt, A-K., (2008) Intersektionell solidaritet [*Intersectional solidarity*]. *Arbetaren* 19, p. 2.
Butler, J., (1990) *Gender trouble: Feminism and the subversion of identity*. New York: Routledge.
Butler, J., (1993) Critically queer. In: *Bodies that matter: On the discursive limits of "sex"*. New York: Routledge, pp. 223–242.
Butler, J., (2004) *Undoing gender*. New York: Routledge.
Butler, J., (2015) *Notes toward a performative theory of assembly*. Cambridge, MA: Harvard University Press.
Candy, L., (2014) Editor's letter. *ELLE*. December. pp. 83–84.
Cornwell, A., and MaxineM., (2006) The politics of rights: Dilemmas for feminist praxis. *Third World Quarterly* 27(7). pp. 1175–1191.
Crenshaw, K.W., (1991) Mapping the margins: Intersectionality, identity politics, and violence against women of color. *Stanford Law Review*. 43(6). pp. 1241–1299. See also: Crenshaw, K., et al. (1995). *Critical race theory: The key writings that formed the movement*. New York: The New Press. pp. 357–383.
Cuperus, R., (2003) The populist deficiency of European social democracy. *Internationale Politik und Gesellschaft* 3. pp. 83–109.
Davis, A., (1983) *Women, race and class*. New York: Vintage Books.
Davis, T., and PostlewaitT., (2003) *Theatricality*. Cambridge: Cambridge University Press.
de los Reyes, P., and Mulinari, D., (2005) *Intersektionalitet: Kritiska reflektioner över (o)jämlikhetens landskap* [*Intersectionality: Critical reflections on the landscape of (in)equality*]. Malmö: Liber.
Eagleton, T., (2011) *Why Marx was right*. New Haven, CT: Yale University Press.
Fraser, N., (2009) *Feminism, capitalism and the cunning of history*. *New Left Review*. 56. pp. 1–11.
Greider, G., (2011) *Ingen kommer undan Olof Palme* [*No one escapes Olof Palme*]. Stockholm: Ordfront.
Halberstam, J., (2012) *Gaga feminism: Sex, gender, and the end of normal*. Boston: Beacon Press.
Hull, A. (Gloria T.), Scott, P.B., and Smith, B., (1982) *All the women are white, all the blacks are men, but some of us are brave*. Old Westburg, NY: Feminist Press.
Jackson, S., (2003) Theatricality's proper objects: Genealogies of performance and gender theory. *In*: DavisT. and Postlewait, T., (eds.). *Theatricality*. Cambridge: Cambridge University Press. pp. 186–213.
Koestenbaum, W., (1995) *Jackie under my skin: Interpreting an icon*. New York: A Plume Book.
Mohanty, C.T., (2003) *Feminism without borders: Decolonizing theory, practicing solidarity*. Durham, NC: Duke University Press.
Mudde, C., (2007) *Populist right-wing parties in Europe*. Cambridge: Cambridge University Press.
Mudde, C., (2010) The populist radical right: A pathological normalcy. *West European Politics* 33(6). pp. 1167–1186.
Mudde, C., (2016) *On extremism and democracy in Europe*. London: Routledge.
Mudde, C., (2017) *Populism: A very short introduction*. Oxford: Oxford University Press.
Müller, J.-W., (2016) *What is populism?*Philadelphia: University of Pennsylvania Press.
Rosenberg, T., (2006) Om socialism, feminism och multisolidaritet [On socialism, feminism, and multi-solidarity]. *In*: Franzén, A., and Larsson, M. (eds.) *Efter ett kvartssekel av nederlag: En debattantologi om arbetarrörelsen och framtiden* [*A quarter of a century of defeat: Debating the*

labour movement and the future]. Stockholm: Byggnads & Socialdemokratiska Studentförbundet, pp. 29–39.

Rosenberg, T., (2016) *Don't be quiet, start a riot! Essays on feminism and performance*. Stockholm: Stockholm University Press.

Senior, J., (2016) Review: 'We were feminists once.' On a movement co-opted. *New York Times*. May 22, www.nytimes.com/2016/05/23/books/review-we-were-feminists-once-on-a-movement-co-opted.html, accessed May 14, 2017.

Sennett, R., (2007) *The culture of new capitalism*. New Haven, CT: Yale University Press.

Taylor, D., (2016) *Performance*. Durham, NC and London: Duke University Press.

Topping, A., (2014) Chanel's Karl Lagerfeld cheered and jeered for 'feminist' fashion statement. *The Guardian*. Sept. 30, www.theguardian.com/fashion/2014/sep/30/chanel-karl-lagerfeld-cheered-jeered-feminist-staement-fashion-catwalk, accessed May 14, 2017.

Ullgren, M., (2017) Meryl Streep förstår hur det teatrala får användas – men inte synas. [Meryl Streep knows how to make use of theatricality – without showing it]. *Dagens Nyheter*. Jan. 10, 4.

Walter, N., (2011) *Living dolls: The return of sexism*. London: Virago.

Zeisler, A., (2016) *We were all feminists once: From riot grrl to cover girl®, the buying and selling of a political movement*. London: Public Affairs.

6

DREAMING OF HOME

A feminist strategy for importing the Nordic model to Taiwan

Chia-Ling Yang

Introduction

> A comprehensive welfare state for all citizens is not a subordinated institution focusing on residual subsidies under the patriarchal capitalist system. [...] In a welfare state for all citizens, the work traditionally done by women becomes important work supported by the national budget and paid work in the welfare system. Accordingly, women become workers and leaders of this important system in the country. When the welfare system creates paid work and power for women, all women's power will be enhanced, and then a leader with women's perspectives in mind will be elected. As a result, there will be fundamental change of traditional gender relations of men-as-superior and women-as-inferior, building a new era for gender equality and diversified gender roles.
>
> *(FSA and Liu 1995: 324–325, quoted in Liu 2015: 4)*[1]

In *The Transformation of the Nordic Experiences in Taiwan* (Liu 2015), Yu-Hsiu Liu, a well-known state feminist who has worked to introduce the Nordic model[2] to Taiwan since the 1990s, quoted words from her book published more than 20 years ago. In the decades since, Liu and other feminist scholars have described the care burden in the family and asked the state to take the responsibility of care for the people. Liu's passage neatly summarises a proposal from Taiwan's feminists for changing welfare policies in what feminists see as a patriarchal state: Taiwan should develop into a welfare state incorporating women's perspectives, which takes responsibility for family care work and creates jobs for women.

Care has been a central topic in feminist theories. Feminist scholarship has criticised the binary divide between public and private and the patriarchal ideology and structural arrangements that constrain women in the private sphere, doing unpaid care work and house chores (e.g. Arendell 2000; Borchorst and Siim 2008; Fraser 2016). Nancy Fraser (2016) depicts three historical stages of 'boundary struggles' that, over the past century in the West, shaped the separation between spheres of production and reproduction: liberal competitive capitalism in the nineteenth century that led to 'housewifisation', while leaving working-class women and poor women of colour with a double burden; state-managed capitalism that, for a few decades after World War Two, provided many workers with a family wage; and by the 1980s, globalising financialised capitalism that commodified and privatised care in two-earner families.

In Taiwan today, there is a 'crisis of care' like the one described by Fraser. Many women have to stay at home in order to take care of children under three years old and the sick and the elderly in the family; and those who work suffer from 'time poverty' and struggle for a balance between work and family. Departing from Fraser's account, however, the current situation in Taiwan seems to combine elements of liberal competitive capitalism, with low participation of women in the labour market, and globalising financialised capitalism, with 68% of childcare for children over three years old provided by the market and more than 160,000 families hiring migrant women from Southeastern Asian countries each year as domestic helpers.[3] Accordingly, Taiwan's feminists are engaged in what Fraser calls boundary struggles, asking for government intervention in the care crisis in the form of new social welfare policies and triggering debates about care work among feminist scholars and activists.

Transnational feminist scholars have called for anti-capitalist struggles with a specific focus on complicated local contexts (e.g. Mohanty 2006). Following transnational feminists' agenda, this chapter examines Taiwan's feminist social welfare movement in Taiwan's complex social context of high commodification of childcare, women's low labour participation, and an on-going birth rate crisis.

In social policy studies, feminist scholars put care at the centre to analyse the relationship between women, the welfare state, the market, and family, and to re-examine welfare state regimes (Daly and Lewis 2000; Sainsbury 2001). As a response to feminist critiques, Gøsta Esping-Andersen (1999) accepts the notion of 'de-familialisation' in welfare states proposed by feminist scholars and concludes that Nordic countries are distinct in maximising the economic independence of women and 'of rather advanced de-familialisation' (66).

When considering countries that retain patterns of familialism, some welfare scholars propose a fourth and fifth regime to be added to Esping-Andersen's three welfare regimes, describing Southern European countries as 'Mediterranean welfare regimes', while East Asian countries follow a 'Confucius Welfare Model'. In these studies, Confucianism is described as a thought system that stresses the notion of family, with an emphasis on duty and obligation (e.g. Jones 1990). However, some scholars stress that Confucianism is not a 'timeless Oriental essence' in East Asian societies that contrasts with Western values. On the contrary, Confucianism has been used by neo-liberals, for example, to support their free-market ideological policy prescriptions by framing welfare as a 'Western' import that harms traditional Confucian values (Walker and Wong 2005: 14). In line with these previous studies' critiques, I want to challenge the Orientalist reading of East Asian welfare states and demonstrate how Confucianism may be used strategically by state feminists to change care policies in Taiwan.

My research focuses on childcare reform in Taiwan since the late 1990s, which was initiated by women's organisations and several feminist scholars.[4] Among the women's organisations, Peng Wan-Ru (PWR) Foundation – led by Yu-Hsiu Liu – has focused on community care. In 2005, the PWR Foundation established the Childcare Policy Alliance, including three women's organisations and the Alliance of Edu-care Trade Unions (abbreviated as Childcarers' Trade Unions in this chapter). The Childcare Policy Alliance advocates for public care and concentrates on childcare policy reform.

In the course of my research, I conducted participatory observations in several meetings held by the Childcare Policy Alliance, including public hearings and seminars about childcare policies when representatives of the Childcare Policy Alliance debated with other interest groups, such as the owners of private childcare institutions. I also interviewed 20 people in the Childcare Policy Alliance, including staff and board members in two women's organisations and the Childcarers' Trade Unions.[5] Additional research materials come from Taiwan's official statistics and feminist scholarship on the Nordic model and government brochures.

Given the space constrains of this chapter, I will concentrate on the PWR Foundation, led by Liu, and analyse how this organisation has used a metaphor of family/home to pave the way to introducing the Nordic model to Taiwan. I will pay particular attention to how the PWR Foundation and feminist scholars engage in building up community-based childcare and their strategies for representing and transforming what is understood as the Nordic model in Taiwan. The metaphor of family/home is especially essential in Taiwan's context, where care work mainly takes place in the private family or in commercial settings, and it demonstrates feminist engagement by redefining the relationship among women, family, and the state. I will employ this productive feminist discourse to rethink the triangle model of the state, market, and civil society central to analysis of care and welfare systems and contemplate links and relationships among the welfare state, the market, the family, and women.

I want to acknowledge that feminists in the Nordic countries have criticised the Nordic model for decades for several related reasons. Firstly, there is still a gap between rhetoric and the everyday experience of most women, which includes a gender-segregated labour market and women's double burden (Eldén and Anving 2016; Elvin-Nowak and Thomsson 2001). Secondly, the model is hetero-normative, with a strong focus on the nuclear family, and too rigid to embrace diversity of sexuality and ethnicity (Dahl 2005; Mulinari 2008; Norocel 2013). Finally, the state institutions and care institutions are inclusive, but highly normative and repressive (Siim 1987; Szebehely 2006). Although I recognise and agree with the critiques of the Nordic model in existing literature, my focus in this chapter is not the Nordic model's strengths and shortcomings, but the ways in which a specific local representation of the Nordic model has been put to work in feminist activism and scholarship in Taiwan.

Women's work and social policy in Taiwan

In Taiwan, there are separate social insurance schemes according to occupation; this is often classified as the 'Bismarkian model' (Walker and Wong 2005; White and

Goodman 1998). Three occupations that are considered by KMT[6] as essential for the stability of the political party and the state – the military, state bureaucrats, and teachers in public schools and universities (abbreviated as 'three essential occupations' in this chapter) – enjoy good social insurance and generous pensions. In 1991, 75% of social welfare expenditures were allotted to this 9% of the population, while the disadvantaged (the poor, handicapped, young, aged, and women) received only 3% (Holliday 2000: 714). In 2009, 54.7% of total expenditures on elderly people (including social insurance, pension, and welfare benefits) were allotted to the three essential occupations, while only 25.8% went to workers, 9% to farmers, 6.2% to basic pension,[7] and 1.4% to elders below the poverty line (Lu et al. 2014: 67–69). Table 6.1 illustrates that the people in the three essential occupations get the most pension; in 2009, 77% of total pension expenditure was allotted to the three essential occupations.

Social welfare has been used by KMT as a means of establishing the legitimacy of its authority, and residual social help stigmatises the disadvantaged groups. Moreover, care is considered by KMT politicians as something provided by a good family with three generations living together. Politicians characterised the introduction of welfare policies as harmful to traditional families.

The lack of universal social welfare particularly affects women in Taiwan, since women's labour participation rate has remained quite low – around 45% – over the past three decades (Wang and Wang 2014). The participation rate first topped 50% in 2012 and is continuing to rise. As of 2016, women's overall participation rate in the labour market had risen to 57.4%, with 78.1% women aged 25–44 in the labour market.[8] Despite these rapid changes, Table 6.2 demonstrates that the ideal of taking care of children under 3 years old at home still prevails (86.6%), but today many more young children are being cared for by grandparents (compared to 82.8% of children cared for by parents and 14.6% by grandparents and other relatives in 1980, Wang and Wang 2014: 49). Because of the lack of affordable childcare services and the gendered division of childcare in the family, women either need to quit their jobs and care for children by themselves, ask for help from relatives, or pay nearly half of their average salary for commercial childcare services

TABLE 6.1 Average pension of various groups in 2009

	Basic pension	*Farmers' pension*	*Workers' pension*	*Three essential occupations' pension***
% of population	46	20	23	10
Average pension NT dollars (US dollars $)*	3,791 ($122)	7,256 ($234)	16,179 ($522)	bureaucrats: 56,383 ($1,819) teachers: 68,052 ($2,195)

Source: Awakening Foundation, www.facebook.com/pg/awakeningfoundation/photos/?tab=album&album_id=10154382837557105, accessed 23 February 2018

Notes: * 1 US dollars=31 NT dollars (Taiwan dollars)

** The military is not included here since it varies a lot according to various rankings among the military group.

TABLE 6.2 How mothers cared for young children in 2016 (%)

Age of child	*Self or partner*	*Grand-parents*	*Other relatives*	*Nannies*	*Private childcare centre*	*Public childcare centre*	*Care at workplace*	*Domestic helpers*
Under 3	47.33	39.31	0.93	10.23	1.71	0.36	0.07	0.05
3–6	24.52	15.6	0.66	2	39.2	16.84	0.2	-

Source: Accounting and Statistics Bureau (2017); table created by the author

TABLE 6.3 Cost for childcare per month (NT dollars and percentage of average salary) for women aged 30–34 in 2016

Age of child	*Average*	*Nannies*	*Private*	*Public*
Under 3	16,007 (50%)	16,479 (51%)	16,724 (52%)	8,313 (26%)
3–6	8,719 (27%)	16,505 (51%)	10,311 (32%)	3,761 (12%)

Source: Accounting and Statistics Bureau (2017); table created by the author

Note: The average monthly salary for women aged 30–34 is 32,155 NT dollars.

(Table 6.3). Not surprisingly, the birth rate in Taiwan dropped to 0.895 child per woman in 2010 and has remained the lowest in the world in recent years. In 2016 the birth rate rose slightly to 1.17 child per woman.

Given the situation faced by women, several non-profits and scholars have banded together to form lobbying organisations, including the Childcare Policy Alliance and the Alliance for Long-Term Care Policy, to advocate for government aid to reduce the family's burden, especially women's responsibility for care work, and to organise workers and initiatives in these areas.[9] Nevertheless, these alliances face difficulties from the state, as well as from the market.

On the one hand, care services have seldom been provided by the state. Although there are critiques of childcare as a commodity in Taiwan (Lin et al. 2011; Liu 2002), the government cannot afford to run more public preschools and hire more staff in these preschools because of the unfair tax system[10] and the excessively generous social welfare programme the three essential occupations enjoy. It is impractical to demand that the government provide care services if there are no changes in the tax system or the social welfare programmes based on different occupational groups. Moreover, most people in Taiwan do not trust the government and are unwilling to pay more taxes because of politicians' corruption.

On the other hand, when two-earner families are not able to take care of children at home, many upper-middle-class parents buy into a myth that is increasingly prevalent in Taiwan of children needing to compete and achieve at young ages. For these families, private for-profit preschools are the main option that provides care services with an emphasis on accelerated learning and academic competition. These expensive private preschools constitute of 68% of care services for children between 3 and 6 years old.[11] Therefore, unlike the trend in Western countries to privatise formerly public care services, childcare in Taiwan is already highly commodified and mainly provided by the market.

In contrast to for-profit afterschool classes focusing on tutoring and exam preparation, the PWR Foundation started community-based afterschool care in the 1990s by training local middle-aged women as the carers and developing programmes based in local elementary schools that focus on play, sports, and daily life activities. Over the past two decades, there have been essential changes in childcare policies in Taiwan because of feminist activism and state feminists' collaboration with the government. Following the successful partnership between the PWR Foundation and elementary schools, afterschool care became a social welfare service regulated by the Ministry of Education in 2001. Also in 2001, the 'support system for nannies in communities' was established; by 2008, working parents could get subsidies for hiring nannies through the community nanny systems.

On the heels of these policy successes, the PWR Foundation opened its first community-based preschool in 2006, designed around the ideal of 'participatory democracy': a collaboration between the local government, scholars, parents, and preschool teachers. After several similar preschool projects in communities and indigenous tribes in the 2000s, non-profit preschools run as collaborations between non-profit organisations and local governments were regulated in 2012, and making similar preschools a permanent state programme became a major policy goal for the Democratic Progressive Party (DPP, oppositional party to KMT) in 2016.

The *Pamphlet on Afterschool Care*, a publication issued by the Ministry of Education and the PWR Foundation (PWR 1997a; 1997b), lays out a community-based care system for Taiwan's citizens from infancy through old age:

> Five areas of universal, community-based social welfare services from age 0 to age 99 are designed: community-based nannies (care for 0–2 year-olds), community-based pre-schools (care for 2–6 year-olds), community-based afterschool care services (care for school-aged children), community-based support services for children, teenagers, and families, and community-based elderly care services.
>
> *(PWR 1997a: 11)*

The PWR Foundation's actions and ideals are clearly modelled on the welfare ideal in Sweden for care 'from cradle to grave', with community-based care as the main sector for universal care services. In the next sections, I will examine the discursive strategies used by feminist scholars and the PWR Foundation in introducing this Nordic model to Taiwan.

Making the state the People's Home

For DPP, advocating to introduce the Nordic welfare model was an effective method for opposing KMT in a pitched political battle where DPP was pressured to produce new policies and social reform (Lee 1996). During the 1992 election of

Parliament members, Wan-I Lin, a professor in social policy, criticised KMT's social welfare policies and suggested that DPP should follow the social democratic model of Sweden and Norway to construct a social welfare state. In his later book, *Welfare States: Historical Comparative Analysis*, Lin quotes Swedish politician Per Albin Hansson's description of 'the People's Home': 'The good society is a society which functions like a good home'; 'in this home, there is equality, thoughtfulness, cooperation, and helpfulness' (1994: 113, 262). Lin goes on to describe the social democratic model of welfare states:

> [The social democratic model] provides social services such as childcare, home services, and care for the elderly, etc., in order to relieve pressures in the family. [...] The state provides care for children, the elderly, and those who are in need of help, and **this de-emphasises the responsibility of care in the family**. The state not only undertakes the heavy burden of social services, but also **allows women to participate in the labour market**.
>
> *(Lin 1994: 128, my emphases)*

Lin's argument highlights the ideal of the 'People's Home' in the Swedish welfare state, de-familialisation, and increasing women's participation in the labour market. Yu-Hsiu Liu has used Lin's representation of the social democratic model of welfare states since the 1990s in her scholarship and work with the PWR Foundation. Consequently, Liu and the PWR Foundation share similar rhetorical strategies; these discourses are the focus of my analysis.

In the concluding chapter of *Women, State, and Care*, Liu states seven key points regarding the 'People's Home'; the first two are: (1) the basic goal of the state is to care for and love its people; (2) the sphere of care and love should expand to the public sphere and fuse public and private spheres so that the state can be the People's Home (FSA and Liu 1997: 265).

In Chinese, the state is called 'Kuo-Chia'. In literal terms, 'Kuo' means 'the state' and 'Chia' means 'the home'. Liu cleverly plays with words to shift the meaning of the state to 'the home' and to blur the boundary between the public and private spheres. Moreover, Liu's preface to *Women, State, and Care* is titled 'From the patriarchal state to the mother state', which is similar to the central argument in this chapter's epigraph. 'The People's Home' is used by Liu to transform the state into the family/home, and the role of the state is further transformed from the figure of a patriarchal father into a mother who cares for and loves her people.

In Taiwan, scholars like Lin and Liu describe the Nordic welfare state as a 'caring state' (Leira 2006). I argue that this discourse is quite different from approaches that tend to separate the state from the private/intimate sphere of the family. The model of separate spheres is one that we are quite familiar with: state, market, and civil society (including the intimate sphere of the family). On the contrary, Lin's and Liu's deployment of a new strategic discourse blurs the division between state and family by making the state into the 'People's Home' or 'mother state'. At the same time, they strengthen the links between state and family by making the state take responsibility for care that is traditionally in the private sphere, typically provided by women. This way of rethinking public-private boundaries and roles can lead to de-familialisation of care work and liberate women from the private sphere for labour and other public roles.

Liu further argues that the state in Nordic countries is different from the state in Jürgen Habermas' theory, and criticises how Habermas characterises the divide between the state and life world:

> In Nordic countries, the state and people's life world are not as contradictory as Habermas describes. On the contrary, the welfare state is the life world, combining the political and economic system and people's identity. [...] In the Nordic countries, identity and/or people's life world are combined with systems in the state. This makes Scandinavian countries different from Western Europe and North America.
>
> *(FSA and Liu 1997: 40–41).*

Liu stresses that feminists and women in Taiwan should ask for equal redistribution and that such a redistribution is related to power, money, and systems that Habermas urges people to avoid. In my opinion, Liu pays special attention to undercutting Habermas' theory because there is widespread public distrust of 'big government' in Taiwan due to on-going government corruption and a recent history of more than 35 years of martial law (1949–1987) under a dictatorial government.

I want to emphasise that this strategic discourse about the state as the People's Home must be situated in the political context of the hostile relationship between Taiwan and China. For decades, national defence dominated the national budget in Taiwan: defence was 70% of the total budget in 1950s, 50% in the 1960s, and remained around 20% in the 1990s. 2009 was the first year that the budget for social welfare (17.9%) exceeded the national defence expenditure (17%). In 2017, the social welfare expenditure is 23.9%, while defence has fallen to 15.5%. I would argue that 'feminising' a masculine state built around the military and national defence is an essential strategy for state feminists as they push the state to allocate more money to social welfare and people's 'life world', which is traditionally women's sphere – and the sphere that Taiwan's government has overlooked. This tactic often hinges on an ambition to revalue traditional women's characteristics and roles, as Liu noted when I interviewed her:

> [Universal provision of social services] can break traditional gender roles assigned to women. It seems to fall into the tradition [of the gendered labour division], but paradoxically it might lead to a more fundamental change. For example, traditional men's areas such as justice and grand narratives are considered to be important, and traditional female characteristics such as care and love are located in the private sphere and are depreciated. Nordic countries

> break the values linking to these dichotomies: to examine their national budget, **it is social services that take up a bigger part of the whole budget, not foreign affairs, trade, and national defence**.
>
> *(Interview with Liu, my emphasis)*

In such a discourse, traditional areas linked to women become important in the culture and in the national budget. In short, women's perspective can become central to the state's decision making, and this shift will inevitably lead towards gender equality.

Interestingly, Liu does not seem to be an essentialist, since she claims that the 'leaders of a caring state or a caring community can be either men or women, as long as they have mothers' psychological attributes, the knowledge and competence of a mother' (FSA and Liu 1997: 269). I would link Liu's argument with discussions of care ethics and feminist psychology (Benhabib 1992; Gilligan 1982). These theories challenge the patriarchal valuation of 'justice' over 'care', linking 'feminine' characteristics of caring and loving to socialised gender roles and the unequal gender division of labour. In other words, the disadvantages of limiting women to the private sphere and the devaluation of care work should be changed, not the care ethics themselves.

Liu's argument not only distinguishes her from other 'male-stream' discussions of the state and family in social theories, but also provides the basis for Liu and other state feminists to cooperate with DPP and the government to provide universal social welfare services on the Nordic model. Liu mentioned in our interview that she introduced the Nordic model to Shui-Bian Chen during his term as Taipei mayor (1994–1998). Liu and several other feminists and welfare scholars designed social welfare policies for Chen as he faced a second election as mayor in 1998, as well as in a later presidential election. After Chen became president in 2000, these scholars served on different committees in Chen's government to formulate and reform social welfare policies, such as afterschool care in 2001, a new labour pension system in 2005, and nannies' subsidies for dual income families in 2008 (see also Liu 2011).

If the patriarchal state is changed into a loving mother figure, according to Liu, it becomes a 'Utopia' (FSA and Liu 1997: 39). For Liu and the PWR Foundation, however, this Utopia is not drawn from nineteenth-century utopian socialism, but from Confucian thinking.

Rethinking Confucianism in social policy studies

Liu's articles connect the ideal world in Nordic welfare states with Confucius' admonition that all in need should be cared for:

> If love and care can be shared by the state and all people, we can accomplish the ideals of 'Great Harmony' in Confucius' The Conveyance of Rites: 'Respect the aged not only in one's family but also in others'; 'love the young

> ones not only in one's family but also in others'; 'widowers, widows, orphans, childless people and the disabled are well cared for.'
>
> *(FSA and Liu 1997: 39)*

Similar passages appear in the PWR Foundation's pamphlets on afterschool care (PWR 1997a: 11, 13) and on the webpage of the Childcare Policy Alliance.[12] It is particularly interesting that state feminists in Taiwan strategically employ Confucianism to introduce the Nordic model since Confucianism has more commonly been used to reinforce patriarchal order in the family and society – especially according to Western observers:

> The ideal family has a place for everyone – and has everyone in his or her place. Filial piety ensures due deference 'upwards'; family honour ensures due care and protection 'downwards'. The ideal family epitomises harmony, solidarity, pride, loyalty as between members of the group. And the ideal family goes on for ever. [...] it is in the image of the ideal family – and hence the well-run household – that the good society is seen as resting not on individuals but on interlocking **groups**, not on equal rights but on ascending orders of duty and obligation, not on 'constructive conflict' – perish the thought – but on the maintenance of stability and harmony at all costs.
>
> *(Jones 1990: 450, original emphasis)*

Nevertheless, I find that Liu's and the PWR Foundation's use of Confucianism is selective: they avoid discussions of filial piety and order in the private family, while emphasising the 'Great Harmony' in public society. Instead of stressing the responsibility of care in the family, they call for cooperation in the local community:

> The ideal where 'children are well raised and the elderly are well provided for' **cannot be realised within the nuclear family**. On the contrary, it needs **cooperation with the local community**.
>
> *(PWR 1997a: 11, my emphasis).*

In my interview with Daisy,[13] a key figure at the PWR Foundation for community-based preschools in Southern Taiwan, she described how she introduced the Nordic model to local people:

> I often gave examples of how I grew up in 'the communal family'. When I was little, my parents were busy, and I was always hanging around in our local community. My parents were even too busy to remember to serve us food. So the neighbour just called me into her house and served me a meal. This is what Yu-Hsiu [Liu] said: 'The communal family can always provide an extra meal for a child in the local community'. So I connected Yu-Hsiu's discourse [...] to my early childhood experiences.
>
> *(Interview with Daisy)*

Daisy's words reveal how Liu's and the PWR Foundation's discourse is understood by PWR staff. Although Daisy is not as familiar with feminist theories as Liu is, her words nevertheless echo socialist feminists' ideals of developing communal living arrangements and collective childcare (Barrett and McIntosh 1982), as well as black feminists' descriptions of family in the black community (Collins 2000[1990]). Socialist feminists have focused on the reproductive labour women carry out in the private sphere and propose communal responsibility for domestic chores. In many U.S. black women's experiences, the family is not limited to a nuclear unit or isolated in the suburbs. Black feminists describe their black community – particularly ties to other women – as a kind of extended family and safety net for raising children together. This expansive, supportive community has functioned, as well, as a central locus for combating U.S. racism. Here I would like to borrow this flexible sense of women's community to reflect on Daisy's words. In many ways, Liu's discourse challenges male-centred theory on the division between the state and family or 'life world'. Yet Daisy's words further criticise the Western-centred dichotomy that divides the public and private sphere: it seems that Daisy transforms the definition of family from the nuclear family in Western industrial society to 'the local community as a big family' where care responsibility is shared.

What separates state feminists' use of Confucianism from traditional Confucianism with its emphasis on patriarchal order within the household is that feminists shift the focus from the private household to the local community and to society as a whole. This strategic move makes the metaphor of family/home refer not to the private sphere of family, but instead to the local community as a communal family gathered in the People's Home. Using Confucianism in this way de-emphasises the family's (or more precisely, women's) private responsibilities, women's labour participation can be enhanced, and the boundaries between the family, the local community, and the state can be changed.

Nevertheless, in theories of civil society, there seems to be no place for the 'local community'. Is local community a synonym for civil society? In the next section, I will probe how state feminists in Taiwan expand and complicate the triangle model of state, market, and civil society by incorporating the concept of participatory democracy.

Communal family with participatory democracy

According to Taiwan feminists' transformation of the Nordic model, the local community is the optimal setting for deploying the social safety net. In feminist scholars' and the PWR Foundation's work, universal provision of social services lies in the 'buffer zone' with a close cooperation between the state/government and civil society.

Before the new policy for afterschool care in 2001, for example, the PWR Foundation had already cooperated with more than 70 schools in eight municipalities for seven years (PWR 1997a: 4) to create an alternative different from expensive private afterschool classes emphasising competition and academic achievements. The PWR Foundation's argument for establishing non-profit after-school care in local communities is as follows:

> Universal social services provide job opportunities and allow people, especially women, to work in the local community. The 'communal big family' of the service system is **not meant to make a profit**. This approach helps care workers get reasonable salaries and can in turn improve the economic condition of care workers' families. Furthermore, it can **avoid the erosion of love labour by profit-making logic**, so that children grow up healthy and the elderly enjoy their old age. In addition, when families in the community get childcare and care services, people of working age do not have to worry about the young and the elderly, and the human power of the working-age multiplies.
>
> *(PWR 1997a: 13, my emphases)*

Similar to Western scholars' claims that the logic of profit-making undermines the social aspects of care work, the PWR Foundation also argues for the ethics of care. The discourse contrasts love with profit-making, and insists that love labour (reproduction, in the Marxian sense) should be effectively taken off the market – differentiated from the logic of profit-making (production) in the free market.

I would like to point out that, here, the characteristics of 'love' not only describe the welfare state and its people, but also become the essence of care work. On the one hand, the emphasis Liu and the PWR Foundation put on 'love' makes the cooperation between the state/government and family possible, since both share characteristics of a loving mother; on the other hand, rhetoric that contrasts love and profit-making draws a clear divide in this three-part model, excluding the market from providing social services. This revises the familiar triangle of the state, market, and civil society (family) into a new form (see Figure 6.1).

Yu-Hsiu Liu mentioned in our interview that this paradigm comes from Wolfgang Streeck and Philippe C. Schmitter's (1985) model of social order. In Streeck and Schmitter's model, people's interaction is divided into three areas with different principles: the first is civil society, with solidarity as its principle; the second is the market, with market competition as its principle; the third is government, with

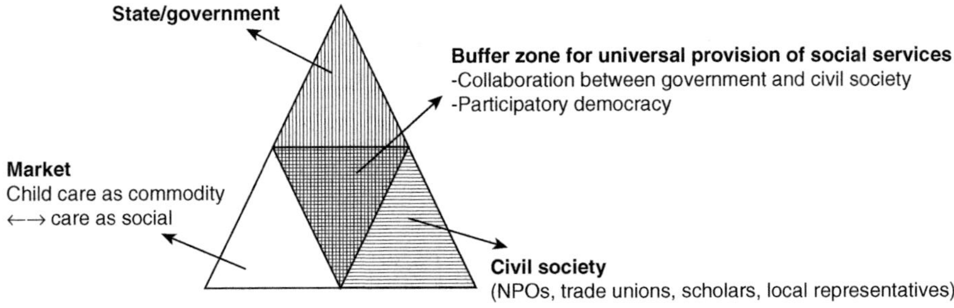

FIGURE 6.1 Collaboration between civil society and the state/government (Liu 2011)

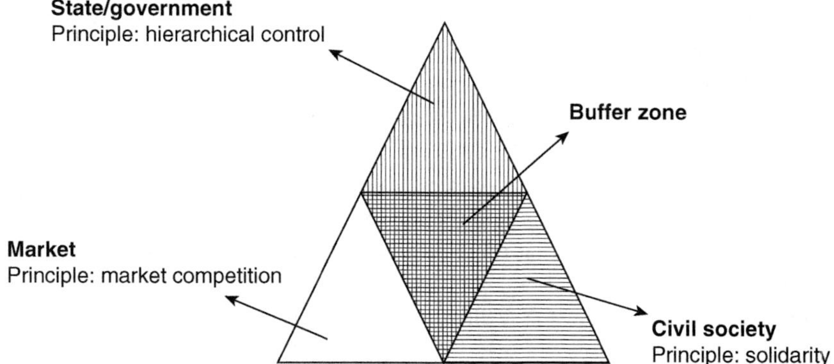

FIGURE 6.2 Guiding principles of co-ordination and allocation (Streeck and Schmitter 1985: 122)

hierarchical control as its principle. Henry Milner (1994) employs this model to explain that social welfare policies for public social services central to people's basic life need to be decided and practised in the buffer zone. Liu (2015) further uses Helga Maria Hernes' notion of 'public-private mix' (1987: 153) to argue for a public service system, so that the care provided in the family or the market can instead be provided by the state and civil society.

Liu also borrows Hernes' notions of 'participatory corporatism' and 'state feminism' (1987: 144–153) to illustrate Nordic democratic corporatism: because of Nordic feminist movements, the Nordic corporatism that traditionally includes labour, employers, and the government extends to social services users like pensioners' and parents' organisations. Such participatory corporatism is used to decide and practise public care policies.

Based on these theories, Liu designed a working paradigm for universal provision of care services: with the government's financial support and a democratic cooperative mechanism for decision making, members of civil society – ranging from individuals and families to trade unions and non-profit organisations – can participate actively in the care system at the level of decision making and practice. The cooperation between the government and civil society can create a buffer zone for the universal provision of care services; it is in this buffer zone that the local community is situated.

However, as Gillian Dalley (1988: 48) points out:

> [Community care] has become a blanket term to cover all sorts of options. [...] On the one hand, there are those who advocate privatised options (especially for solving the problems of care); on the other, are those who advocate socialised or collectivised options.

What distinguishes this new feminist design of community-based care in Taiwan from the voluntary sector in most Western countries is that, in Liu's model, the de-familialisation of care work results in paid jobs in the community, and the threshold to these jobs is not high, especially for middle-aged housewives. Moreover, when local-based care services release women from the responsibility of childcare and from the heavy economic burden of purchasing commercial childcare, women gain a chance to participate in the labour market. When I observed at one of the PWR Foundation's community-based preschools, Daisy encouraged mothers of preschool children, especially housewives, to join job-training programmes for women offered by PWR so that these housewives can take steps towards returning to the labour market or join it for the first time.

Feminist reforms of Taiwan's welfare state promote not only de-familialisation, following Esping-Andersen (1999: 44–45), but also the commodification of women's labour. According to Esping-Andersen, familialism leads to low birth rates, the waste of human power, a decrease in family income, and thus to a decrease in the tax base and more poverty (ibid: 51–70). This is the constellation of problems that Taiwan currently faces. Scholars (Lin et al. 2011; Liu 2006) and the PWR Foundation (1997a: 6–8) argue in favour of socialising care work on the Nordic model as a way to solve the problems of Taiwan's low birth rate and waste of (women's) human power.

Nevertheless, it is worth carefully examining the proposals of state feminists and the PWR Foundation. Although Liu calls for care services as the national budget's top allocation in her vision of the 'loving state', in reality, the PWR Foundation seems to promote a pragmatic, cost-cutting approach to providing care services, similar to a 'loving mother' practising frugality and 'home economy' to keep the family budget balanced. In the case of the community-based, non-profit preschools, the government only offers non-profit organisations some financial support in the beginning to establish locations for community-based care and – following the principle of 'participatory democracy' in partnership with civil society – some on-going bureaucratic control to ensure quality of care. I would like to point out that, while this pragmatism makes it easier for the government to start a new childcare plan without fundamental changes to the tax system and expensive social welfare programmes, it does make for a meaningful and lasting change in the national budget if such community-based care services can expand with more support from the government.

Secondly, although state feminists challenge the artificial dichotomy between public and private spheres and the concept of the nuclear family, they accept a binary contrast between 'profit-making' and 'love'. According to my interviews of members of the Childcarers' Trade Unions, Taiwan's owners of for-profit childcare centres and preschools already use the discourse of 'love labour' to justify the difficult working conditions and to discourage care workers from demanding higher salaries. These owners often distinguish childcare workers from other workers, since 'the essence of care is love' – so if the workers demand better conditions or more money, they are by implication degrading the value of love.

Finally, it is difficult for the government to distinguish non-profits from profit-making companies, since for-profit companies can establish NGOs that funnel money to the parent companies. This already started happening in 2001, when government-regulated afterschool care in elementary schools began. Most after-school care in elementary schools is currently provided either by the schools' young practice-teachers or by NGOs that neither follow non-profit logic nor train the local women as care workers. These NGOs are often created by the owners of private for-profit childcare centres, so that these entrepreneurs can extend their businesses into elementary schools as low-cost places to boost profits and reach new consumers.

According to the Childcare Policy Alliance's press conference on Father's Day[14] 2016, there are only 41 non-profit preschools – about 6.5% of all preschools in Taiwan. We need further research on how to expand current efforts and create meaningful change in childcare policies in Taiwan, in order to plan the next steps in the transformation of the nation's welfare state regime. We also need to continue to rethink divisions and connections between the state, market, and civil society and this system's impacts on women and families.

Conclusion: the big communal family

Following transnational feminists' agenda, I have paid attention to local complexities of feminist struggles over the boundary of public/private and production/reproduction. Feminist efforts to bring the Nordic model to Taiwan has required weaving a social safety net that blends policy ideas from abroad with Taiwan's own complex historical and political contexts. In an aggressively 'masculine' state with a long-term dictatorship in living memory and hostile national relations with China, state feminists have made surprising progress – to look at the state as 'feminine', with a mother's care values and responsibilities. This tactic allows feminists to cooperate with the state to combat the high commodification of childcare in the market – an effort that is still in progress. Taiwan's feminist struggles over the crisis of care have pushed back against social contexts of housewifisation, the domination of commercial childcare services, and the growing number of migrant women working as domestic helpers, by advocating for both de-familiarisation of care and re-commodification of women's labour.

Importantly, in a society that continues to value its Confucian tradition, state feminists have employed Confucianism strategically as a legitimated cultural tradition in their efforts to 'import' the Nordic model. Wielding the metaphor of the state as 'the People's Home' and the local community as 'the big communal family', state feminists in Taiwan take an authoritative Confucian discourse and use it for something new: to call for the establishment of community-based childcare supported by a strong collaboration between civil society and the state.

In my assessment, state feminists' rhetorical transformation of the state from a patriarchal father into a loving mother has two meanings corresponding to feminists' continuous 'boundary struggles'. Firstly, it follows the feminist slogan 'the personal is political': when the state's intervenes in providing care services, women's care responsibilities in the private sphere can be socialised and politicalised.

Secondly, it simultaneously flips this motto on its head, so that 'the political is personal': when the state is a loving mother, suddenly politics is no longer dominated by traditional masculine values that privilege military spending and situate justice only within the public sphere. On the contrary, the state connects strongly with people's life world, and the traditionally feminine characteristics of care and love become central to state policies. With these two strategic moves, the divide between public and private is blurred.

The metaphor of 'the big communal family', I argue, complicates the traditional model of care analysis. 'The big communal family' lifts the care burden from individual nuclear families and transforms Marxist duties of reproduction – women's daily grind of care – into local opportunities for housewives to join or return to the labour market. The buffer zone created by the state and civil society becomes the area in between the private and public spheres, which serves as an important platform for state feminists to promote non-profit organisations based on women's interests, women's engagement in civil society, and productive collaboration with the state.

Notes

1 All translations of Chinese quotations from references and interviews are mine.
2 In Liu's articles, 'the social democratic model', 'the Scandinavian model', and 'the Nordic model' are used simultaneously. In this chapter, I use 'the Nordic model'.
3 Domestic helpers are live-in domestic workers who take care of the elderly and the sick. Employers often ask them to take care of the children as well as to do house chores. See Table 6.2 for detailed statistics.
4 This chapter is part of my research results of two research projects: 'Translating the "Nordic model" to Confucianism: Women's organisations in Taiwan' (a case study in the research project 'Imagining change: Women and the creation of civil societies in the Arctic, Asia, Latin America and Europe', financed by The Swedish Research Council in Sweden, 2011–2015) and 'Construction, translation and competition of childcare discourses: Engagement of women's groups in policy making in Taiwan' (financed by the Ministry of Science and Technology in Taiwan, 2014–2016).
5 I did not interview the third women's organisation in the Childcare Policy Alliance since its participation in the Alliance was not as active as the other three organisations.
6 The political party led by Chiang Kai-Shek that governed Taiwan after World War Two, replacing the previous Japanese governance (1895–1945) in Taiwan.
7 The basic pension system was introduced in 2008 and covers 46% of the population (unemployed people are excluded from welfare benefits based on occupations) but it is not mainly financially supported from tax but from personal insurance.
8 The average age of first childbirth was 27 years old in 2016 in Taiwan. Accordingly, the age group of 25–44 years old includes those who are most likely to give birth and have small children. Data source: Accounting and Statistics Bureau (2017).
9 The burden of care in the family includes childcare and care for the elderly and the sick. However, this chapter only focuses on childcare and does not cover the heavy burden of elder and sick care in Taiwan.
10 According to Accounting and Statistics Bureau, personal income tax constitutes 23.6% of total tax revenue, which was higher than business income tax (20.7%) in 2016. Taiwan Labour Front (Lin et al. 2011) notes that in the past two decades, the percentage of income tax of total tax revenue rose from 23% in 1990 to 47% in 2010, while property tax decreased from 27% to 12.5%. In short, national finances are

suffering because the government does not collect sufficient taxes from entrepreneurs and the very wealthy.

11 There were 6,310 preschools in 2016, among them only 2,002 public preschools. Ministry of Education, http://depart.moe.edu.tw/ed4500/cp.aspx?n=1B58E0B736635285&s=D04C74553DB60CAD, accessed 22 June 2017.

12 The webpage of the Alliance for Childcare Policy: http://cpaboom.blogspot.tw/(in Chinese), accessed 23 February 2018.

13 In this chapter, I use pseudonyms for all research participants except for Yu-Hsiu Liu, who is a well-known feminist in Taiwan.

14 According to the interviews, the Childcare Policy Alliance chose Father's Day to have a press conference in order to deconstruct the gendered division of childcare.

References

Accounting and Statistics Bureau, (2017) *Report on Women's Marriage, Fertility, and Employment*. Taipei: Accounting and Statistics Bureau.

Arendell, T., (2000) Conceiving and investigating motherhood: The decade's scholarship. *Journal of Marriage and Family*. 62(4). pp. 1192–1207.

Barrett, M., and McIntosh, M., (1982) *The Anti-Social Family*. London: Verso.

Benhabib, S., (1992) The debate over women and moral theory revisited. In: S. Benhabib (eds.), *Situating the Self: Gender, Community and Postmodernity in Contemporary Ethics*. Oxford: Blackwell. pp. 178–203.

Borchorst, A., and Siim, B., (2008). Woman-friendly policies and state feminism: Theorizing Scandinavian gender equality. *Feminist Review*. 9. pp. 207–224.

Collins, P.H., (2000 [1990]) *Black Feminist Thought*. New York: Routledge.

Dahl, U., (2005) Scener ur ett äktenskap: Om heteronormativitet i svensk jämställdhetspolitik. [Scenes of marriage: About heteronormativity in Swedish Gender Equality Policy]. In: Kulick, D., (ed.). *Queer i Sverige* [*Queer in Sweden*]. Stockholm: Natur och Kultur. pp. 48–71.

Dalley, G., (1988) *Ideologies of Caring: Rethinking Community and Collectivism*. London: MacMillan Press.

Daly, M., and Lewis, J., (2000) The concept of social care and the analysis of contemporary welfare states. *The British Journal of Sociology*. 51(2). pp. 281–298.

Eldén, S., and Anving, T., (2016) New ways of doing the 'good' and gender equal family: Parents employing nannies and au pairs in Sweden. *Sociological Research Online*. 21(4). pp. 1–13.

Elvin-Nowak, Y., and Thomsson, H., (2001) Motherhood as idea and practice: A discursive understanding of employed mothers in Sweden. *Gender and Society*. 15(3). pp. 407–428.

Esping-Andersen, G., (1999) *Social Foundations of Post-industrial Economies*. Oxford: Oxford University Press.

Fraser, N., (2016). Contradictions of capital and care. *New Left Review*. 100. pp. 99–117.

FSA (Feminist Scholars Association) and Liu, Y.-H., (eds.). (1995) *White Paper on Women's Conditions in Taiwan in 1995*. Taipei: China Times.

FSA (Feminist Scholars Association) and Liu, Y.-H., (eds.). (1997) *Women, State and Care*. Taipei: Fembooks.

Gilligan, C., (1982) *In a Different Voice: Psychological Theory and Women's Development*. Harvard: Harvard University Press.

Hernes, H.M., (1987) *Welfare State and Women Power: Essays in State Feminism*. Oslo: Norwegian University Press.

Holliday, I., (2000) Productivist welfare capitalism: Social policy in East Asia. *Political Studies*. 48(4). pp. 706–723.

Jones, C., (1990) Hong Kong, Singapore, South Korea and Taiwan: Oikonomic welfare states. *Government and Opposition*. 25(4). pp. 446–462.

Lee, M.-T., (1996) *State Machine, Political Transition, and Social Welfare: A Study of the 'Old-Age Pension' Campaign in Taiwan (1992–95)*. Hsin-Chu: National Tsing-Hua University (in Chinese).

Leira, A., (2006) Parenthood change and policy reform in Scandinavia, 1970s-2000s. In: Ellingsaeter, A.L. and Leira, A. (eds.), *Politicising Parenthood in Scandinavia: Gender Relations in Welfare States*. Bristol: Policy Press. pp. 27–51

Lin, T.-H., Hong, J.-S., Li, J.-H., Wang, C.-C., and Chang, F.-Y. (2011) *Generations in Disaster: Risk in Domination of Entrepreneurs, Povertization and Low Birth Rate*. Taipei: Taiwan Labour Front.

Lin, W.-I., (1994) *Welfare State Regimes: A Historical Comparison and Analysis*. Taipei: Strong Current Publishing.

Liu, Y.-H., (2002) Caught between globalization and the female role: The dilemma of women in Taiwan. *National Policy Quarterly*. 1(2). pp. 85–116.

Liu, Y.-H., (2006) Child care system in Nordic Europe. *Journals of Children and Adolescence Welfare*. 10. pp. 7–22.

Liu, Y.-H., (2011) Taiwan's transformation of Scandinavian universal care and full employment policies and decision-making mechanisms. *Journal of Women's and Gender Studies*. 29. pp. 5–79.

Liu, Y.-H., (ed.) (2015) *The Transformation of the Nordic Experiences in Taiwan*. Taipei: Fembooks.

Lu, J.-D., Li, S.-J., Wang, S.-I., and Chen, C.-R., (2014) *Research on Ways of Provision of Social Welfare Services in Taiwan*. www.ndc.gov.tw/News_Content.aspx?n=E4F9C91C F6EA4EC4&s=05CDC57761692634 (Accessed 23 February 2018)

Milner, H., (1994) *Social Democracy and Rational Choice. The Scandinavian Experience and Beyond*. London: Routledge.

Mohanty, C.T., (2006) *Feminism without Borders: Decolonizing Theory, Practicing Solidarity*. Durham, NC and London: Duke University Press.

Mulinari, D., (2008) Women friendly? Understanding gendered racism in Sweden. In: Melby, K., Ravn, A.-B., and Wetterberg, C.C. (eds.), *Gender Equality and Welfare Politics in Scandinavia*. Bristol: The Policy Press. pp. 167–182.

Norocel, O.C., (2013) 'Give us back Sweden!' A feminist reading of the (re)interpretations of the Folkhem conceptual metaphor in Swedish radical right populist discourse. *Nora: Nordic Journal of Feminist and Gender Research*. 21(1). pp. 4–20.

PWR (Peng Wan-Ru Foundation), (1997a) *Pamphlet on Afterschool Care: Ideals*. Taipei: Ministry of Education and Foundation for Enhancement of Women's Rights.

PWR (Peng Wan-Ru Foundation), (1997b). *Pamphlet on Afterschool Care: Practices*. Taipei: Ministry of Education and Foundation for Enhancement of Women's Rights.

Sainsbury, D., (2001) Gendering dimensions of welfare states. In: Fink, J., Lewis, G., and Clarke, J. (eds.), *Rethinking European Welfare: Transformations of European Social Policy*. London: The Open University and Sage Publications. pp. 115–129.

Siim, B., (1987) The Scandinavian welfare states: Towards sexual equality or a new kind of male domination. *Acta Sociologica*. 30(3). pp. 255–270.

Streeck, W., and Schmitter, P.C., (1985) Community, market, state—and associations? The prospective contribution of interest governance to social order. *European Sociological Review*. 1(2). pp. 119–138.

Szebehely, M., (2006) Organizational changes and everyday realities: A comparative study of home-care services in Scandinavia. *Tidsskrift for Arbejdsliv*. 8(1). pp. 49–66.

Walker, A., and Wong, C.-K., (eds.). (2005) *East Asian Welfare Regimes in Transition: From Confucianism to Globalisation*. Bristol: The Policy Press.

Wang, P., and Wang, S.-Y., (2014) Development and difficulties in care policies in Taiwan: 1990–2012. In: FSA (Feminist Scholars Association) and Chen, J.-H. (eds.), *White Paper on Women's Conditions in Taiwan in 2014.* Taipei: Fembooks. pp. 29–76.

White, G., and Goodman, G., (1998) Welfare Orientalism and the search for an East Asian welfare model. In: Goodman, R., White, G., and Kwon, H-J. (eds.), *The East Asian Welfare Model: Welfare Orientalism and the state.* London and New York: Routledge. pp. 3–24.

7

MAKE(ING) ROOM IN TRANSNATIONAL SURGES

Pakistani Khwaja Sira organising

Erika Alm

Introduction

Copenhagen, Denmark: A TV station journalist interviews a group of activists from Pakistan who are in town for Copenhagen Pride 2015. One of the activists remarks on the visibility of gender variant people in Pakistani culture: "If you visit Pakistan, you will see, you see transgender people everywhere! Because the hijra and transgender culture is very common in Pakistan". Another activist delivers a powerful analysis: "Here in Denmark, some transgendered people, they did not come out properly, and they are not much visible [...] So, this [their visit to Denmark] is very good thing. Maybe they learn a few things from us" (Agger 2015). This scene highlights some of the themes explored in this chapter: the reformulation of gender variant narratives and lives as integrated parts of Pakistani culture; the construction of an imagined transnational trans* community; and activists challenging hegemonic notions of political agency and social justice as phenomena that emanate from the North and West and travel to other parts of the world.[1]

This chapter takes its departure in recent scholarly and activist writing on gender variant subjectivities, experiences and organising in transnational discursive and material entanglements structured by colonial, neoliberal surges (Sood 2009; Winter et al 2009; Cotton 2011; Aizura 2012; Lamble 2013; Shakhsari 2013; Snorton and Haritaworn 2013; Boellstorff et al. 2014). The aim is to explore strategies that members of the Pakistani Khwaja Sira community – part of a broad transnational gender variant community – deploy when organising for social justice. The chapter draws on interviews, conducted alongside my colleague Lena Martinsson, with members and leaders of four different Khwaja Sira lead organisations, two group interviews with unorganised Khwaja Siras, and two interviews with prominent activists currently not connected to a specific organisation. Some of the activists were interviewed more than once. The location of the activists varies from major cities to rural areas. Some of the activists have experience of working for organisations that have had international donor funding, while others have not. However, the question of what it means to orient activist work toward securing funding engages them all. For contextualisation, the following have been given weight in the analysis: interviews with members of two NGOs that describe themselves as allies to the Khwaja Sira community, and one unorganised self-proclaimed ally; interviews with Pakistani feminist activists regarding how to establish strategies for social justice work in a transnational activist setting (Alm and Martinsson 2016); Pakistani media material; and the litigation documentation of a case in the Pakistani Supreme Court pertaining to the rights of Khwaja Siras. The first interviews were conducted in early 2012, at a time when the practice of providing national identity cards for gender variant citizens was well on its way to being implemented, after the Supreme Court had commanded the provincial governments to take action in securing the constitutional rights of their gender variant citizens.

Scholars working on trans* and decoloniality, such as Tom Boellstorff, Mauro Cabral, Aniruddha Dutta and Svati P. Shah, have emphasised the importance of accounting for other spatial scales than the transnational one, asking us to consider for example regionality and urbanisation processes (Dutta 2013; Boellstorff et al. 2014; Shah 2014). They have warned against tendencies to construct universal gender variant subjects that are unmarked by, for example, class (Shah 2014: 636–637), and urged us to think about the ease with which gender variant subjects from the global South and East "circulate across the transnational routes of the industrial-academic complex, reified as the objects of colonial knowledge" (Boellstorff et al. 2014: 436). Hence, there is a need for studies that look at the co-constitution of transnational and local conditions for gender variant activism without determining a priori the translocal (Brickell and Datta 2011; Greiner and Sakdapolrak 2013) assemblage as an overdetermined effect of the unfolding of colonial globalisation processes.[2] Anthropologist Anna Tsing's (2005: 1) understanding of transnational connections as something that gets charged in "sticky materiality of practical encounters" can function, methodologically, as a point of departure for an analysis that brings the sometimes unpredictable manifestations of translocal discourses and practices to the fore without reifying them as predetermined once and for all by coloniality and globalisation.

Activist work, especially if done through organisations, is often oriented toward the state and its institutions and practices. It is also, however, oriented toward civil society, the intersection of the public and the political sphere, sometimes grounded in imagined communities of belonging (Anderson 1983; Yuval Davis 2006; Alm and Martinsson 2016). Given that the dynamics between civil society and the state have changed with the NGOization of civil society (Lang 1997; Bernal and Grewal 2014), it is essential to pay attention to the effects this might have on activist work. Some researchers claim that the expansive sphere of NGOs weakens state sovereignty, partly because the social contract between states and citizens is undermined when NGOs take the position of the welfare state in providing solutions in contexts where citizens' basic needs, such as housing and education, are not fulfilled

(Bernal and Grewal 2014: 4). However, the very form of the non-governmental organisation might well help produce the state by making the state visible through differentiation (see Mitchell 1999). As the constitutive outside of state sovereignty, the NGO takes on its own form of governmentality. In the words of Bernal and Grewal (2014: 8): "In this way the NGO form, somewhat paradoxically, derives power from working with the biopolitical logic of the state".

Terminological matters and the medical gaze

The establishment and spread of terminology is a messy, affective and performative matter, and it is one of the ways in which organising in a neoliberal, globalised setting plays out. Scholarly conversations around travelling terminology have highlighted the problems that come with the universalisation of terms that are firmly rooted in both Anglo-Saxon language contexts and the sociocultural contexts associated with the post-industrial, highly secular societies of the Northern and Western hemisphere where issues of sexuality and gender identity often are articulated in terms of identity politics. There is always the risk of overwriting local terminology and imposing hegemonic understandings of, for example, gender binarity (Massad 2002; Morgensen 2009). Universalising certain terms risks minoritising other terms that are then understood as grounded in a specific cultural or geographical context.

> Many denominations circulate currently as examples of a geographically neutral category – transgender, or trans* – and terms such as trasvesti, hijra, fa'afafine, and meti or katoey become doubly local, localised in their own culture and in relation to the international scope of transgender as a culturally nonspecific umbrella term.
>
> *(Boellstorff et al. 2014: 436)*

In Pakistan, activists, government officials and the general public use a plethora of terms. Some of the most commonly used terms are Khwaja Sira, eunuch, hijra, mukhanas, khushra, khotki, transgender and third person. Some are mainly used in official documents. For example, third person is often used in legislative and policy texts. Others, such as hijra and khotki (spelled kothi in the Indian context), are used in different international contexts. The latter are both terms used in the subcontinent with etymological roots in Hindi and Urdu (Dutta 2012, 2013; Redding 2015; Shah 2015). Transgender, with its etymological roots in English, is the most common term in transnational human rights and medical contexts, and in LGBTQ rights activism. The terms are entangled, which in itself speaks to the fact that local terminology is already entangled with transnational spreading of terms.

The terminology used in research contexts, by Pakistani researchers and by researchers from other parts of the world studying Pakistani material, is not the same as that used in activist contexts. In research articles, the terms hijra and eunuch are common (Rehan, Chaudhary and Shah 2009; Rehan 2011), while the activists interviewed refer to the community with the terms Khwaja Sira and transgender. Social anthropologist Faris Khan situates the former – Khwaja Sira – as deriving from narratives about a socially and culturally privileged position during the reign of the Moguls, and talks about the latter as a colonial term (Khan 2014, 2016). This tension between Khwaja Sira (as an indigenous term to Pakistan) and transgender (as a term loaded with colonial baggage) has been pointed out to me during conversations with Pakistani intellectuals (Alm and Martinsson 2016). However, most of the Pakistani activists interviewed use the terms interchangeably. The leader of a Khwaja Sira organisation in Karachi is explicit in how she uses transgender as a way of connecting her cause to transnational struggles. Transgender is also the term used by the Pakistani physicians working on HIV/AIDS prevention programmes targeting Khwaja Siras. When asked about the chosen terminology, the clinicians referred to international medical and public health discourses, as well as to the need for a common terminology in order to be able to cooperate and make alliance with scholars.

Judging by the fieldwork that this chapter is based on, and previous research, this tension – between, on the one hand, terms that are thought of as indigenous and, on the other, terms that have travelled transnationally – is being negotiated and enacted as part of organising. 'Linguistic labour' (Pigg 2001) is an everyday activity for the activists interviewed. Aniruddha Dutta (2013) provides an example of how instrumental the use of the term transgender is in the inclusion and exclusion processes of work for social change targeting gender variant and same-sex desiring subjects in Eastern India:

> Bridging the analysis of 'global queering' with a critique of hegemonic usages of 'transgender', I argue that the transgender category expands into India through institutionally constrained intersections between regional cultural tendencies and transnational activist discourses, exerting a certain globalizing force without simply being a homogenizing or colonizing imposition.
>
> *(Dutta 2013: 498)*

Transgender has become the term par excellence for gender variant people, used in transnational and translocal contexts alike (Towle and Morgan 2006; Dutta 2012, 2013; Boellstorff et al. 2014; Shah 2015; Khan 2016). The term has evolved out of the critique directed at the diagnostic term transsexualism – a term coloured by the pathologising framework of psychiatric management of gender variant expressions. Due to this history transgender is often used in medical contexts and thus has connotations of medicalising (while not necessarily pathologising) discourses and practices. These connotations are noteworthy, given the fact that transnational trans* activism and advocacy has been dominated by conversations about the importance of depathologisation and access to trans* specific health care. To question the pathologisation of gender variant people – and how their needs are mediated and restricted by medical diagnostic systems – is one of the major questions on the agenda of trans* organisation in Europe and the Americas. It is also high up on the transnational agenda, both in transnational policy-making organisations and institutions such as the United Nations (UN) and EU, and in transnational organisations specifically focusing on trans* health such as the World Professional Association for Transgender Health (Sood 2009; Winter 2009; Gorton 2013).

Pathologisation of gender variant people is not an issue that Khwaja Sira leaders mention when asked about the most pressing issues for their communities. However, both activists and their allies express explicit resistance toward medicalising discourses in general and pathologising ones in particular when asked about translocal expressions, such as the discussed – but only partially implemented – requirement for gender variant people to submit to medical examinations as a prerequisite for ID cards. As one activist stated, "Why should doctors have a say? This is about my feeling, my belonging". The leader of a Karachi organisation has fought the Sindh government on this particular issue. She argues that if genital examination or hormonal testing should be a prerequisite for gender variant citizens, then it ought to be a prerequisite for everyone. In a news article from 2010, she is quoted as saying, "No one has the right to tell someone else what they are. I know what I am" (*The Express Tribune*, June 13, 2010). Another activist, who testified before the Supreme Court in 2009, talks about the medical examinations as "just another door for corruption" and expresses great doubt as to what the medical profession might have to say about the issue. She claims there is a self-regulating function that challenges people who claim to be part of the community but not necessarily are, saying jokingly, "Call *me* about this, I am the medical board, I can tell if you are a Khwaja Sira or not". Her comment addresses a narrative about the community that is common in the interviews, namely that there are tensions within the community about who qualifies for inclusion. These tensions are, however, not primarily related to embodiment, but to identity and solidarity.

So, what might look like a 'stopping device' (Ahmed 2007) – the use of a terminology that ties into not only colonial universalising tendencies, but also a transnational discourse that prioritises conversations about depathologisation over, for example, questions of housing or education – does not necessarily function as stopping; it might actually enhance the reach of the organisations that use it. By using a term that is common in transnational trans* activist rhetoric and transnational policy organisations, the Pakistani activists are tapping into what Sally Engle Merry (2003) has called the 'international civil society'. This approach gives precedence to human rights and empowerment as the main focus of struggles for social justice and social change, while still negotiating what this transnational influence might entail and resisting, for instance, the primacy of the pathologisation discourse.

The problematisation of pathologisation echoes in the interviews with the allies. A journalist that has written extensively on the plight of the Khwaja Sira community describes the demand for medical examinations as discriminatory: "Why are you examining them extra? They are not trouble makers". The allies that work within the medical framework as physicians and psychiatrists – clearly part of an international medical community – speak frankly about the issue of pathologisation of gender variant people, stating that they doubt the need for a psychiatric diagnosis: "They don't have a disease. They have problems with culture". One of the clinicians admits that DSM – the *Diagnostic and Statistical Manual of Mental Disorders* developed by the American Psychiatric Association and used in large parts of the world – is culturally coded and as such not possible to apply universally without serious consideration. The psychiatrist in the group taps into the transnational, medical narrative of gender dysphoria, talking about "the intensity of the desire to be a woman" (which is the core of the transsexual narrative), but he also acknowledges that the Khwaja Sira community holds a unique cultural position in Pakistani society as a position beyond the gender binary. He describes this through a quotation from a member of the community they work with: "I am not a man, not a female, I am a hijra". This says something about the intersection of global and local terminologies and the very creation of translocal adaptations that then speak back to, and rearticulate, the terminology that is understood and used as universal, neutral and not culturally situated. These negotiation processes, enacted by the psychiatrist and the community member to whom he refers, can be understood as decolonising processes – as decentring the colonial, violent epistemic discourses that uphold notions of scientific knowledge as modern, objective and evidence-based, yet as possible to abstract into a universal category (Wynter 2003; Mignolo 2007).

Follow the money: Conditions for organising in neoliberal times

While the pathologisation of gender variant experiences is not at the centre of the conversations with Pakistani activists, another aspect of the medicalisation of gender variant citizens is foregrounded, namely the discourses and practices around HIV/AIDS prevention and how they orient work toward improving the living conditions for the community. The importance that transnational HIV/AIDS intervention programmes have come to have for gender variant organising around the world cannot be understated, since they present one of the few opportunities to attract funding for outreach work (Dutta 2012, 2013; Khan 2014; Shah 2015; Khan 2016).

HIV/AIDS has become one of the major health care related issues on the Pakistani state agenda, due to successful lobbying from international activists, patient organisations, pharmaceutical companies and commercial actors. The government has launched national prevention programmes, and one of the target groups is Kwhaja Siras. Khwaja Siras are described as the second most prone group to infection, and as such a threat to the social health of the nation. The other risk groups are men who have sex with men, drug users, sex workers and truckers (Rehan, Chaudhary and Shah 2009; Rehan 2011). The Pakistani state is staging itself as a welfare state through the launching of HIV/AIDS prevention programmes and the ratifying of international policy documents on HIV/AIDS prevention (for the Nepalese example, see Pigg 2001). This performance is bridging national and transnational narratives of epidemic threats, securitisation and state accountability, toward its own citizens and the citizens and states of the world. Queer scholars such as Scott Morgensen (2009), Karen Booth (2010) and Stacey

Leigh Pigg (2001) have pointed out that the discourses and practices of HIV/AIDS prevention are formulated and enacted per neo-colonialist notions and patterns, targeting not only so-called underdeveloped countries, but also indigenous people as sources of an epidemic, and implicitly as threats to the welfare of the global North and West.

Activists describe the orientation toward HIV/AIDS as problematic, highlighting the stigmatisation that comes with it. In the words of a Karachi-based activist, "Khwaja Siras are thought of as spreading disease. We are thought of as filth". According to the activists, the intervention programmes work sub-optimally, since the aim of the programmes is to simply locate infected people to prevent the disease from spreading, but there is no follow up or treatment programmes in place. One of the major problems, as identified by a Karachi-based activist, is that large amounts of funding are spent on salaries instead of going to the communities in need. The same activist talks about the discrimination that HIV-positive people are facing at the hands of physicians in hospitals, but also at the hands of people who are running the prevention programmes, who she claims have no interest in honouring the knowledge about HIV/AIDS prevention indigenous to the Khwaja Sira community. These people have "no sense of empathy for people with HIV", she says. Representatives of a Lahore-based organisation add that the scholarly work done on Khwaja Siras is a liability since it tends to focus on sex work. This focus on sex work further stigmatises the community and influences, for example, health care workers, to reduce Khwaja Siras to sex workers prone to HIV infection.

While a global framework for doing social justice work within NGOs has emerged in our neoliberal times, it is very clear that this framework does not control the everyday practices of organising (Bernal and Grewal 2014: 13). This is evident in the pragmatism that the Pakistani activists express when asked about how the orientation toward HIV/AIDS has affected their work; the baseline is as follows: If this is where the funding is available, this is the issue we invest in. However, there is an obvious frustration among the interviewed activists with the fact that it is so much easier to get funding for an HIV/AIDS prevention project than for projects that focus on empowerment and education. This is the case even when they can present well-developed project ideas, such as the one with mobile schools for Khwaja Sira children in Karachi, a project that takes its departure from the everyday experiences of street harassment and sexual violence and provides a solution to isolation and disempowerment. As an Islamabad-based activist concludes, "We need to create projects around this [housing, employment, education] rather than AIDS, AIDS, AIDS".

A Karachi-based activist expresses frustration with the way that the focus on HIV/AIDS prevention has affected not only the general public's opinion of Khwaja Siras but also her organisation's relation to the NGOs with which they have cooperated. She describes how organisations that are neither grounded in the community nor led by Khwaja Siras are exploiting their connections with her organisation. They invite her to meetings, making sure to document the interactions, and then leave her behind when the funding comes through. Funding that is targeting the Khwaja Sira community ought to go through Khwaja Sira organisations, she says, insisting on being more than a token for international NGOs that have little or no knowledge about the local conditions. "We know our own lives and histories the best. Why can't the international community understand this?" Her organisation, and others like it, is not lacking in infrastructure; however, that is often an argument put forth by regional, fairly large NGOs that claim to be working on behalf of the Khwaja Sira community when they argue as to why they ought to get funding instead of the local Khwaja Sira organisations. She is especially frustrated with organisations that claim to be facilitating community building. She argues that they are corrupt, recounting an episode when she was contacted by a donor that asked if her organisation could "handle finances" on a project that she had never heard of but evidently had been described as being part of. She never saw any money, nor did she hear anything from the organisation that supposedly was facilitating the project on behalf of the Khwaja Sira community. She identifies the problem as that of accessibility, not visibility. It is not that the potential donors cannot find community-based organisations like hers; they are highly visible. As she says of herself, "You can google me and find me directly, people know me, I am an ambassador; people recognise me and say, 'We have read about you.' The international community knows me". It is rather that the donors do not have access due to their lack of knowledge in, for example, the local languages. So, the donors tend to bet their money on the organisations that are fronted by people who speak fluent English – people who will function seamlessly in the transnational circuit. The Karachi-based activist is not the only activist that does this analysis, but her formulations are particularly astute: "If I don't speak English, does this mean that I don't know how to work with projects?"

The questions raised in relation to donor money – namely, who secures funding and who embarks on alliances with researchers – often tie into the previously mentioned tensions around who ought to be included in the Khwaja Sira community and on what grounds. Khwaja Siras describe their own community as inclusive of a range of gender and sexual non-conforming practices and subjectivities (Khan 2016).[3] Khan (2016) argues that one of the strategies used by Khwaja Sira activists consists of not being explicit about what constitutes the grounds on which the community is forged, i.e. that keeping an air of ambiguity around what sets Khwaja Siras apart from the rest of the population, in terms of gender identity, sexual preferences and sexual behaviours, can be understood as resistance toward a cisnormative society. This ambiguity can be articulated in other, more conflictual, ways as well, for example in conversations about funding. Several of the activists, particularly the ones that have been active for a longer period of time, declare that there are false Khwaja Siras, people that pose as Khwaja Sira in order to be able to claim money targeting the community. Dutta details similar conversations in Eastern India, where projects funded by the government and international development agencies have been instrumental in creating tensions among gender and sexual non-conforming people (Dutta 2013). The introduction of transgender and men who have sex with men (MSM) as two separate categories – both based in terminology and notions about gender and sexual identities that are endemic to the global West and North and hence potentially colonising – has generated specific problems for those who do not fit neatly into either category: "[S]ome activists claimed that existing MSM interventions already had many *kothis* who were transgender, while others opposed any MSM-transgender conflation and alleged that MSM leaders were masquerading as transgender to obtain funding" (Dutta 2013: 496).

The search for funding and the handling of money also bring conversations about the inherent volatility in being oriented toward money to the fore. These are conversations about trustworthiness, and how accusations of corruption can be raised both by community members and by people outside the community. One of the Islamabad-based activists even states that "[i]t is good that we are not getting money", since this means that she cannot be accused of corruption. She identifies the project form, and the fact that funding is more or less only available through NGOs, as one of the largest obstacles in social justice work. This is an analysis she shares with the majority of the activists interviewed. One of the women's rights activists interviewed during previous fieldwork expressed similar concerns about Pakistani women's rights movements becoming increasingly focused on finding funding and formal power. Politicians, government administrators and dominating NGOs, she said, are appropriating struggles being fought on the grassroots level and rearticulating them in terms not recognisable by the ones fighting on the streets. She talked about how many NGOs function like multinational companies, and that the fraternisation between politicians, government officials and people working in NGOs is corrupting people on all levels. Pertaining to her own work, she had tried to make sure that the projects run by her organisation are not dependent on external financing, so as not to be limited by particular forms of reporting back to donors. The motto had been "don't run with the money". As has been shown, one of the most common critiques toward the NGO form, expressed by both Khwaja Sira and feminist activists interviewed, relates to the way in which funding orients social justice work toward particular issues. The NGOization of civil society and activism ties into processes of neoliberalism and globalised capitalism, with effects that tend to depoliticise collective struggles and put focus on individual entrepreneurship and cultural awareness rather than on distribution of capital and political power (Bernal and Grewal 2014). In a global system where the notion of a liberal state is the hegemonic one, the binary between the public and the private sphere is still prolific. Hence, the NGO form creates a specific position for political action: "[T]he NGO (defined by its lack of official status and its position as outside the state) politicises and globalises the private as an organised entity, but also as a private entity that is not a profit-making enterprise" (Bernal and Grewal 2014: 8).

However, as scholarly and activist work has shown, there is no clear-cut differentiation between public and private, between state and civil society (Bernal and Grewal 2014). Two LGBTQ activists, interviewed during previous fieldwork, described how they related to international donor and state initiatives, concluding that they did what they could to stay under the radar of the Pakistani state, since state recognition, even in the form of funding, comes with surveillance. One of them described Pakistan as a negligent state in its combination of being a failed welfare state and a highly successful violent state (Alm and Martinsson 2016). These descriptions of Pakistan as a country with a weak state which leaves activists with little choice but to turn to international donors if they want funding – having to negotiate transnational terminology and agendas – raise questions about what the conditions are for those activist movements that develop a strong distrust toward the state as part of their strategies for resistance and social justice work.

Making history: The construction of the respectable gender variant citizen

The critical discourse around donor reliance (Bernal and Grewal 2014) seems to build on an idea about social justice work, and perhaps also political agency, as conditioned by autonomy, self-sufficiency and neutrality. One of the ways in which this type of critique might play out in the complex landscape of translocal negotiations of transnational and national conditions for organising is that it risks giving precedence to organisations that have a formalised relation to the state and display a concrete knowledge about the governmental, political system, despite the scepticism toward the state expressed by many activists. This double-bind has particular effects on the conditions for gender variant organising, not just in the global South and East but in the North and West as well. Social justice work for the rights of gender variant people is likely to be looked upon with suspicion for challenging the cisnormative status quo since administrative systems – so fundamental for the nation state as an economically productive and reproductive entity – take their departure from the gender binary. Given this fact, gender variant organising often addresses the state as one of the interlocutors. Therefore, on the one hand, it runs the risk of getting caught in a politics of recognition with the state (Butler 2004), while on the other hand it risks being dismissed by other social movements for buying into liberal identity politics, despite the systemic critique of cisnormativity as a structural problem (see for example Spade and Mananzala 2007; Spade 2011). The dynamics of translocal organising cannot be reduced to such schematics though, and this section details how the Khwaja Sira activists interviewed tap into a plethora of national and transnational discourses in their negotiations to make room for themselves. One of the strategies used for emphasising the importance of the rights of gender variant people is to frame issues of economic discrimination, social stigmatisation and violence in a historical narrative of the decline of cultural recognition as an effect of the construction of the Pakistani nation. Several of the Khwaja Siras activists talk about how the community has had the very specific cultural role of entertainers, performing ceremonial dancing at the births and weddings of sons (see also Khan 2014, 2016). These narratives of origin and descent are also often retold in media and governmental official documents, such as the ones documenting the litigation in the Supreme Court case on the human rights of gender variant citizens (Human Rights Case NOS.63 of 2009).

Such narratives could be interpreted as grounded in nostalgic constructions of a lost historic period, similar to the narratives about gender variant people produced in the global West and North, when scholars and activists look for more tolerant, preindustrial societies with 'natural' gender systems that transcend the gender binary. Such endeavours tend to not only exotify and reify gender variant subject positions in the global East and South but also locate them in a primordial context through a neocolonial politic of contemporaneity (Towle and Morgan 2006; Boellstorff et al. 2014). In one sense the historical narratives of Khwaja Siras can be understood to tap into nostalgic, culture-conservative notions of a cultural space and place, describing the respect for Khwaja Siras as dependent on them serving the particular function assigned to them and hence of them staying put in the designated place. But the activists make power-sensitive analyses of social change, where the tale of the Mogul Empire mainly functions as a way to anchor the contemporary problems as consequences of modernity and hence as acute and necessary to address by politicians. One of the allies talks about the decline in respect for Khwaja Sira culture as related to processes of modernisation, in which old customs lose their social function and the makeup of societal status changes, thereby making certain characteristics or abilities more defining, such as the ability to speak fluent English. A group of unorganised Khwaja Siras based in rural Sindh mention the urbanisation processes, noting how they, in combination with the accessibility and affordability of CD players and karaoke machines, have challenged the cultural role of Khwaja Siras as entertainers; perhaps such effects of technological developments have had more impact in rural contexts than urban ones (Boellstorff et al. 2014). The general analysis is that the loss of job opportunities has had an impact on the social position of Khwaja Siras, with deteriorating cultural recognition and enhanced social stigmatisation. Some activists tap into narratives about the conditions for the construction of the Pakistani nation state as an explanation, claiming the partition of 1947 as a defining moment. When asked the direct question of what historical events led to the decline in cultural status for Khwaja Siras, an Islamabad-based activist laconically replies, "The British happened". The traces of the colonial British Empire in the subcontinent is a theme that is reiterated in the interviews, as well as in media coverage and some research articles.

The narratives that tap into the modernisation project as a national project – a project that at least potentially has the function of providing its citizens with social justice on the grounds of building a strong nation state – expose another type of political volatility that the activists identify as a respectability discourse. There is, especially in the media material, a tendency to talk about the solution to social stigmatisation as that of disciplining disobedient, unruly subjects into good citizens. The jurist Mohammad Aslman Khaki, who was pivotal in the litigation in the Supreme Court resulting in the 2009 decision, describes his vision of assimilating Khwaja Siras into mainstream society: "These ID cards are supposed to be the first step in the transformation of the Khwaja Siras from beggars and sex workers on the fringes of society to industrious citizens employed as tailors, cooks and health workers contributing to the nation" (*The Express Tribune*, 13 June 2010). Politicians ought to view Khwaja Siras as resources for the nation, not despite the particular life situation many of them live under, but because of it: "I believe that they are the golden asset of the nation because they are not tied down by their families. All they need is two square meals a day, some rest and work" (*The Express Tribune*, 13 June 2010). This type of calculation with citizens' lives as both expendable and bendable, formable to fit the model of productive citizenship, is prevalent in the documentation of the Supreme Court litigation. The court insists on the necessity to register Khwaja Siras, not only in order for them to be able to claim their formal rights and for their local governments to reach out to them, but also for Khwaja Siras to be accounted for, as if they constitute a liability to society and the nation (Human Rights Case NOS.63 of 2009). There are reports of how the local governments have failed to get their numbers straight, and in the media Khwaja Siras are characterised as highly mobile and untraceable through family bonds.

The issuing of ID cards, which was celebrated nationally and internationally as a victory for the civil rights of Khwaja Siras, can also function as a normalising apparatus if the demands for medical examinations that were made in the Supreme Court are carried out. Khaki is quoted in a newspaper article describing the arguments for medical examinations: "'Their gender needs to be determined on objective medical grounds,' says Khaki. 'It's not enough to simply say that they have a feminine soul'" (*The Express Tribune*, 13 June 2010). Opposing such medicalising and disciplining approaches to the community – the effects of biopolitics (Foucault 2008) – Khwaja Sira activists have engaged in counter-discourses to the social pressure to conform, expressed for example in the way that a group of unorganised Khwaja Siras in Islamabad addresses the discourse of respectability when talking about why they believe it to be their right, as citizens, to beg:

> It is our right to beg, the state is not giving us any security [...] We understand that the government is trying to abolish begging, but it should not do that for Khwaja Siras, because we don't have any other option, because we have to live so far from family due to harassment. [...] We don't mean to insult Pakistan by discussing these problems.

One of the Karachi-based activists proclaims that she thinks the government ought to issue certificates for Khwaja Siras that would decriminalise commercial sex work, stating that the criticism she is getting for not coming down hard on sex work within the community is unfair and ungrounded: "If I can't help them with money, I have to let them do sex work". To refute the intimate ties of discourses of respectability and citizenship, and hence resist assimilation as a prerequisite for citizenship, is a strategy with long-standing traditions. In contemporary India, hijra activists have taken allegations of not measuring up to respectability and civility and turned them into arguments that strengthen the community. They have done this by arguing that this presumed unrespectability – often formulated as not having proper ties to their families – makes them less vulnerable to corruption (Dutta 2012: 126).

Activists counter the discourses that portray Khwaja Siras as not worthy of social respect with narratives about the lack of governmental and social support. Narratives that focus on the failure of the government can be found in the Supreme Court litigation as well, combined with the respectability discourse. The following example is from one of the first hearings: "[T]hey are citizens of Pakistan but their fundamental rights are being violated inasmuch as in some of the cases, the she-males are compelled to live an immoral life including offering themselves for dancing [...] the Government is bound to protect their rights and provide them opportunities" (Human Rights Case NOS.63 of 2009). During the litigation, arguments were also put forth that point toward poverty and a lack of economic support as the main causes for stigmatisation and discrimination. The activists interviewed take their departure from this type of analysis, and some of them were instrumental in the litigation process, providing the jurists with their arguments. However, as shown in this chapter, they also express a lack of trust, not only in the government but also in the state. They feel as though the government only *talks* about social change but never bothers with any real politics. Some of the activists point toward the lack of political interest in their situation as one of the major problems and say they see no change in sight. The promises made in the Supreme Court decision about community centres and employment in the government agencies, for example as tax debt collectors, have not been implemented on a large scale. Nor has the rhetoric of access to free health care and education, or the help to claim inheritance, translated into action.

A Karachi-based activist that has been working in the governmental sector for some time and experienced the work conditions first hand points to the fact that no Khwaja Siras have been offered a permanent position. All are working on a contract basis, and some have even resigned because of this discrimination. "Government is corrupt", she concludes. Narratives about governmental corruption are, as shown, commonplace among both activists and allies. Yet, in their calls for human and civil rights they are interpellating not only the transnational community of trans* activists and advocates, or the circuit of international donors, but also a state that has not recognised them as citizens. A very concrete example can be drawn from 2016, when a campaign was launched in the district of Khyber Pakhtunkhwa by a regional organisation. Khyber Pakhtunkhwa is known as one of the most conservative regions of Pakistan, and was around this time the site of several highly publicised murders of Khwaja Siras (*Daily Times*, 1 June 2016, *Daily Times*, 2 June 2016). The campaign targeted the Pakistani Census of 2016, and consisted of photos of people holding placards demanding state recognition of gender variant people as citizens, making their voices and votes count. The placards, with rainbow-coloured frames, insisted, "Count transgender persons as equal citizens. #endtransphobia".

In conclusion, the activists interviewed have developed multiple strategies for handling the double-bind to the state. On the one hand, there are the pushbacks toward the negligent state and its economy of abandonment (Povinelli 2011).

These can be traced in the activist critique of the respectability politics inherent in the assimilation model and their scrutinising of the state rhetoric of redistribution that does not pay up. On the other hand, there are the narratives of origin and descent that play into constructions of a cultural continuum of the geographic place now known as Pakistan, and campaigns like the one just referenced that use liberal notions of citizenship to bolster claims for rights. A longstanding activist, well known in national and international contexts, delivers her analyses of two aspects of the complexities of negotiating for room in her translocal context, with its intersection of transnational, national and local interests. Firstly, she puts her finger on the politics of paying homage to discriminated, abjected citizens only after their death. "If I will die, they will use me as an example and say, 'She was so important for the movement.' They will use my picture". In her case, the proponent is the government, and her formulation is shorthand for what trans* scholars have talked about as transnecropolitics, using Achille Mbembe's (2003) concept of necropolitics to describe how patterns of colonialism and racism make certain gender variant bodies and lives only recognisable as human after death (Lamble 2013; Shakhsari 2013; Snorton and Haritaworn 2013; Boellstorff et al. 2014: 436). Secondly, she reacts dismissively toward efforts to define the Khwaja Sira community itself as an effect of state interventions; such suggestions have come from intellectuals as part of a critique of the assimilation project initiated by the state. They bear resemblance to critiques of the role of homonationalism in reifying notions of the liberal, respectable, upstanding gay citizen (Puar 2007). When asked about the significance of the Supreme Court decision of 2009 for the constitution of the community, she laconically states, "I was Khwaja Sira before, and I am one now". Her razor-sharp analyses of the necropolitical approach of the negligent and violent state apply to the transnational circuits as well, to the use of the figure of the suffering gender variant person in transnational trans* activism and trans* scholarship. Cabral (in Boellstorff et al. 2014) addresses this necropolitical "reduction of trans* people to potential or real victims" as something that affects gender variant people's possibilities to participate in processes that determine their life situations:

> We are never supposed to be in the room – except as corpses, or bodies in danger of extinction, exhibited for progressive consumerism, frequently oriented toward funding. And even when trans* issues – often codified, in a reductive way, as 'gender identity issues' – occupy a growing portion in international LGBTI activism, that expansion is not translated into the circulation of critical knowledge produced by trans* people.
>
> *(Boellstorff et al. 2014: 436)*

"They can learn from us. We can change the world": Transformative strategies

Two of the Lahore-based activists interviewed were part of the group of Pakistani activists attending Copenhagen Pride 2015 mentioned at the beginning of this chapter. They talk about how they were invited to Danish schools to speak to youth, and learned that the Danish youngsters had preconceptions that Pakistan is a conservative country in terms of gender and sexual politics, and that they were surprised that Pakistani gender variant people lived such visible lives. The activists were in turn surprised by the youth's lack of knowledge about the living conditions of Danish gender variant people. One of the activists laughs at the memory of the encounters they had with the students and recounts a specific conversation in which one of the students asked her what her motives were for travelling to Denmark. She recites her answer: "We are here to learn from you and perhaps teach you as well". Then she turns toward us and says, "They can learn from us. We can change the world!".

This type of statement hinges on analyses made by several of the interviewed activists, on the importance of civil society as an arena for activist work. The changing relations between NGOs and states, and the NGOisation of civil society, has created new figurations of political subjects; for example, Bernal and Grewal (2014) have argued that organisations that demand to be recognised as contributing to social change through their work on empowerment and capacity-building produce a different type of political subject than organisations that demand capital and political redistribution. The intricacy of strategies deployed by activists in their approach to the state is mirrored in an equally complex approach to civil society. When asked about their everyday work, the activists stress the importance of community-based sensitising work and the need to politicise the intersections of the public and private spheres. Some of them have tried to obtain political influence by running for office in their respective provincial governments. The leader of a Karachi-based organisation describes how she, despite not succeeding in obtaining a place in government, has earned social credibility by being rooted in a tightly knit community. She is, through her organisation, reaching out not only to other gender variant citizens of Karachi but to a broader imagined community of the impoverished – those in need of someone to fight for their rights to fresh water, safe housing, equal education and efficient health care. The aim of the organisation is, as she expresses, to sensitise civil society to the plights of Khwaja Siras and other disenfranchised groups, such as homeless children living on the streets. A group of Lahore-based activists describe similar approaches in their efforts to make Khwaja Siras understand that they are being discriminated against, to raise their consciousness of the ills that society is putting them through. The organisation these activists are members of cooperate with a national LGBT NGO that, among other things, works with HIV/AIDS prevention. Sharing the space with the better established organisation provides them not only with the means to influence the implementation of prevention programmes but also with the possibility to arrange sensitising workshops for the community members who come to be tested. In addition to employing their connections with other organisations to reach out to the community, they talk about approaching religious leaders as channels to the general public. Having noticed that some religious leaders are tapping into the narrative that says Khwaja Siras used to have social respect, the activists think of these religious leaders as potentially helpful in raising awareness of the contemporary situation for the community: "We should invite Ulamas and other religious leaders to our quarters so that they see how we live. [...] We need to communicate our message to the religious leaders".

Engaging with religious discourses as a way to educate both the own community and the general public is a strategy used by other activists as well. This strategy takes its departure in an analysis that acknowledges the importance of religious communities and institutions in civil society, and the role of religion in the average citizen's life as the basis for communities of belonging with specific meaning-making functions. Making sense of one's rights through religious discourses is a strategy used by, for example, the unorganised Khwaja Siras in rural Sindh who have turned to local religious leaders for help, referring to their lives as sacred by creation: "We are by God. Please help us". This type of rhetoric is also found in the Supreme Court litigation, when the litigator argued for the sanctity of gender variant citizens' lives with reference to the Quran and Allah: "They are creatures of Allah Almighty, therefore, their social life is to be respected" (Human Rights Case NOS.63 of 2009).[4] The litigator uses religious discourses to identify patriarchal systems (although not named as such) as mechanisms of oppression: "Their male relatives, instead of looking after them as part of their religious, moral and legal duty, prefer to expel them from their homes" (Human Rights Case NOS.63 of 2009).

Some of the activists are very explicit in their analyses of patriarchal systems and hegemonic masculinity as culprits in the discrimination of gender variant people. Several of them also talk about strategies to combat patriarchy, particularly mentioning not only public pedagogy – in the form of community outreach programmes of different types – but also formal education as vehicles for social change. While describing educational institutions as bastions of patriarchy and discrimination, they have not given up on pedagogy as a strategy. Some of them believe the government ought to instate separate schools for Khwaja Siras to provide them with safe spaces for education, while others demand that all educational institutions should be inclusive in the truest sense, as anything else would simply send "the message that we are not as human as they [members of mainstream society] are". The faith in the transforming power of knowledge and education can be traced in activists' ways of talking about the need to reform the school system and curricula as well. In the words of a long-time activist in the women's movement:

> With astute material we can reclaim a space for things that are suppressed by dominant discourse. Through education we can foster a generation that can envision a different future. It is an act of faith, to instigate change like this, because you can't tell ahead what will come out of it.

This chapter has explored the theoretical and empirical potentials in understanding gender variant activism as articulated and enacted in a globalised, transnational setting while trying to pay attention to the significance of context-specific conditions for activist work. It has focused on the complex negotiations of Khwaja Sira activism as navigating strategies of redistribution and inclusion, assimilation and resistance, in a translocal context far more complex than colonial notions of political subjectivities in the global South account for. During the summer of 2017, social and traditional media was buzzing with excitement over two separate events: the opening of a Khwaja Sira-led school for Khwaja Siras who have been ostracised from the public school system, and the introduction of two bills in the Senate on the rights of gender variant people.[5] The launching of these two different types of activist interventions into the discrimination of gender variant citizens of Pakistan – both rooted in Khwaja Sira activism and aimed at the politics of abandonment – is the legacy of Pakistani gender variant organising.

Notes

1 The terminology used in this chapter is a compromise. To not isolate Khwaja Sira activism as only affecting and engaging with the Pakistani context, and to be able to show the transnational connections and work done by the activists, a heuristic term to connote practices and subjectivities that do not fit the gender binary is needed. For this purpose, I have chosen the term 'gender variant' (see also Dutta 2013). Gender variant does not connote an identity position; it is a descriptive term that gathers practices and people identified by cisnormative systems as falling outside of the gender binary. Such identification processes are context specific and in no way universal (for a critique of gender binary systems as violent colonial traces, see for example Lugones 2007, 2010). In addition to gender variant I use 'trans*' when I am referring to the transnational discourses that use the terms 'transgender' and 'trans*' to connote specific experiences, expressions, subjectivities and activism.

2 Clemens Greiner and Patrick Sakdapolrak argue that the term translocality can be used to point toward the co-constitutionality of the transnational and the local, and at the same time capture the moments of re-articulations when the local and the transnational merge into a situated assemblage (Greiner and Sakdapolrak 2013).

3 "In the contemporary period, *khwaja sira* serves as an umbrella term consisting of several overlapping sex and gender subcategories that, according to my research consultants, may include individuals with congenital genital irregularities (*khunsa*), feminine males who situationally cross-dress (*zennana*), and *zennanas* who excise their male genitalia and assume a more permanent feminine presentation (*hijra*)" (Khan 2016: 159).

4 Local religious leaders have responded to the call for arms, issuing a fatwa (a religious decree) on the rights on Khwaja Siras, as reported by *Dawn* ("Pakistan: Fatwa allows Transgender Marriage", *Dawn*, 27 June 2016).

5 "The Transgender and Intersex persons (Promotion and Protection of Rights) Bill 2017" and "The Transgender Persons (Protection of Rights) Criminal Law (Amendment) Act 2017" have been developed by a taskforce headed by Senator Rubina Khalid in close cooperation with activists from all regions of Pakistan. (*The Express Tribune*, 14 July 2017).

References

Agger, R., (2015) *Tre transkønnede aktivister fra Pakistan vil hjælpe danske ligesindede med at springe ud* [Three trans activists from Pakistan want to help Danish counterparts to come out]. *DR, DK.* www.dr.dk/nyheder/indland/video-transkoennede-pakistanere-til-copenhagen-pride-hvor-er-de-danske-henne

Ahmed, S., (2007) A phenomenology of whiteness. *Feminist Theory*. 8(2). pp. 149–168.

Aizura, A., (2012) Transnational transgender rights and immigration law In: Enke, A., (ed.). *Transfeminist Perspectives in and beyond Transgender and Gender Studies*. Philadelphia: Temple University Press. pp. 133–151.

Alm, E., and Martinsson, L., (2016) The rainbow flag as friction: Transnational, imagined communities of belonging among Pakistani LGBTQ activists. *Culture Unbound*. 8(3). pp. 218–239.

Anderson, B., (1983) *Imagined Communities: Reflections on the Origin and Spread of Nationalism*. London: Verso.

Bernal, V., and Grewal, I., (eds.). (2014) *Theorizing NGOs: States, Feminisms, and Neoliberalism*. Durham, NC: Duke University Press.

Boellstorff, T., Cabral, M., Cárdenas, M., Cotten, T., Stanley, E.A., Young, K., and Aizura, A.Z., (2014), Decolonizing transgender: A roundtable discussion. *TSQ: Transgender Studies Quarterly*. 1(3). pp. 419–439.

Booth, K., (2010) A magic bullet for the 'African' mother? Neo-imperial reproductive futurism and the pharmaceutical 'solution' to the HIV/AIDS crisis. *Social Politics: International Studies in Gender, State and Society*. 17(3). pp. 349–378.

Brickell, K., and Datta, A., (eds.). (2011) *Translocal Geographies: Spaces, Places, Connections*. Farnham: Ashgate.

Butler, J., (2004) *Undoing Gender*. New York: Routledge.

Cotton, T., (ed.). (2011) *Trans Gender Migrations: Bodies, Borders, and the (Geo)politics of Gender Trans-ing*. New York: Routledge.

Daily Times (1 June 2016) *Transgender community demands separate residential colonies*.

Daily Times (2 June 2016) *No country for a transgender person*.

Dawn (27 June 2016) *Pakistan: Fatwa allows transgender marriage*.

Dutta, A., (2012) Claiming citizenship, contesting civility: Institutional LGBT movement and the regulation of gender/sexual dissidence in West Bengal, India. *Jindal Global Law Review*. 4(1). pp. 110–141.

Dutta, A., (2013) Legible identities and legitimate citizens: The globalization of transgender and subjects of HIV-AIDS prevention in Eastern India. *International Feminist Journal of Politics*. 15(4). pp. 495–514.

Foucault, M., (2008) *The Birth of Biopolitics: Lectures at the Collége de France, 1978–1979*. Basingstoke: Palgrave Macmillan.

Gorton, R.N. (2013) Transgender as mental illness: Nosology, social justice, and the tarnished golden mean. In: Stryker, S., and Aizura, A.Z. (eds.).*The Transgender Studies Reader 2*. London: Routledge, pp. 644–652.

Greiner, C., and Sakdapolrak, P., (2013) Translocality: Concepts, applications and emerging research perspectives. *Geography Compass*. 7(5). pp. 373–384.

Human Rights Case NOS.63 of 2009, Supreme Court of Pakistan, 14.07.2009.

Khan, F., (2014) *Khwaja Sira: Culture, Identity Politics, and "Transgender" Activism in Pakistan*. Surface Dissertations Paper 56. Syracure University.

Khan, F., (2016) Khwaja Sira activism: The politics of gender ambiguity in Pakistan. *TSQ: Transgender Studies Quarterly*. 3(1–2). pp. 158–164.

Lamble, S., (2013) Retelling racialized violence, remaking white innocence: The politics of interlocking oppressions in Transgender Day of Remembrance. In: Stryker, S., and Aizura, A.Z., (eds.). *The Transgender Studies Reader 2*. London: Routledge. pp. 30–45.

Lang, S., (1997) The NGOization of feminism. In: Scott, J.W., Kaplan, C., and Keates, D. (eds.). *Transitions, Environments, Translations: Feminisms in the International Politics*. New York: Routledge.

Lugones, M., (2007) Heterosexualism and the colonial/modern gender system. *Hypatia*. 22(1). pp. 186–209.

Lugones, M., (2010) Toward a decolonial feminism. *Hypatia*. 25(4). pp. 742–759.
Massad, J., (2002) Re-orienting desire: The gay international and the Arab world. *Public Culture*. 14(2). pp. 361–385.
Mbembe, A., (2003), Necropolitics. *Public Culture*. 15(1). pp. 11–40.
Merry, S.E., (2003) Human rights law and the demonization of culture (and anthropology along the way). *Polar: Political and Legal Anthropology Review*. 26(1). pp. 55–77.
Mignolo, W., (2007) Delinking: The rhetoric of modernity, the logic of coloniality and the grammar of de-coloniality. *Cultural Studies*. 21(2). pp. 449–514.
Mitchell, T., (1999) Society, economy, and the state effect. In: Steinmetz, G. (ed.). *State/Culture: State-Formation after the Cultural Turn*. Ithaca, NY: Cornell University Press. pp. 76–97.
Morgensen, S.L., (2009) Indigenous AIDS organizing and the anthropology of activist knowledge. *New Proposals: Journal of Marxism and Interdisciplinary Inquiry*. 2(2). pp. 45–60.
Pigg, S.L., (2001) Languages of sex and AIDS in Nepal: Notes on the social production of commensurability. *Cultural Anthropology*. 16(4). pp. 481–541.
Povinelli, E., (2011) *Economies of Abandonment*. Durham, NC: Duke University Press.
Puar, J.K., (2007) *Terrorist Assemblages: Homonationalism in Queer Times*. Durham, NC: Duke University Press.
Redding, J.A., (2015) From 'she-males' to 'unix': Transgender rights and the productive paradoxes of Pakistani policing. In: Berti, D., and Bordia, D., (eds.). *Regimes of Legalities: Ethnography of Criminal Cases in South Asia*. Oxford: Oxford University Press. pp. 258–289.
Rehan, N., (2011) Genital examination of hijras. *Journal of Pakistan Medical Association*. 61(7). pp. 695–696.
Rehan, N., Chaudhary, I., and Shah, S.K., (2009) Socio-sexual behaviour of hijras of Lahore. *Journal of Pakistan Medical Association*. 59(6). pp. 380–384.
Shah, S.P., (2015) Queering critiques of neoliberalism in India: Urbanism and inequality in the era of transnational "LGBTQ" rights. *Antipode*. 3. pp. 635–651.
Shakhsari, S., (2013) Shuttling between bodies and borders: Iranian transsexual refugees and the politics of rightful killing. In: Stryker, S., and Aizura, A.Z. (eds.). *The Transgender Studies Reader 2*. London: Routledge. pp. 565–579.
Snorton, C.R., and Haritaworn, J., (2013) Trans necropolitics: A transnational reflection on violence, death, and the trans of color afterlife. In: Stryker, S., and Aizura, A.Z. (eds.). *The Transgender Studies Reader 2*. London: Routledge. pp. 66–75.
Sood, N., (2009) *Transgender People's Access to Sexual Health and Rights: A Study of Law and Policy in 12 Asian Countries*. Kuala Lumpur: Asian-Pacific Resource and Research Centre for Women (ARROW).
Spade, D., (2011) *Normal Life: Administrative Violence, Critical Trans Politics and the Limits of Law*. New York: South End Press.
Spade, D., and ManazalaR., (2007) The nonprofit industrial complex and trans resistance. *Sexuality Research and Social Policy: Journal of NSRC*. 5(1). pp. 53–71.
Spivak, G.C., (2004) Righting wrongs. *The South Atlantic Quarterly*. 103(2/3). pp. 523–581
The Express Tribune, (13 June 2010) *Dragging the line*.
The Express Tribune, (14 July 2017) *Two bills tabled in Senate for transgender rights*.
Towle, E.B., and Morgan, L.M., (2006) Romancing the transgender native: Rethinking the use of the 'third gender' concept. In: Stryker, S., and Aizura, A.Z. (eds.). *The Transgender Studies Reader 2*. London: Routledge. pp. 666–684.
Tsing, A.L., (2005) *Frictions*. Princeton, NC: Princeton University Press.
Winter, S., (2009) Cultural considerations for the World Professional Association for Transgender Health's standards of care: The Asian perspective. *International Journal of Transgenderism*. 11(1). pp. 19–41.

Winter, S., Chalungsooth, P., Teh, Y.K., Rojanalert, N., Maneerat, K., Wong, Y.W., Beaumont, A., Wah HoL.M., Gomez, F.C., and Macapagal, R.A., (2009) Transpeople, transprejudice and pathologization: A seven-country factor analytic study. *International Journal of Sexual Health*. 21(2). pp. 96–118.

Wynter, S., (2003) Unsettling the coloniality of being/power/truth/freedom: Towards the human, after man, its overrepresentation – An argument. *CR: The New Centennial Review*. 3(3). pp. 257–337.

Yuval Davis, N., (2006), Belonging and the politics of belonging. *Patterns of Prejudice*. 3. pp. 197–214.

8

PUTTING (LEFT) POLITICS BACK INTO (WESTERN) FEMINIST THEORY

Conversations with feminist activists and scholars in Argentina[1]

Diana Mulinari

Introduction

In the last few decades feminist scholarship has been widely transformed by the contributions of black, anti-racist, aboriginal and postcolonial intellectuals/activists (Collins 1991; Anthias and Yuval-Davis 1992; Sandoval 2000; Oyewùmì 2005; Rivera Cusicanqui 2010). These interventions have, up to a certain point, challenged and contested the implicit Eurocentrism at the core of European Gender Studies. However, and despite these contributions, Gender Studies as an academic discipline continues to reinforce the myth that Europe is a self-contained entity. Notwithstanding discourses on global feminism, the production of feminist theory is regulated through a clear division of labour, where the centre produces theory and the periphery provides empirical illustrations (Connell 2007).

Transnational feminism as a theoretical frame was established during the late 1990s, taking a point of departure in knowledge systems and epistemologies of resistance evolving from women's struggles against neoliberal capitalism (Alexander and Mohanty 1997; Grewal and Kaplan 2002; Mohanty 2003). Several scholars point to the tension between scholarship on transnational feminist organising (Naples and Desai 2002; Ferree and Tripp 2006) and transnational feminist knowledge production as a normative analytical frame (Fernandes 2013).

The strength of transnational feminist genealogies is located in its agenda for the production of a theoretical practice, by means of doing theory by thinking through the flesh (Moraga and Anzaldúa 1981), valorising the knowledge arising from feminist activist practice at the peripheries. Central to a transnational feminist genealogy is to illuminate and act upon the diversity of anti-imperialist, anti-colonial, anti-racist and anti-capitalist feminists' struggles understood as epistemic sites of fundamental value for feminist scholarship (Swarr and Nagar 2010; Conway 2017).

The aim of this chapter is to contribute to the transnational feminist practice of unlearning privilege regarding the power to define what theory is and who is a theorist by learning from others situated at the margins of hegemonic feminist scholarship. The aim of the chapter is to name, identify and analyse the production of feminist knowledge by diverse feminist activists in Buenos Aires, Argentina, learning from the way they construct their (feminist) past, explain their (feminist) present and argue about their (feminist) future.

Feminists in Argentina are located in a wide range of social movements, networks, organisations and institutions – from lesbian feminist collectives and trans* work cooperatives to women activists in trade unions and occupied factories to women leading black and indigenous movements; from university Women's Studies programmes to mainstream political parties.

The chapter is organised as follows. The chapter begins by presenting the methodological and theoretical frame exploring scholarships of hope and transnational/Third World feminism. Following this, three different angles of feminism in Argentina are provided through an analysis of diverse subject positions among activists and scholars who define themselves as feminists.

Methodology

Skissernas[2] ('Sketches') is an art museum situated in the city of Lund, Sweden, very near the university where I am employed. I love the place, with the opportunity it offers of following the labour process of individual artists through the exhibition of the several sketches produced before the finished artwork. Sometimes I prefer the sketches to the finished art-piece. As yet, there is no 'Skissernas museum' for feminist scholarship where the writing process with its manuscript revisions is exhibited instead of only the final published version.

I faced serious problems in writing this chapter, which has changed quite dramatically from sketch to finished text. It was the kind of text that made me unhappy. A text that I always put on hold, and to which I returned with a feeling of duty more than one of pleasure or passion in the writing. I have written other texts that were painful or challenging, but this one was sluggish. The text did not go my way. When I presented what I thought was a nearly finished version to my colleagues, they commented carefully and engaged with me by suggesting that, while particular sections were very interesting, the analytical scope framing the chapter needed further development. They were absolutely right; the text had no point (although they would never articulate their criticism in that way because they are generous and caring colleagues).

Something was wrong with the text, and I believe it was its aim: I did not want to write about feminism in Argentina. I could not write about feminism in Argentina. There is no need to write about feminism in Argentina. There are thousands of excellent feminist scholars writing about the topic (Di Marco 2010; Tarducci 2012; Barranco 2013; Bellucci 2014). Their work falls outside the scope of 'feminist theory' because many of them seldom publish in English (in a context where publishing internationally means publishing in English via UK or US publishing houses). The issue is one of translation. Or, rather, the issue is the hegemony of English as the language of social theory. Hopefully a transnational feminist agenda will help us to speak and work in academia in different languages.

The text was much easier to write when I changed the aim. While the first sketch was about feminism in Argentina, this final product is about what I have learned from feminist struggles and feminist knowledge production in that country.

The analysis evolving from the collected empirical material is grounded in considerable personal-political reflection. I had been forced into exile in 1977 during the military dictatorship (1976–1983) and have been active in the struggle for human rights in Argentina,[3] sharing today the Argentinean feminist movement's agendas and societal visions. In other words: this is a text shaped by my having 'taken sides' with human rights and feminist activists (Armbruster and Laerke 2008), or rather, by my 'outsider within' position.

This text is, however, not solely located within a black feminist autobiographical tradition (Anzaldúa 1999; Cosslett et al. 2000) but enters into a dialogue with the practice of feminist ethnography, following the activities of diverse feminist groups during four visits to Buenos Aires in 2010, 2012, 2014 and 2016 (two months each) and the powerful voices of fifteen feminist activists from diverse backgrounds and locations within the Argentinean feminist movement.

Travelling back and forth between Argentina and Sweden demands an ability to translate not only theoretical debates and political agendas, but also my own positionality changes when crossing the Atlantic: a woman of colour in Sweden (despite my privileged position as professor), a human rights activist in Argentina (despite my experience of state terrorism, a white middle-class privileged settler). I thought to conclude the paragraph with a consideration of embodying a feminism identity in both contexts.

But, the meaning of being a feminist, in the Global North and the Global South, is radically different, as well as in my shifting location within these, up to a certain extent, epistemological communities of belonging.

Feminist philosopher Maria Lugones (1987) identifies different ways of being at ease in the world. On the one hand, she argues for a way of embodying privilege, being at ease in the world by being confident, a fluent speaker; another is to be normatively happy with the norms and values of the society. On the other hand, the author identifies two other forms of being at ease in the world: being at ease in the world because one is together with people one loves (even within worlds one dislikes) and being at ease in the world (even within worlds one dislikes) because one is together with people who share similar memories.

A feminist project departs from the refusal to be normatively happy (Ahmed 2009) and from the refusal to speak the language of power fluently. It departs also from the need of communities of friends to share old memories and to create new ones. But most of all, it departs, following Lugones, from the suspicion (or the knowledge) that those who are too comfortable, too at ease in the world (even the feminist worlds), lack the desire to travel among and within worlds.

Southern Theory: The making of scholarships of hope

> Silence. Whispers. Uncomfortable body shifting. Had I done something wrong? This is happening on one of my courses in Gender Studies after a discussion of Saskia Sassen's book *Expulsions* (2014). "I do not like this book. It makes me feel powerless," one of the students from Ecuador commented, trying to break the compact silence. "It is as if everything was better in the Sixties." "Not for us," another student of indigenous background from Bolivia nearby whispered. "She writes as if what we do every day in Argentina, in Brazil, everywhere, does not matter," another added. "There is nothing in the alternatives she discusses about el buen vivir [the good life] here, and that is also political economy,"[4] concluded the whole group.[5]

I disagreed with the students. Saskia Sassen is one of my favourite contemporary thinkers and her book has been widely read and positively received among critical scholars and intellectuals globally. I had included *Expulsions* in the course literature because I believed that Saskia Sassen's reconceptualisation of political economy is a vital one. Her work is theoretically ground-breaking when arguing for the entrance of a new phase of capitalism, a new phase she names as 'exclusion'. I was also impressed by her methodological boldness in using a variety of datasets and case studies to explore carefully and systematically four expressions of this expulsion logic: the shrinking of the economic spaces, the new rush for African land, the financialisation of everything and environment destruction. My first reading of the students' (most of them from Latin America) resistance towards *Expulsions* was that they were not especially familiar with political economy as a specific genre, and I tried in my response to their criticisms to locate Sassen's work within this particular tradition. However, a second and more reflective reading of the students' evaluation of the book forced me to listen to their criticism, or, rather, to move from an explanation based on the students' ignorance towards one that explored their epistemological and emotional location in the Global South.

My second reading located their criticism in their identification with historical legacies, forms of resistance and alternative epistemologies outside the scope of Sassen's narrative. I began to understand their reactions.

Sassen provides a traditional (and only too familiar) temporal perspective defining post-war Keynesianism as a space of incorporation that shifted towards neoliberalism, and now towards a phase of expulsion (Sassen 2014: 28–29). Despite the strengths of Sassen's work there is a solid epistemic continuity with Eurocentric modes of reading the social, as well as a (white) nostalgia for the European welfare state. This binary (and normative) opposition between the good old days of the European welfare state and the poverty of the neoliberal project, and the cruelty of expulsion, excludes the centrality in the European racial regime of overexploitation of indigenous people, land and migrant labour at the core of what Sassen conceptualises as a productive and prosperous time. Expulsion is regulated through a narrative where universal truths about capitalism are told through the (privileged) location of the West. Expulsion is located within a genre of (white) nostalgia that decreases our ability to identify other futures; black feminist scholars in their criticism of Nancy Fraser's connection between neoliberalism and feminism identity this as white feminist fatigue syndrome (Bhandar and Ferreira da Silva 2013).

I came to understand the students' responses as a criticism towards a specific genre in Western social science production of dystopic stories, often based on the marginalisation and exclusion not only of other forms of knowledge but other emotional regimes, particularly those of hope.

There is, however, an incipient field of scholarship of hope: the emergence of studies that explore democratic alternatives to capitalism is broad (Wright 2012; Hall et al. 2015), some of them strongly inspired by the work of feminist scholars (Federici 1999). Wendy Harcourt (2014) convincingly argues that while neoliberal cultures always prioritise capitalist profit, global struggles against this regime (anti-colonial/anti-imperial, peasant, ecological, labour, women's, peace and justice, anti-globalisation, etc.) have provided new societal visions and new hopes. The author argues that "there is profound meaning and hope for global transformation in the struggles carried out by people in places looking at the articulation between the global and the local" (Harcourt 2014: 1308).

An understanding that the social is shaped by both the cruelty of capitalism and also by the strength of its democratic emerging alternatives is at the core of this chapter.

Transnational (feminist) solidarity

> There are many kinds of prejudices, and maybe one of the most difficult to challenge is the fascination of the Global North with the spirit of mobilisation and resistance, which goes for all social movements, including feminism, in Argentina. This taking and being in the streets. But what this *gringolandia* does not see is the hours and hours, and months and even years of meetings and assemblies and more assemblies and more documents and comments on those documents beyond and through the being in the streets. For example, in the document we define ourselves as anti-capitalists, and that was no problem because *el pueblo feminista* [the feminist people] is very leftist, but it took five meetings to try to find a language that was not only against capitalism but also for something else. I think we succeeded, but it was a lot of discussions. Maybe it was easier before, when everything good was embodied in the word 'socialism'. But the term does not help any more. There is an immense intellectual work in Argentina, in Latin America, trying to think of alternatives to heterocapitalism, alternatives from the left. I sometimes hope that we can provide some elements to this work.
>
> *(Ariceli)*

This quote, from a well-established feminist intellectual that I interviewed, identifies the labour process and the knowledge production around and beyond the feminist mobilisations in the Global South that the Global North visualises and celebrates. This everyday labour of conversation, dialogue and disagreement, vital in the construction of the epistemological bases of transnational feminism, is shaped, according to Ariceli, by an identification with the left.

The central challenge is the naming of these possible (anti-heterocapitalist) futures in a context where, while the meaning of the term 'left' may be vague and often contested, the term is a strong signifier of Latin American genealogies of political struggle, from the Cuban Revolution to the so-called turn to the left in the region with the leadership of Morales, Chávez, Kirchner, Lula da Silva, Tabaré Vazquez and Correa in the last few decades. The left, or rather left genealogies, name also the social identities and communities of belonging at the core of these processes, from rural workers in Bolivia to urban workers taking over factories in Argentina, to feminist scholars like myself identified with the Global South.

Most of the scholars I spoke to understand knowledge production as production of emancipatory knowledge. Many of them (nearly all of them) see their participation in social movements as a central strategy to learn from other knowledge-producing organisations outside academia.

Here are three illustrations of these practices: some of the scholars I met combine their title of professor with feminist slogans at the foot of their e-mails, supporting the struggle for the right to state-subventioned abortion. Others wear diverse feminist pins when going to faculty meetings or any other formal university event. The pins transform them from gender scholars into feminist activists, "from solemn academics into feminist troublemakers", in the words of one of my informants. Finally, feminist scholars seldom participate as individuals but as members of different organisations, seldom speaking as 'experts' but often as representing their organisations. The scholars I spoke to defined their location as public intellectuals or their vocation for intellectual activism from an epistemological standpoint based on the politics of place. They often argued that *this is how things are in the 'South'* or, rather, how *'we' do things in the 'South'*. The notion that the North has the privilege of delinking from the field of the political was very present in my material as well as the notion that this privilege decreases the ability of scholars from the Global North to think in terms of possible futures. It is the privilege of political disembodiment, so fundamental to academia in the Global North, that creates a scholarship that systematically conceals the Eurocentrism that is constitutive for its epistemological and analytical frames through which they read (and impose) their version of the truth to others (Gutierrez Rodriguez et al. 2010).

Feminist decolonial scholar Silvia Rivera Cusicanqui (2004) is highly critical of the US-located decolonial theory. She argues and convincingly shows a process of appropriation and exclusion of intellectual work made earlier, particularly in Bolivia, in the process of translation into English and location within US universities. But what Rivera Cusicanqui considers is the most dangerous effect of US-located decolonial theory is the depoliticisation that is at the core of its abstraction. There is nothing within decolonial theory that supports and nurtures our people's struggles, our people's dreams, the author concludes. Claudia de Lima Costa (2013) develops a similar argument, suggesting that when ideas and practices travel from the Global South to the Global North, or, rather, when concepts are dislocated, their potential for epistemological ruptures decreases and they are depoliticised.

I came to Sweden as a young woman escaping from state terrorism in Argentina. Like all other survivors, I bear the inscriptions of those many hands that, by risking their lives, saved mine. I also bear the memories of those (many) Swedish welfare employees, from social workers to teachers, who were there for us, doing a little bit more (or a little bit less?) than they had to. Their smiles, their presents (a teddy-bear for my daughter) and their laughter protected and healed me. And I felt for many years also protected by the beautiful parade on international solidarity on 1st May and by the people marching in solidarity with 'our' struggles in Latin America. However, I would promptly learn that international solidarity (*à la* Swedish) had its colonial emotional frame. It was based on demands of binary oppositions such as evil military/good democratic activists and framed through racist desires such as democratic, gender equality Sweden/authoritarian, patriarchal Latin America.

When the Latin American (often male) heroes negotiated, when (leftists') dreams were institutionalised or crushed, that is to say when things got dirty, the Swedes of the international solidarity movement moved on, in search of other struggles, other objects, maybe worthier of their solidarity.

One of the most painful experiences regarding transnational solidarity was to go through the death of the Cuban leader Fidel Castro when I was in Sweden. I was sad, a feeling I shared with many feminists in the Global South and many Latin Americans in the Swedish Diaspora who had been forced into exile during military dictatorship or forced migration during post-dictatorship neoliberal regimes in recent decades.

I did expect the right to do what they did – to speak about Fidel as a dictator and Cuba as a country in chaos – but I did not expect that the Swedish left and the Swedish feminists would produce long interventions regulated through colonial disappointment (such as: "I supported the Cuban Revolution but I was forced to distance myself when…") in an emotional regime that could be conceptualised as one of (white) colonial purity.

The feminists (even those identified as anti-racists or from postcolonial traditions) were absolutely silent, despite the impressive development of queer and trans* rights in Cuba. This silence followed the already established tradition of being silent over the development of queer and trans* rights in countries such as Argentina and South Africa, when these developments resisted providing the Global North (or global feminism embodied in the Global North) with an active role.

One of my (Swedish/white/feminist) friends tried to be kind, commenting that she understood that I was sad because, well… I was a Latin American. As if being Latin American was a childhood sickness people never get rid of, or a rather melodramatic emotional disability that hinders rational thought in specific situations. We were allowed to mourn within a paternalistic colonial boundary.

But the inability among the Swedish left and Swedish feminists to learn from mourning rituals within the Latin American community made me really feel (really understand) how Eurocentric knowledge is produced through a systematic resistance to learn from others. The construction of the Latin American community (and of many feminists from the Global South) mourning Fidel as ignorant, romantic and emotional denied even the possibility of a political subject position outside Eurocentric binary oppositions: either Fidel Castro was an authentic revolutionary or Fidel Castro was a dictator. Either Cuba was a success or it was an undemocratic regime. In Sweden, as in many other countries in Northern Europe, the theoretical and political identification with the historical legacy of the left is difficult to acknowledge within a context where Marxist theory is highly stigmatised in academia (Eagleton 2012) through code-words such as 'deterministic', 'simplistic', 'structuralist', 'essentialist'. In my case, my mourning was considered not only emotional but, particularly being a scholar, vulgar.

Maybe the Swedish-colonial-white subject position is based on the ability and the privilege to leave in search of "more revolutionary, more authentic, more pure" struggles. I/we could not leave Cuba and its revolution, because we had family, friends, lovers, hopes and dreams there. We knew each and many of the shortcomings of the Cuban Revolution through the suffering of Cuban people we loved. So we chose to stay with them and their struggle. Maybe the Swedish-colonial-white subject position is based on the desire for authentic resistant subjects who are never successful in their struggle towards the redistribution of global power. "They like us when we resist but do not win," a very good friend of mine commented when trying to explain the Global North's love affair with the Zapatistas. I thought she was exaggerating. But maybe she was right.

Feminist scholar Seodu Herr (2014) explores the differences between the tradition of Third World feminism, which she reads as being neutral or even approving of nation states and (Third World) nationalism, and the tradition of transnational feminism that as a theoretical frame often challenges both nation states and the (patriarchal) frame of both anti-imperialist and anti-colonial struggle (Alarcón et al. 1999). To a certain extent Chandra Mohanty´s shift (Mohanty 1997) from the term 'Third World feminism' to 'transnational feminism', or rather from a focus on a Third World anti-imperialist agenda towards global anti-capitalist feminist practices, was a response to the violent presence of neoliberal global capitalism. Transnational feminism is not a monolithic field. It covers both postmodern-influenced scholarship that Seodu Herr identifies *and* systematic and institutional analysis of power as argued by Chandra Mohanty in her criticism of postmodern transnational feminism's inability to address the struggles against colonialism and for national liberation that are central for feminism (Mohanty 2013: 969).

My identification with the epistemic community of Third World/transnational feminism bridges my theoretical and political identification with leftist genealogies from Franz Fanon (1961/2004) to Jose Carlos Mariátegui (1928/2010) (and its serious shortcomings) for feminism today. I/we mourned Fidel Castro in my/our location in Third World feminism/transnational feminism or, rather, as a leftist Third World/transnational feminism.

Feminism stories: Feminism genealogies

> And again and again ['y dale y dale'] with Julio Lopez and Julio Lopez. And each of us cares for Julio but we wanted to put the focus on femicide.

The quote is the concluding remark of Mariana, a young woman who identified herself as a trans/feminist activist. We are a group of five hundred women waiting to begin (one of the many) demonstrations demanding a state response to the increasing level of sexualised violence; what Latin American/Argentinean feminism defined as *femicidios* (Segato 2013). The systematic police brutality against trans* persons working in prostitution is also on the agenda.

For half an hour Mariana, together with other organisers, has been trying to sort out the slogans and flags of different groups. Members of human rights organisations have arrived in solidarity with the feminist mobilisation but also demanding 'Memory, Truth and Justice' for Julio Lopez, one of the survivors of state terrorism and concentration camps, who was kidnapped (and disappeared) in September 2006, a few days before he was due to testify in court. The photos of the disappeared that human rights groups often carry are seen together with the photos of the women/trans* who have been killed in the last few years. Mariana´s parents were persecuted during the military dictatorship and forced into internal exile. I can see how fractured she is between these two powerful social movements, moving between her loyalties to the human rights movements (with their pictures of the hundreds of women disappeared during the dictatorship) and her loyalties to the feminist movement (with their pictures of women/trans* killed by the 'violence machista/lesbo and transfóbica').

Women played a central role in the struggle against the dictatorship (Taylor 1997; Bellucci 1999) and their role was fundamental in the resistance against neoliberal agendas in the 1990s. Participation in these social movements, scholars argue, paved the way for a vital agenda that linked social rights to gender rights (Flori 1988; D'Atri 2007). Di Marco (2010) uses the notion of the *pueblo* feminist ('the feminist people') to grasp these heterogeneous social movements towards a shared identity as feminists forged together in response to the powerful Catholic Church and the institutionalised machismo in the country (Montesino 2002). In 2003, after twenty years of what human rights activists define as impunity, the democratic transition president Nestor Kirchner challenged the complete impunity regarding human rights violations that had been committed by the military dictatorship, revoking the amnesty laws and opening the path for the prosecution of human rights violators (Sikkink 2008). Also in 2007, a bill to legalise abortion was introduced to Congress, after years of feminist mobilisation and the creation in 2005 of the National Campaign for the Right to Legal, Safe and Free Abortion (Sutton and Borland 2013). Parallels between the two events were made both by the human rights movements and by the feminist movement.

In *Why Stories Matter*, feminist scholar Clare Hemmings (2011) provides a solid critique of how the past has been told within Western feminism. Feminism's genealogies in Argentina are often contested and rewritten by feminists themselves. Should the roots of Argentinean feminism be traced back to Bartolina Sisa, born in what is today Bolivia, an indigenous woman leader of the anti-colonial struggle and today a central figure for a decolonial feminist movement, or should they be located in the commitment and the dreams of the thousands of women migrants of European background escaping hunger and pogroms, who embodied emerging forms of socialist and anarchist feminism? And how can 'our history' be told at the crossroads between the powerful mobilisation and support of working-class women for Eva Perón in the 1940s and the similarly powerful mobilisation of (bourgeois) feminists against women's vote provided by the Perón administration?

In the following section, explorations of how these genealogies are named will be illustrated through the voices of Valeria and Amelia, self-identified feminists, both of them in their late fifties, both of them working with feminist issues – Valeria within the municipality and Amelia in a non-governmental organisation.

Valeria speaks of a feminism defined by not being 'gringo':

> We have a different feminism here, not a gringo one. Our history is one of powerful, courageous women. This generation of feminists grew up with anarchist or socialist grandmothers who maybe could not speak fluent Spanish but could sing the *International* in Yiddish. They grew up with the memory of the female *guerrilleras* of the Seventies, with the Mothers in the Plaza and with working-class women in the Nineties' barricades against neoliberalism. What they learned is that the place of women is in the streets demanding rights. What they learned is that they will be hated, that those who have power will try to destroy them, will call them bad mothers and communist whores as they did with our comrades in the Seventies, or creasy old women as they called the Mothers of the Plaza. They know that together we will survive.

Valeria's genealogy identifies one of the first articulations of a feminist agenda in the country shaped by socialist and anarchist ideas and framed within the experience of the working class (most of them European migrant women), with Virginia Bolten screaming: "Ni Dios, ni patrón, ni marido" ('No God, no boss, no husband'), calling for solidarity with women workers' strikes (Barranco 1990).

I have to confess that I reacted (bad girl – missed the sociological course on methods) when Valeria spoke of a gringo feminism. Both because what she calls 'gringo' feminism in the Global North is where I am located and it hurt to be confronted with this kind of feminism genealogy that excluded the diversity of feminisms in the Global North, but also because her narrative about feminism in Argentina excluded the serious conflicts within the movement regarding class, race and sexuality. While I did not tell her everything that I am now telling the reader, she did understand that I felt uncomfortable. The following shows the way through which Valeria reframed and further developed her story:

> I use 'gringo' for this stupid, superficial feminism, the one that supports women because they are women even if they can destroy the planet. We have that kind too here in Argentina: a "gorilla" feminism, that hated Evita and now hates Cristina Kirchner.[6] The one that goes around in Latin America counting bodies and writing articles criticising Evo (she is referring to Evo Morales, the president of Bolivia) if they find some place where women and men are not equally represented. And I am not saying that gender equality is not important, but... I use 'gringo feminist' to name those who focus on

> women over everything else, over social justice for everybody. We have a popular feminism here, we have an indigenous feminism here. Our struggle is against transnational corporations even if they are all women on their board of directors.

The vivid contrast between the experience of loss that working-class women felt with 'Evita's' death and the celebration of her death among privileged women (and particularly among feminists) who had boycotted the Perón administration's 1947 reform that gave the vote to women puts the issue of class at the core of Argentinean feminist agendas (Carlson 1988).

What Valeria argues is that the roots of Argentinean feminism are located in the political struggles of the 1970s and the transgression of gender norms by the women active in the struggle (González and Kampwirth 2001; Martínez 2009) and not in the feminism that organised against women's vote because they feared that working-class women would use the vote to support Eva Perón and that in 2017 voted in a right-wing neoliberal government against the former president Cristina Kirchner.

Valeria's genealogy – from women anarchists, through women in the guerrilla movement, to the Mothers of the Plaza and the 'piqueteras' (the working-class women picketing the streets in the 1990s against neoliberalism) (Monteagudo 2011) – is a genealogy not only of brave women but of women who name feminism through leftist ideologies, even though Valeria uses the term 'courageous' to name the tradition.

Amelia provides a slightly different reading: one focusing on women's vulnerability. The military dictatorship understood the political and social upheavals of the 1970s as produced by a cancer that they were called to extirpate, particularly the infected tissues. Central to these interventions was the reorganisation of male and female roles and the punishment of female political prisoners. Amelia identifies not only with the powerful, courageous women in Argentinean history but also with the violence that these women suffered as women (Taylor 1997; Hirsch and Smith 2002). It is through this genealogy, one that links the military dictatorship with patriarchy, that she identifies the continuities between slogans of the human rights organisations and slogans of the feminist movement today.

> Take the Not One Less [*Ni una menos*] or the We Want Ourselves Alive [*Vivas nos queremos*] or the green scarf of the campaign for the right to abortion that comes from us, from the white scarves that the Mothers and Grandmothers have, or rather from our struggle. The issue of life and death. That is a very sensitive thing in Argentina. It is where the memory arises from. New struggles and new agendas but with old scars.

The feminists' mass mobilisations of Not One Less[7] organised in 2015 as a campaign against gender violence was framed in an anti-capitalist agenda, linking the violence against women's and trans*' bodies to capitalist exploitation and appropriation of land and water. It is at the crossroads between the struggle for human rights – the rich, broad and contradictory experience of the Argentinean left – and women's rights that feminist knowledge systems evolve in the Argentinean context.

In Argentina the left and the right continue to be powerful boundaries creating (feminist) epistemological communities of belonging. This anti-imperialist and socialist legacy has shaped Latin American feminist knowledge productions and practices, putting transnational struggles against neoliberalism at the core of feminist agendas and making Argentinean feminists aware of the intersections between imperialism/colonialism/capitalist exploitation and gender and sexuality.

One of the most dangerous forms of epistemological racism (Grosfoguel 2003) is the representation of the Argentinean (and Latin American) feminism movement and knowledge production outside the frame of everyday anti-imperialist and left politics in a broad sense.

Epistemologies of hope: Unlearning racist legacies

Suelí Carneiro (2001) asserts that the legacy of European hegemony that objectified black men and women continues to pervade the Latin American cultural imagery. However, racism has been until recently a marginal, theoretical issue. Issues of racism (Bidaseca and Vazquez Laba 2013) are raised by black and indigenous feminist activists, whose access to academia and to Gender Studies is limited.

What follows is an analysis of an event that is an attempt to challenge this amnesia. The event took place in what had been one of the cruellest clandestine detention and torture centres during the dictatorship, today a memorial centre with diverse cultural and political activities: the ex-ESMA.[8] The date was 20 March 2016, four days before the commemoration of the military coup that would mobilise more than half a million people in the streets of Buenos Aires with slogans of 'Never Again' and 'Memory, Truth and Justice'. Bearing in mind the violent repression against activists of indigenous background in Argentina occurring under the right-wing neoliberal government elected in 2015, the participants will not be identified by name.

There are no more than fifty persons in the room, this sunny Sunday afternoon. The panel is composed of three representatives of indigenous organisations and two anthropologists. In the audience is 'us'. The 'us' comes in different categories: young people interested in indigenous struggles, feminists and environmental and human rights activists. But what makes the 'us' is our whiteness – even though nobody in this room would name it. The first panellist identifies the extensive and racist knowledge of the other at the core of social science and humanities. Of the thousands of books written about his community, only one has been written by a scholar of indigenous background. The presentation changes in form and content when he recounts a recent event in which more than fifty persons died during the hottest summer months because of their lack of access to drinking water. And, he continues, looking to the audience: "This is a genocide; they killed women and children, also. It happens to us, what happened to you, but it happens all the time."

What he is trying to say in his gentle voice is that there have been other genocides before 'ours'. What he is not saying is that our whiteness has impeded our understanding of the links between the two. I know, as does every other feminist and human rights activist in the room, that the Argentinean nation state is based on a genocide – that of its indigenous population. The innocent phrase "We come from the boats" and the vision of European anarchist and socialist workers, many of them of Jewish origin, provides a sense of innocence to our position: despite the (progressive) ideologies of our grandparents, we are grandchildren of white settlers. I can feel 'us' in the room receiving the powerful criticism. Nobody moves.

Another intervention is from a very experienced activist with Mapuche background. He argues that the same family names of those destroying his land are at the core of the country's leadership today. He identifies the connections and describes new forms of collaboration and solidarity between the Mapuche and the people of the valleys in the southern part of Argentina, defending the water supply from transnational corporations. The room begins to breathe; this is a language we know, *our* language, *our* struggle. But before he concludes his intervention, he (as an aside) comments that it is the first time that he and his companions have been to the former ESMA. Nobody has invited them before. He concludes with the following words: "We respect your suffering, but you do not see ours."

The workshop continues. The three of them are more to the point now. "It is not that we do not want to engage with your suffering," one of them says. "It is that what happened to you has happened to our communities so many times." Genealogies of struggles are fundamental, and our inability to feel the connection says something about the shortcomings of social movements in Argentina, among others the human rights and the feminist movements.

How come they had never been invited? How come that, despite indigenous populations marching every 24 March with the slogan "There have been other genocides", we did not get it? Or rather, the connection demanded such a radical shift in our worldview that we applauded the activists and then went on with our business and with our "suffering".

The representatives were men, not because women were marginalised but because women are the ones leading the struggles of their communities for the protection of land and water. The list of indigenous and rural women leaders assassinated in Latin America over the last decade is appalling.[9]

The imprisonment of Milagro Salas, leader of rural and indigenous communities in the northern part of the country, by the newly established right-wing neoliberal government has created an impressive wave of feminist solidarity, her liberation being one of the central points in the document produced for the feminist *Not One Less* mobilisations:

> We bring with us the experiences, the discussions and the social bonds that we have built between all of us in the *Encuentros* (National Feminist Meetings) and

> in years of popular organisation in diverse areas. We recognise ourselves in the Latin American, native and Afrodescendant struggles: we emphasise the role of women in the community struggles for life and territories. We honoured those killed: Bety Cariño in Mexico (2010), Berta Cáceres in Honduras (2016), Laura Leonor Vasquez Pineda (2017) and at least 41 girls burned alive by the State of Guatemala on March 8, we embraced their families as we embrace the people of Brazil, who are suffering the consequences of a right-wing and sexist institutional coup.
>
> *(www.pagina12.com.ar/41947-ni-una-menos, accessed 12 August 2017).*

These emerging voices confront Eurocentrism in Argentinean feminism, as Itati, an indigenous woman leader in a meeting organising a national mobilisation for the right to abortion, declared:

> What the *compañeras* do not want to understand [she is referring to the urban/white feminists] is that our bodies are our land, our bodies are our water. Our bodies are our communities. Our healers have always helped us [in the interruption of unwanted pregnancies], and because of this they have been burnt alive, put in jail and assassinated. We will support you, but we will not march with the slogan "My Body, My Decision." Because for us it would be our body, our land, our decision.

It is these indigenous and rural women leaders who, after more than fifteen hours of discussion in the Latin American congress of the Liga Campesina[10] that took place in Buenos Aires, decided to identify themselves and their movement as feminist, making indigenous feminism popular and communitarian feminism as the future of feminism in Argentina. The struggle against racism and the solidarity with indigenous populations resisting global capitalism have been incorporated not only into most feminist documents but into the worldviews of a new generation of feminists.

Epistemologies of hope: Towards a Che Guevara with red lips

Much has happened in the country since *Kiss of the Spider Woman (El beso de la mujer arana)* by the Argentinean writer Manuel Puig was published in 1976. The plot of the novel explores a central paradox: how leftist revolutionary organisations that embodied an agenda of societal transformation reproduced heteronormative and homophobic discourses and practices. The plot is organised through the meeting of two prisoners, a political activist and a gay man, focusing particularly on the forms of intimacy created, with the tortured political activist challenging his prejudice, and the gay man being killed by the police for being loyal to the political activist's needs.

Most observers would point not only to the brutal dictatorship but also to the difficult transition to the democracy inscribed in a neoliberal frame during the 1990s. Most scholars would also identify the centrality of social movements challenging neoliberalism for the electoral success of the Kirchner administration. Feminism was a particularly vital and wide-ranging player during the three decades bridging these diverse movements. The legal recognition of trans* rights was expressed in the Gender Identity Act (GIA) approved by the Senate on 9 May 2012, which removes requirements to declare change of gender on legal documents and allows access to gender-affirming treatments through the public health system if desired (Rucovsky 2015).

Since the start of the democratic administration in 1984, diverse groups of feminist-identified organisations, from union activists to lesbian collectives, have successfully connected the human rights struggle, so fundamental for the democratisation process, with women's and GLTTTBI agendas demanding social, political and sexual rights (Bellucci and Rapisardi 1999; Pecheny 2003). I use the term GLTTTBI following activists who often argue that the notion of 'queer' is too academic and denies the identities their members so strongly have fought for (Brown 2002; Berkins 2003). The acronym GLTTTBI refers to gay, lesbian, transvestite, transsexual, transgender, bisexual and intersex people. Mainstream media and public discourses use the notion of movement for the diversity (*el movimiento por la diversidad*).

Particularly over the last ten years GLTTTBI's massive mobilisation has succeeded in creating alliances between human rights activists and gender and sexual rights, in a context where Cristina Kirchner was elected as president. When many GLTTTBI activists speak of 'the gained decade' they express both a support for the Kirchner administration and an acknowledgement of the radical transformation of everyday life through the passing of laws such as for same-sex marriage (*matrimonio igualitario*) and gender equality, one of the most successful in recognising trans* persons' rights globally.

While it could be argued that trans* rights in Argentina are inscribed within a transnational agenda of global queer citizenship, it could also be argued that the specific ways through which the articulation of these rights are legitimised and acted upon are a product of local histories inspired by socialist anti-imperialist worldviews fundamental in the struggles against neoliberalism. The emergence of broad forms of collaboration between GLTTTBI and the human rights organisations took place through the shared experience of struggles against neoliberalism and resistance to police violence in the 1990s.

> You are not going to believe me, and it is nearly impossible to believe; now we go on singing "Las Madres de la plaza, las trans las abrazan" ["Mothers of the Plaza, the trans embrace you"] and everybody is happy. But ten years ago, things were different. Well, the thing is that we were going to have one of our first meetings for the cooperative and it was decided that it could be in the Mothers' house. And there I was going around the block, one, two, three times, and it rained, and I am sure that the *compañeros* [comrades] inside thought that I was *la yuta* (the police/slang). You're going around... But I did not dare to enter. I felt that the people in the human rights – well, you know,

> you are one of them, you… they are very well-educated… and all their courage; all their suffering. But then from nowhere one of the Mothers came my way and commented that I was going to get a pulmonary infection with so much rain and so few clothes ([laughs]… yes… she commented on my clothes style) and welcomed me.

Alicia is a trans* activist and I have been re-reading this quote many times over: on the one hand because she is (unconsciously?) making a clear boundary between who she is and who I am (the human rights people). She is locating me where she thinks I belong, with the 'very well-educated' human rights people. There is so much generosity in her story. I can see her, in her impossibly high heels, going along the streets around the Mothers' building, the rain pouring down, and her hesitation over crossing an unspoken boundary. Focal to the boundary-making is the representation of the human rights activists as well-educated (read middle-class and white).

Core to her narrative is also the inscription of the trans* movement as within those who love the Mothers. When writing themselves into the notion of the people, by adapting the slogan 'The people embrace the Mothers' into 'The trans embrace the Mothers', the trans* movement in Argentina takes a stand beyond sexual rights towards a societal vision located in other central political identities:

> We have seen the suffering in our families; some of us have experienced hunger. And you also know very well that I work in the cooperative following my principles. I did it much better during the night…. Some of our families have neglected us… and the Mothers, many of you people also, experienced that too. I am not a trans for the TV shows, we are *pueblo* [the people]… And of course … I am the best stone-thrower ever….

She always makes me laugh. And I laughed also during that conversation, not only because of the way she told stories but also because I had a great respect for her ability in confronting the police. I got back to her that same evening, just to tell her how much I have learned from how she created bridges between our different backgrounds and experiences. The creation of communities of belonging is at the core of the forms of resistance for groups suffering stigmatisation. Some trans* persons are expelled from their families, and, while it is true that many families responded with solidarity to the tragedy of family members being imprisoned, in exile or disappeared, some families distanced themselves from the members who suffered political persecution during the dictatorship. Alicia is making this powerful connection: that of creating new families that transgress biological kin.

In her study of women's reproductive social movements in Argentina, social anthropologist Lynn Morgan (2015) suggests that, while global social movements' genealogies are highly complex, activists themselves trace their roots to homegrown social justice histories and politics rather than to the diffusion or importation of US or global feminism movements.

The links between some 'GLTTTBI' networks and organisations and left-wing social movements and human rights organisations have always been strong. Alicia provides several reasons for this. On the one hand, she argues for a self-definition that entangles a trans* identity inscribed in working-class experience. But she also opens discussion for other fundamental links with the human rights struggle, among others her experience (expressed by the throwing of stones) of the repressive state, through her confrontation with the police, but also what she names as her principles, that is, her political choice of working in a cooperative despite being more economically successful in prostitution. In Argentina, sex- and gender-based political movements have long drawn attention to the link between the political economy of sexuality *and* the repressive practices of the state. Lohana Berkins (recently deceased), who was one of the most key figures of the trans* movement, and Maria Rachied, identified as lesbian, have run for legislative seats on left-wing tickets. Julio Talavera, an activist prominent in the HIV/AIDS movement, has for a long time also been one of the leaders of HIJOS (Children of the Disappeared).

I have to acknowledge that the first time I encountered the figure of the legendary Che Guevara with red lips I was not convinced. We were celebrating (or rather waiting with thousands of others outside the Parliament) the passing of the new law on gender identity. A very young activist must have felt my consternation at this Che with red lips, and asked: "Do you think he would be here with us? Do you think he would like it?" I smiled because my spontaneous answer would have been no. The Latin American left, while done by many people with different bodies, is masculinistic and heteronormative in its form and content.

Maybe I was wrong. Actually I *was* wrong. When the Lohana cooperative participates in demonstrations with the slogan 'We want a trans*person to democratise the unions'; when new Che Guevara posters appear everywhere on social media with the slogan 'FURIA Transvesti', I not only smile but think that Che Guevara with red lips is undoubtedly a better myth.

Beyond the Che Guevara with red lips is the production of Southern Theory, knowledge production in which social movements speak, challenge, listen and learn from each other and from the historical and mythical left which most of them recognise as its difficult and problematic roots, towards new communities of belonging.

Hope is a Che Guevara with red lips, in a pin with the colour of the rainbow flag.

Conclusion

A core argument developed through these pages is that the body of feminist knowledge produced at the margins deserves more investment in scholarship dialogues than rhetorical acknowledgements of the role of women's resistance in the Global South. A transnational feminist vision needs to acknowledge and take as a point of departure the centrality of the Latin American and Argentinean left broadly understood as crucial for the development of feminism in the Argentinean context, and cardinal for the feminist epistemologies and knowledge production.

A fundamental, nearly foundational, experience of left politics in a broader sense locates Argentinean feminism within an anti-capitalist agenda. The naming of social conflict through the left-right frame is often excluded in the ways through which postcolonial and decolonial feminism are taught as newly established academic fields in European academia.

While Argentinean feminism is transnational in its language and agenda, it is regarded as extremely Global South/*sudaca* [11] in its frame, particularly in the centrality of the field of politics in shaping and defining the form and content of feminism. In other words, feminist knowledge in Argentina challenges post-political emotional regimes at the core of Western knowledge production. Central to the contribution of Argentinean feminism to transnational feminist theory is the creation of regimes of hope that acknowledge and recognise earlier socialist and anti-imperialist struggles and locate the violence against women's and trans*' bodies at the crossroads between repressive states and profit-ridden markets.

Notes

1 Thanks to feminist scholars /feminist activists Mabel Belucci, Ana Gonzalez, Maria Alicia Gutierrez, Maria Eugenia Morey, Florencia Portenio, Elsa Schvartzman and Monica Tarducci, and to the feminist inspired artists ´collective *Mujeres Publicas* for everything I learned and continue to learn from them.
2 www.skissernasmuseum.se/en/calendar/introduktion-till-museet-32/
3 Scholarship on human rights struggles in Argentina in response to the 1976–1983 civic-military dictatorship that brutally 'disappeared', murdered, tortured, imprisoned and forced into exile thousands of citizens is extensive (Arditti 1999; Calveiro 2008).
4 Buen vivir (Sumak Kawsay) www.theguardian.com/sustainable-business/blog/buen-vivir-philosophy-south-america-eduardo-gudynas
5 Thanks to the student group, who allowed me to publish class discussions.
6 'Gorilla ' is a pejorative political term that is used to name those who are against, first, Perónism and recently, the Kirchner administration.
7 www.jacobinmag.com/2017/03/argentina-ni-una-menos-femicides-women-strike/. See also www.pagina12.com.ar/41947-ni-una-menos (accessed 12 August 2017).
8 See www.espaciomemoria.ar/english.php (accessed 12 June 2017).
9 www.newyorker.com/news/news-desk/the-death-of-berta-caceres (accessed 15 August 2017).
10 http://fmriachuelo.com.ar/2015/04/05/soberania-alimentaria-vi-congreso-de-la-coordinadora-latinoamericana-de-organizaciones- (accessed 15 August 2017).
11 *Sudaca* is an offensive and derogatory term for people with origin in Latin America.

References

Ahmed, S., (2009) *The Promise of Happiness*. Durham, NC: Duke University Press.

Alarcón, N., Kaplan, C., and Moallem, M., (1999) *Between Woman and Nation: Nationalisms, Transnational Feminisms and the State*. Durham, NC: Duke University Press.

Alexander, M.J., and Mohanty, C.T., (eds.). (1997) *Feminist Genealogies, Colonial Legacies, Democratic Futures*. New York and London: Routledge.

Anthias, F., and Yuval-Davis, N., (1992) *Racialized Boundaries: Race, Nation, Gender, Colour and Class and the Anti-Racist Struggle*. London: Routledge.

Anzaldúa, G., (1999) *Borderlands: The new Mestiza. La Frontera*. San Francisco: Aunt Lute Books.

Arditti, R., (1999) *Searching for Life: Grandmothers of the Plaza de Mayo and the Disappeared Children of Argentina*. Berkeley: University of California Press.

Armbruster, H., and Laerke, A., (2008) *Taking Sides: Ethics, Politics and Field Work in Anthropology*. New York: Berghahn Books.

Barranco, D., (2013) Pulsiones feministas/pasiones del conocimiento [Feminists' desires/passions of knowledge]. *Debate Feminista*. 48(24) October. pp. 195–200.

Barranco, D., (1990) *Anarquismo, Educacion y Costumbres [Anarchism, Education and Customs]*. Buenos Aires: Contrapunto.

BhandarB., and Ferreira da Silva, D., (2013) *White Feminist Fatigue Syndrome*. Available at: http://criticallegalthinking.com/2013/10/21/white-feminist-fatigue-syndrome/ (Accessed 29 August 2017).

Bellucci, M., (1999) Childless motherhood: Interview with Nora Cortiñas, a Mother of the Plaza de Mayo, Argentina. *Reproductive Health Matters*. 7(13). pp. 83–88.

Bellucci, M., (2014) *Historia de una Desobediencia: Aborto y Feminismo. [History of a Disobedience: Abortion and Feminism]*. Buenos Aires: Editorial Capital Intelectual.

Bellucci, M., and Rapisardi, F., (1999) Alrededor de la identidad: Luchas políticas del presente [Around identity: Political struggles today]. *Revista Nueva Sociedad*. 162. pp. 40–53.

Berkins, L., (2003) Un itinerario político del travestismo [A political path of trans rights]. In: Maffia, D. (ed.). *Sexualidades Migrantes: Género y Transgénero [Migrant Sexualities: Gender and Transgender]*. Buenos Aires: Feminaria Editora.

Bidaseca, K., and Vazquez Laba, V., (2013) *Feminismos y Poscolonialidad: Descolonizando el Feminismo desde y en América. [Feminism and Postcoloniality: Decolonizing Feminism from and in America]*. Buenos Aires: Ediciones Godot.

Brown, S., (2002) Con discriminación y represion no hay democracia: The gay and lesbian movement in Argentina. *Latin American Perspectives*. 29(2). pp. 129–134.

Calveiro, P., (2008) *Poder y Desaparición. [Power and Disappearance]*. 2nd edition. Buenos Aires: Colihue.

Carlson, M., (1988) *¡Feminismo! The Woman's Movement in Argentina from its Beginnings to Eva Perón*. Chicago: Academy Publishers.

Carneiro, S., (2001) Ennegrecer al feminismo: La situación de la mujer negra en América Latina desde una perspectiva de género [Blackening feminism: The situation of black women in Latin America]. Paper presented at the International Seminar on Racism, Xenophobia and Gender organised by Lolapress, Durban, August 27–28; also (2005) *Nouvelles Questions Féministes* 24(2).

Collins, P.H., (1991) *Black Feminist Thought: Knowledge, Consciousness and the Politics of Empowerment*. New York: Routledge.

Connell, R., (2007) *Southern Theory: The Global Dynamics of Knowledge in Social Science*. Cambridge: Polity Press.

Conway, J., (2017) Troubling transnational feminism(s): Theorising activist praxis. *Feminist Theory*. 18(2). pp. 205–227.

Cosslett, T., Lury, C., and Summerfield, P., (2000) *Feminism and Autobiography: Texts, Theories, Methods*. London: Routledge.

D'Atri, A., (2007) Re-politicization of the women's movement and feminism in Argentina: The experience of Pan y Rosas. In: Durán, L., Payne, N., and Russo, A. (eds.). *Building Feminist Movements and Organisations: A Global Perspectives*. London: Verso. pp. 13–24.

Di Marco, G., (2010) Los movimientos de mujeres en la argentina y la emergencia del pueblo feminista [Women´s movements in Argentina and the emergence of the feminist people]. *Aljaba* [online], 14. Available at: www.scielo.org.ar/scielo.php?script=sci_arttext&pid=S1669-57042010000100003. (Accessed 9 June 2007)

Eagleton, T., (2012) *Why Marx was Right*. Reprint edition. New Haven, CT: Yale University Press.

Fanon, F., (1961/2004) *The Wretched of the Earth*. New York: Grove Press.

Federici, S., (1999) Reproduction and feminist struggle in the new international division of labor. In: Dalla Costam, M., and Dalla Costa, G.F., (eds.). *Women, Development, and Labor of Reproduction: Struggles and Movements*. Trenton, NJ: Africa World Press. pp. 47–82.

Fernandes, L., (2013) *Transnational Feminism in the United States: Knowledge, Ethics, Power*. New York and London: New York University Press.

Ferree, M., and Tripp, A.M., (eds.). (2006) *Global Feminism: Transnational Women's Activism, Organizing and Human Rights*. New York and London: New York University Press.

Flori, M., (1988) Argentine women's organizations during the transition to democracy. *Feminist Issues*. 8. pp. 53–56.

González, V., and Kampwirth, K., (eds.). (2001) *Radical Women in Latin America: Left and Right*. University Park, PA: Penn State University Press.

Grewal, I., and Kaplan, C., (2002) *Scattered Hegemonies: Postmodernity and Transnational Feminist Practices*. Minneapolis, MN: University of Minnesota Press.

Grosfoguel, R., (2003) *Colonial Subjects*. Berkeley, CA: California University Press.

Gutierrez Rodriguez, E., Boatca, M., and Costa, S., (2010) *Decolonizing European Sociology*. London: Ashgate.

Hall, S., Massey, D., and Rustin, M., (ed.). (2015) *After Neoliberalism?: The Kilburn Manifesto*. Dagenham, UK: Lawrence and Wishart. Available at: www.lwbooks.co.uk/journals/soundings/manifesto.html (Accessed 3 July 2017)

Harcourt, W., (2014) The future of capitalism: A consideration of alternatives. *Cambridge Journal of Economics*. 38(6). pp. 1307–1328.

Hemmings, C., (2011) *Why Stories Matter: The Political Grammar of Feminist Theory*. Durham, NC: Duke University Press.

Herr, R.S., (2014) Reclaiming Third World feminism: Or why transnational feminism needs Third World feminism. *Meridians*. 12(1). pp. 1–30.

Hirsch, M., and Smith, V., (2002) Feminism and cultural memory: An introduction. *Signs*. 28(1). pp. 1–19.

de Lima Costa, C., (2013) Equivocation, translation, and performative intersectionality: Notes on decolonial feminist practices and ethics in Latin America. *Anglo Saxonica*. 3(6). Available at: http://works.bepress.com/claudiadelima_costa/3/ (Accessed 18 August 2017)

Lugones, M., (1987) Playfulness, "world"-travelling, and loving perception. *Hypatia*. 2(2), Summer. pp. 3–19.

Mariátegui, J.C., (1928/2010) *7 Ensayos de Interpretación de la Realidad Peruana* [*Seven Essays of Interpretation of the Peruvian Reality*]. Lima, Perú: Biblioteca Amauta.

Martínez, P., (2009) *Género, Política y Revolución en los Años Setenta: Las Mujeres del PRT-ERP*. [*Gender, Politics and Revolution: The Women from PRT-ERP*]. Buenos Aires: Imago Mundi.

Mohanty, C.T., (1997) Women workers and capitalist scripts: Ideologies of domination, common interests, and the politics of solidarity. In: Alexander, M.J., and Mohanty, C.T., (eds.). *Feminist Genealogies, Colonial Legacies, Democratic Futures*. New York: Routledge. pp. 3–29.

Mohanty, C.T., (2003) *Feminism without Borders: Decolonizing Theory, Practicing Solidarity*. Durham, NC: Duke University Press.

Mohanty, C.T., (2013) Transnational feminist crossings: On neoliberalism and radical critique. *Signs*. 38(4). pp. 967–991.

Monteagudo, G., (2011) *Politics by Other Means: Rhizomes of Power in Argentina's Social Movements*. Dissertation. Available at: http://scholarworks.umass.edu/open_access_dissertations/420 (Accessed 2 July 2017)

Montesino, S., (2002) Understanding gender in Latin America. In: Montoya, R., Frazier, L.J., and Hurtig, J. (eds.). *Gender's Place: Feminist Anthropologies of Latin America.* Basingstoke, UK: Palgrave Macmillan. pp. 273–280.

Moraga, C., and Anzaldúa, G., (1981) *This Bridge Called My Back: Writings by Radical Women of Color.* Albany, NY: Kitchen Table Press.

Morgan, L., (2015) Reproductive rights or reproductive justice: Lessons from Argentina. *Health and Human Rights.* 17(1). pp. 36–47.

Naples, N., and Desai, M. (eds.). (2002) *Women's Activism and Globalization: Linking Local Struggles and Transnational Politics.* New York and London: Routledge.

Oyewùmì, O., (2005) *African Gender Studies: A Reader.* Basingstoke, UK: Palgrave Macmillan.

Pecheny, M., (2003) Sexual orientation, AIDS, and human rights in Argentina: The paradox of social advance amidst health crisis. In: Eckstein, S., and Wickham-Crowley, T., (eds.). *Struggles for Social Rights in Latin America.* New York: Routledge. pp. 253–271.

Puig, M., (1976/2002) *El Beso de la Mujer Arana* [*The Kiss of the Spider Woman*]. Madrid: Seix Barral.

Rivera Cusicanqui, S., (2010) The notion of 'rights' and the paradoxes of postcolonial modernity: Indigenous peoples and women in Bolivia. *Qui Parle: Critical Humanities and Social Sciences.* 18(2). pp. 29–54.

Rivera Cusicanqui, S., (2004) La noción del "derecho" o las paradojas de la postmodernidad colonial. Indigenas y mujeres en Bolivia. [The notion of rights and the paradox of post-colonial modernity: Indigenous peoples and women in Bolívia]. *Revista Aportes Andinos.* 11. Aportes sobre diversidad, diferencia e identidad.

Rucovsky, M. (2015) *Trans* Necropolitics: Gender Identity Law in Argentina. Sexualidad. Salud y Sociedad.* Centro Latino-Americano em Sexualidade e Direitos Humanos (CLAM/IMS/UERJ). Available at: ISSN 1984–6487 (Accessed 12 July 2017).

Sandoval, C., (2000) *Methodology of the Oppressed.* Minneapolis, MN and London: University of Minnesota Press.

Sassen, S., (2014) *Expulsions: Brutality and Complexity in the Global Economy.* Cambridge, MA: Belknap Press: an imprint of Harvard University Press.

Segato, R., (2013) *Territorio, Soberanía y Crímenes de Segundo Estado: La Escritura Sobre el Cuerpo de las Mujeres Asesinadas de Ciudad Juárez* [*Territory, Sovereignty and Crimes of Second State: The Writing on the Body of the Murdered Women of Ciudad Juárez*]. Buenos Aires: Tinta y Limón.

Sikkink, K., (2008) From pariah state to global protagonist: Argentina and the struggle for international human rights. *Latin American Politics and Society.* 50(1). pp. 1–29.

Sutton, B., and Borland, E., (2013) Framing abortion rights in Argentina´s Enucentros Nacionales de Mujeres. *Feminist Studies.* Spring. 39(1). pp. 194–234.

SwarrA., and Nagar, R., (eds.). (2010) *Critical Collaborations: Transnational Feminist Practice.* New York: State University of New York Press.

Tarducci, M., (2012) La antropología feminista hoy: Desafíos teóricos y políticos en un mundo globalizado [Feminist anthropology today: Political and theoretical challenges in a globalized world]. *Cuadernos de Antropología Social.* 36. Available at: www.scielo.org.ar/scielo.php?script=sci_arttext&pid=S1850-275X2012000200001 (Accessed 26 February 2018).

Taylor, D., (1997) *Disappearing Acts: Spectacles of Gender and Nationalism in Argentina's "Dirty War".* Durham, NC: Duke University Press.

Wright, O.E., (2012) *Envisioning Real Utopias.* London: Verso.

EPILOGUE

Diana Mulinari and Lena Martinsson

"We should write something about the context", we said to each other and began to laugh. 'Context' is a term often used within the social sciences and the humanities to name the background shaping the analysis. We laughed because as feminist scholars and activists we carry the so-called context in our bodies and on our backs. And most readers know, most readers feel the 'context' these days.

Naming the context as an evil one is without a doubt not very academic. However, Europe's response to the needs of people forced to leave their countries destroyed by the greed of financial capitalists cannot be named in other ways.

Europe as an idea, as an identity and as a political project, seems incapable of practices of solidarity and care; in other words, Europe is suffering from a crisis of solidarity. This context was important for some of us when we decided to write a book about hope, about learning from feminists' struggles and knowledge production, about a possible future beyond Eurocentric dystopic notions on a lost modernity, the militarisation of national borders and the greed of financial capital.

Impressive numbers of people have resisted both ideologies of hate and invitations to belong to closed communities, among them many activists identifying as feminist, working for transnational forms of solidarity and alternative understandings of home and belonging. During these (feminist) struggles, we carried with us a conviction that hope, visions and imaginaries about the future, locally as well as transnationally, are emerging in (feminist) places around the world. This leads us to three concluding points:

We are inspired by a transnational feminist agenda where the Global South is not an object of theory and an illustration of Western academic anxieties but a space for the development of vital, fundamental knowledge evolving from feminist practices and forms of resistance. We would like to suggest that a de-colonial agenda takes a point of departure in local and translocal knowledges and in their ability to provide multivocal explorations and often clear-cut solutions. The epistemologies produced within and through these feminist struggles challenge the arrogance of Western feminist academic debates and agendas. This is not an argument for relativism but an argument for the need to explore who has the power to define what is a fundamental topic or a vital theoretical issue within feminist academic agendas. In line with this, we also find it important to study the unavoidable transnational sphere as a political space for border-struggles, conflicting positions, (dis)connections and imaginaries.

What we are calling for are forms of feminist knowledge production with a scholarly commitment and engagement in the practice of unlearning privilege and learning from feminist communities of struggle in diverse peripheries and borders.

We read a decolonial agenda as one that nurtures the travel of insurgent knowledge, protecting its political agendas and visions, challenging and interrupting forms of Western academic appropriation and critically exploring processes of productive translation that create spaces for thinking together and through others.

We depart from acknowledging the privileged position of some of us as located in the Global North, but underline our identities as migrant women, trans*, queer and human rights activists, hoping that our position at the margins and in diverse peripheries opens up a possible dialogue with other scholars in similar contexts within a transnational arena.

We argue for a decolonial agenda that opens the possibility of a subject position at the cross-roads between a (feminist) activist and a (feminist) academic identity, creating forms of solidarity and scholarly dialogue from the location of diverse margins both in the Global North and the Global South.

Finally, hope. Hope because of the many feminist-inspired struggles that find their way in between, through hegemonic discourses, borders, and neoliberal forces. Hope, because of the many alternative alliances and counter-hegemonies forms of knowledge production that have been discussed and analysed in the different chapters

Scholarships of hope challenge white Western (feminist) political depression and their dangerous sceptical agendas over our (feminist) ability to transform science and change the world. Scholarships of hope grow in the shadows of thousands of peripheries and voice the powerful sense of possibilities and the vitality of shared futures.

INDEX